Technological Change and Industrial Development

(Indian Experiences)

TECHNOLOGICAL CHANGE AND INDUSTRIAL DEVELOPMENT

(INDIAN EXPERIENCES)

RACHNA MUJOO

A.P.H. PUBLISHING CORPORATION
5, ANSARI ROAD, DARYA GANJ
NEW DELHI-110 002

Published by
S. B. Nangia
A.P.H. Publishing Corporation
5, Ansari Road, Darya Ganj
New Delhi-110002
☎ 3274050
Email : aph@mantraonline.com
Website : www.aphbooksindia.com

ISBN 81-7648-246-3

2001

Typesetting at
NEW APCON
25/2, Panchsheel Shopping Centre
New Delhi - 110 017
☎ 6490802
6494336

Printed in India at
Efficient Offset Printers
New Delhi-110 035

Preface

Economists have always been in search of factors responsible for growth of a nation. Led by pioneering work of Schumpeter, a number of studies analysing the experiences of developed countries have identified the technological change as the most crucial factor for making significant contribution to the national economic growth. Whereas in case of developing countries generally constrained by shortage of capital, the need for efficient utilisation of the resources particularly capital has often been emphasised. Several studies have been pursued for assessing and analysing the impact of technological change in India, the most popular and illustrative in recent times being those of B.N. Goldar and Isher J.Ahluwalia. By virtue of its nature, these studies, in spite of being highly data intensive, have fairly drawn certain significant and meaningful policy implications, which could, no doubt, play activating role in development of the industrial sector. Since these studies have heavily depended upon the macro level data only, and the regional dimension is sidetracked from the focus of analysis, they provide no or little treatment to the growth of organised industries at the micro level. In order, therefore, to bridge this gap, the present study entitled as 'Technological Change and Industrial Development : Indian Experiences' was undertaken by the author of this book at the Giri Institute of Development Studies (GIDS), Lucknow for the award of Ph.D. degree in Economics.

The study basically aims at analysing the inter-relationship between differentials in technological progress and those of differentials in output and employment growth of the organised industrial sector in Uttar Pradesh both at the State and the regional levels during the reference period of 1974 –1986. Besides, the analysis has also been carried out for twenty industry groups and the four categories delineated out of them on the basis of their capital labour ratios of the final year, i.e., 1985-86. Production functions are estimated, using the rich cross-section and time series data base of the study. Although the study suffers from one basic limitation of not utilising the latest ASI data of the year 1990-91 owing to its non-availability till completion of this study, the emerging conclusions and recommendations appear to have remained as revealing and rewarding as would have been after using such data.

Indeed the study has succeeded in painting out the unrosy scene of the organised manufacturing sector of the U.P.'s economy , which has experienced a sluggish productivity growth during whole of the reference period as witnessed by the movement behaviour of total factor productivity (TFP) indices and estimated production functions. However, in sub-period-II (1980-81 to 1985-86), as a result of significant technological advancement, the organised manufacturing sector has experienced appreciable increases in output growth simultaneously with downsizing of the employment growth, depicting finally a clear cut conflict between the two. To partake with the national level objective of efficiency and equity , it would, therefore, be desirable to follow two pronged approach for manufacturing purposes; first to promote the organised sector for maximisation of output growth and second to gear up the tempo of the unorganised sector for creation of maximum possible employment opportunities.

Moreover, inter-category analysis has clearly demonstrated that industry groups constituting the 'medium high capital intensive' category are undoubtedly best suited to industrialisation of U.P.'s economy in terms of both technological progress and increases in output and employment growth. The two industry groups rated to be outstanding in terms of both technological advancement and increased output and employment growth are 'manufacture of electrical machinery, apparatus, appliances and supplies and parts' and ' manufacture of food products'.

Finally, while trying to dig out ground realities of the industrial scenario within the State, the regional analysis has pointed out that in respect of technological progress, the three backward regions (Eastern, Uttranchal and Bundelkhand) of the State are much better placed as compared to those of the developed ones, i.e., the Western and the Central. Of the three backward regions, Bundelkhand has demonstrated exceptionally good performance with neutral technological progress and economies of scale. This provides us a clear cut indication of a much wider scope for industrialisation of less developed regions of the State.

It gives me an immense pleasure in recording gratitude to my supervisor. Dr. R. T. Tewari, Ex-Adviser, Economic Planning, Government of Uttar Pradesh, Lucknow, for his valuable guidance, useful suggestions and fruitful discussions, not only at the time of drafting the thesis, but throughout the period of conceiving this study. But for his untiring and unstinted support and constant encouragement this work would not have seen light of the day.

I am also indebted to several other individuals, my colleagues and friends whose support, comments and suggestions have been of great help. I am personally grateful to Prof. B.K. Joshi, the then Director of GIDS, Lucknow for his institutional support throughout the period of this study. I would particularly like to thank Prof. R.K. Singh, Department of Statistics, Lucknow University , for his suggestions in accomplishing the statistical analysis, and to Mr. R.L. Raina, Ex-General Manager, UPDESCO , Lucknow, for his constant encouragement and for making relevant data readily available at times of need. I would also like record my appreciation to a dear friend Ms. Ishrat Hasnain, GIDS, Lucknow for her help and co-operation from beginning to the end of the study.

I wish to express my thanks to librarians of GIDS, IIM, SPI and LU located in this city of Nawabs for extending their support to me for availing full benefits of the literature.

Thanks are also due to Mr. S.K. Ghosh and Ms. Aparna Sharma for data processing on computers and also Mr. K. Mathews for preparing the typescript.

My sincere acknowledgement is due to ICSSR, New Delhi for providing me the short-term partial assistance to complete the work.

Finally, I express a deep sense of gratitude to my parents, especially to my Father late Prof. H.N. Mujoo, who is no longer with us to share the glimpse of our happiness at this occasion. But the feeling of his constant presence and encouragement will ever remain as a source of inspiration to me throughout my life. I would also like to record sincere gratitude to my husband, Mr. R.C. Tikoo, whose silent but continued support against all odds made this study possible. Last but not the least, I would also like to express the heartiest affection to my little son Rakshit, who remained quite amusing throughout the period of finalising the manuscript for publication of this book.

RACHNA MUJOO

Lucknow University.
Lucknow, 2000

Contents

List of Tables

List of Appendix Tables

CHAPTER 1

Introduction

Historically, the technological progress has been recognised as one of the major sources of economic growth from the time of classical economists. However, they were of the view that technological change involved only a temporary disturbance in the equilibrium and, therefore, laid emphasis on the increases in the quantities of conventional inputs, i.e., land, labour and capital and treated them as factors of growth. But what made technological progress the central focus of discussion in recent years was the pioneering work of Schumpeter in early twentieth century and the empirical findings in case of developed countries indicating that a sizeable portion of output growth could not be attributed to increases in factor inputs.

In spite of its overwhelming importance, the term technological progress is sometimes understood in a very abstract manner. Abramovitz has aptly referred to it as a 'measure of our ignorance'. To a larger satisfaction, it may, however, be defined as advances in the knowledge related to art of production. Such advances may take the form of a new product, a new process or a new mode of organisation, marketing and management. In addition to these, looking to the perspective of developing countries, its conceptualisation may also include minor changes and improvements made in the process of assimilating and adapting the imported modern technology.

Technological change assumes greater significance for developing countries being constrained by shortage of resources, particularly the capital. It, therefore, becomes imperative for these countries to make use of this scarce resource with a greater efficiency and in a manner which could ensure maximum possible exploitation of existing factor endowments.

Technological progress by unleashing the latent productive potential leads to increases in production, productivity and thereby sectoral incomes of an economy. In labour surplus developing countries, the need of the hour is to absorb more and more additional labour force in the non-farm sector and to reduce the burden on agriculture. Appropriate technology enables the modern sector to expand faster with the same level of investment, besides widening the scope of generating additional employment opportunities for growing labour force.

Application of technology suiting the factor endowments has a favourable impact on both the output growth and employment growth. In backward areas or the so called 'late comers', the technological advancement in the productive sectors of the economy mainly agriculture and industry, are expected not only to augment the productivity levels but also enhance the scope of employment. This, in turn, will lead to lifting the areas from morass of backwardness, besides promoting balanced regional development.

India's planning has already covered a longer period of its journey. And a massive investment has already been made to achieve the National level goal of rapid economic growth. As a sequel, there might have been a significant progress not only in overall development but also in development of the key sectors of the economy. Industrialisation is the main vehicle through which rapid economic development can be achieved. This line of thought has been emphasised since India's Second Five Year Plan, resulting in heavy investment over a wide spectrum of industries accompanied by all-round efforts including technological advancement. This shows a wider scope for a study which could analyse the role of technological change in the process of overall development, particularly in the context of industrial sector.

The economy of Uttar Pradesh is mainly agrarian. It is also characterised as one of the industrially backward States. According to the Annual Survey of Industries (ASI) report, the total capital investment in the organised industrial sector of U.P. during 1985-86 was Rs.4266.42 crores and the total employment was of the order of approximately 5.61 lakhs. The total State income during the same year at the current prices was Rs.24,785 crore, out of which the total share of industrial sector was Rs.3154.61 crore (i.e 12.7 percent only). Moreover, the share of organised industrial sector in the total industrial income was as high as Rs.1639.69 crore (i.e. nearly 52 percent). Apart from the industrial backwardness, the State also suffered from alarming nature of inter-regional disparities in levels of industrial development, which might, *inter-alia,* be due to inter-regional differentials in technological progress. This made the study more relevant in the context of Uttar Pradesh. Moreover, looking to the past literature, there had hardly been any study carried out on this theme in the context of Uttar Pradesh. To bridge this gap, it was, therefore, decided to undertake the study of 'Technological Change and Industrial Development :Indian Experiences'.

1. OBJECTIVES

Main objective of the study would, therefore, be to analyse the technological change and its role in development of the organised industrial sector in Uttar Pradesh during the period 1974-75 to 1985-86. The specific objectives of the study are listed below:

(i) To analyse the investment pattern and the plan allocations of outlays for development of the industrial sector in Uttar Pradesh;

(ii) To study and analyse the inter-relationship between the changes in technology and those of output growth and employment separately for each of the industry groups and whole of the manufacturing sector in the State; and

(iii) To assess and analyse the relationship between the inter-regional differentials in technological progress and those of output growth and employment in whole of the organised industrial sector at the disaggregative level.

2. ISSUES

(i) To what extent the technological advancement has been effective in accelerating the development of organised industrial sector in U.P.;

(ii) Whether technological progress has led to an improvement in regional pattern of development of the organised industrial sector. Whether the disparities in levels of industrialisation have started showing a tendency of convergence;

(iii) To what extent there has been a technological advancement in various industry groups during the period of the study (1974-75 to 1985-86). Moreover, as a result of this advancement, what kind of changes have taken place over the period in various industry groups mainly in terms of output growth and employment; and

(iv) Whether the technological progress has brought about a favourable impact on both the output growth and employment of the organised industrial sector in U.P. during the reference period.

3. METHODOLOGY

The analysis of technological change and development of organised industrial sector of Uttar Pradesh in the present study has been carried out at the State as well as the regional levels. The State level analysis primarily concerns with whole of the organised industrial sector, twenty industry groups (two-digit level) and four categories of these industry groups delineated on the basis of capital-labour ratios of the final year (i.e. 1985-86). However, owing to paucity/insufficiency of data, the regional level analysis of the organised industrial sector is confining to the five economic regions of Uttar Pradesh (i.e. Western, Central, Eastern, Uttaranchal and Bundelkhand).

To measure technological change during the reference period, efforts have been made to find out estimates of partial and total factor productivity indices, besides working out estimates of the Cobb-Douglas and the CES production functions. Partial productivity indices of labour and capital would show efficiency in use of the factor inputs overtime. To throw light on overall efficiency in factor use, Kendrick, Solow and translog indices of total factor productivity have also been estimated.

Total factor productivity indices are based on the restrictive assumptions of perfect competition and constant returns to scale. For relaxing these assumptions, the estimated parameters of production function have also been worked out through regression analysis. The unrestricted Cobb-Douglas production function provides estimates of elasticities of output with respect to labour and capital, returns to scale and neutral technical progress. One of the major shortcomings of the Cobb-Douglas production function is that it assumes elasticity of substitution to be equal to one. Elasticity of substitution is an important parameter having empirical implications not only on the substitutability of factors but also on economic growth, income distribution and resource allocation. The conflict between the output growth and employment growth can be traced back to low substitutability of the production structure. Therefore, to overcome this drawback, side relations derived from the CES production function are also estimated. Here, elasticity of substitution can assume any constant value between 0 to ∞.

Although the State of Uttar Pradesh is one of the most backward states of the country, incessant efforts for development via industrialisation, particularly since the Fifth Plan are expected to have brought about significant structural changes in the State economy. And obviously because of this, efforts have been made to assess and analyse the development of organised industrial sector of State as well as the regional levels in terms of the trend growth rates of both the output and the employment. It may, however, be added that details of the methodology followed are given in the third chapter of 'Data Sources And Methodology' of the study.

4. SOURCES OF DATA

The present study is based on the data collected from secondary sources only, the chief one being the various issues of Annual Survey of Industrues published by the Government of Uttar Pradesh. Relevant data have also been compiled from the statistical Abstracts of Uttar Pradesh and various issues of Reserve Bank of India Bulletins. Besides, the other sources include various Plan documents of the Government of India and Uttar Pradesh and the relevant reports of the Economics and Statistics Division of the State Planning Institute, Lucknow.

5. ORGANISATION OF THE STUDY

The entire study is arranged in seven chapters. Having described the broad framework of the study in this introductory Chapter, the Chapter-II attempts to recapitulate various concepts of technological change, besides incorporating review of the literature available on the subject. A detailed description of the data sources, choice of variables and the methodology followed for measuring technological change is provided in the Chapter-III. The capital being major constraint in developing countries, efficient allocation of resources among competing ends is deemed to be most crucial. Therefore in the Chapter-IV, attempts have been made to shed light on the theoretical issues shaping investment pattern and analyse Plan allocations of outlays for development of the industrial sector in Uttar Pradesh. The Chapters V and VI constitute core of the study. Using the relevant econometric tools/models, the inter-relationship between the technological change and performance of the organised industrial sector including various industry groups at the State-level during the reference period is analysed in the Chapter-V. Whereas the Chapter-VI is mainly devoted to the analysis of the relationship between inter-regional differentials in technological change and those of the performance of the organised industrial sector as a whole in U.P. at the regional or disaggregative levels. Finally, the main conclusions emerging out of the analysis in various chapters alongwith meaningful policy implications are accommodated in the Chapter-VII.

CHAPTER 2

Technological Change: Recapitulation of the Concept

Economists have duly recognised the central role that technological change has to play in economic development. The importance of improvements in machinery was recognised way back in 1776 by Adam Smith in his *Wealth of Nations*. Subsequent classical economists also found it crucial to development. Malthus, for example, thought that production could increase through accumulation of capital, fertility of land and use of labour saving inventions. Similarly, Ricardo also felt that the invention of machines increases the amount of goods in a society and 'contributes very much to the ease and happiness of mankind'.[1] Despite these thoughts, the importance of technological change to growth remained secondary as compared to traditional inputs in the classical school of thought.

Marx, on the other hand, clearly recognised the importance of technical innovations in the development of capitalist system. Thus, he states in the *Communist Manifesto* that 'the bourgeoisie cannot exist without constantly revolutionising the instruments of production'.[2] Like Marx, Marshall also was very clear as far as the importance of technical progress is concerned. In his *Principles of Economics*, he conceived the importance of 'knowledge' as the chief engine of economic progress.[3] However, technological progress was brought to notice in the early twentieth century by the work of Schumpeter, who sought in it the explanation of the short term instability and long term dynamics of the capitalist system.[4] According to him, the 'fundamental impulse that sets and keeps and capitalist engine in motion comes from the new consumers' goods, the new methods of production or transportation, the new markets, the new forms of industrial organisation that capitalist enterprise creates'.[5]

Technological change has been used in several ways to describe a variety of phenomena; but two broad interpretations corresponding to macro and micro-fields can be outlined. First, the term is used to refer to the effects of changes in technology, or in other words, the role of technological progress in economic growth. Second, the term is used to refer to changes in technology itself, where technology can be defined as useful knowledge relating to art of production. Any change in this knowledge implies technological change. Hence, in its second form technological change includes knowledge creating activities of research and development, invention, innovation and the spread of technology depends upon its subsequent diffusion.[6]

1. EFFECTS OF CHANGES IN TECHNOLOGY

Technological change has been defined directly or indirectly in terms of its effects on productivities of inputs. Mansfield (1968, pp. 10-11) offers its direct definition as follows:

'Technological change is the advance of technology, such advance often taking the form of new methods of producing existing products, new designs which enable the production of products with important new characteristics and new techniques of organisation, marketing and management.'

However, technological change is, often, conceived through its indirect definition. Schumpeter (1939, pp. 87-88), to whom technological change was synonymous with innovation gives its indirect definition as: 'we will now define innovation more rigorously by means of the production function....This function describes the way in which quantity of products varies if quantity of factors vary. If, instead of quantities of factors we vary the form of the function, we have an innovation'. Schumpeter laid a great stress on discontinuous nature of technical progress, a process characterised by major breaks, giant discontinuties, which startle the society with their appearance.

An opposed to this is a school of though that lays emphasis on continuous nature of technical progress. A major proponent of this school is Usher (1954), who opines that major inventions emerge from cumulative synthesis of relatively simple inventions, each of which requires an individual 'act of insight'. Therefore, the continuously occurring large number of changes of small magnitude result in a single big change.

But Schumpeter's emphasis on major breakthroughs had a great impact on the entire generation of economists concerned with productivity and technological change. Compare, for example, the following definition given by Solow. 'I am using the phrase 'technical change' as a short hand expression for *any kind of shift in the production function*'.[7]

Testing empirically, with the tool of production function, various economists found technological change to be the most important source of output growth. But, what greatly proved to be decisive were the findings of Fabricant (1954), Abramovitz (1956) and Solow (1957). They found out that 80 to 90 percent of output growth per head in the U.S. economy could not be accounted for by increase in capital per head, thereby, giving this credit to technological change. Many other studies have also reached a similar conclusion. Denison (1962a), with a slightly dissimilar approach, where he decomposed the sources of growth into a large number of elements, also reached the conclusion that technological change is very important factor of growth. However, in his study technological change contributed only about 40 percent (as against 80-90 percent of above mentioned studies) of the total increase in per capita income. Analogously, almost the similar conclusions were arrived at by studies on some European economies.[8]

However, it would be wrong to ascribe this large contribution to technological progress alone, as there are some other factors also contributing to growth. These are technological progress in the narrow sense, economies of scale, external economies, improvements in health, education and the skill of the labour force, better management and the movement of labour force from low productivity to high productivity sectors. This is the reason why the names given to this group have ranged from 'output per unit of input', 'efficiency index', 'total factor productivity', 'change in productive efficiency', 'technical change', and the 'measure of our ignorance'. To emphasise the nature of this concept, it has also been called a 'residual'.[9]

Attempts were, therefore, made in the subsequent researches to firstly, disaggregate the residual factor, measuring the factor inputs in conventional manner; and secondly, labour and capital inputs were adjusted for changes in quality and composition so that much more measured growth could be attributed to increases in factor inputs.[10]

A major attempt on disaggregating the residual has been made by Denison (1962a, 1962b, 1967). He decomposed the sources of growth into a large number of elements. Apart from taking into account the contribution of factor inputs, factors affecting the quality of labour, such as, education, shorter work days, etc., were also incorporated. As identified by him, the importance of advances in knowledge and the role of economies of scale were the most significant findings in estimating the components of residual.

The second line of thought was carried out by making a distinction between the 'embodied' and 'disembodied' technical changes; between innovations that are incorporated in new capital goods and labour force and those that are not. Earlier, in the works of Solow, Abramovitz and others, the technological change was taken as a unexplained residual meaning, thereby, that it is disembodied. But, further researches led by Solow (1960) attempted to search for a solution where technological change is embodied in the latest vintage of capital (i.e. the current year investment). Analogously, technological change can be said to be embodied in the latest vintage of labour (i.e. improvements in the productive efficiency of new workers due to education, training, etc.).

Apart from making a distinction between 'embodied' and 'disembodied' technological changes, a distinction is also made between exogeneous (or autonomous) and endogeneous (or induced) innovations. The first view treats technical change as an unexplained phenomenon, an increase in production being simply attributed to the passage of time. In the endogeneous technical change, the expansion of technical possibilities is explained explicitly by one or more economic factors, such as, (a) long term changes in prices of the factors or production, (b) learning processes concerning production and (c) investment in education and research.[11]

Neo-classical economists viewed technological progress as an exogeneous variable treating it as 'manna from heaven'. But it was subsequently realised that 'technical progress does not occur by accident but through deliberate diversion of resources to activities which generate progress in pursuit of fame and profit, or both'.[12] In the modern growth models, Kaldor and Mirlees followed by others have tried to incorporate technological change as an endogeneous variable into the economic system. Kaldor and Mirlees (1962) have related technical advancement to capital accumulation where knowledge grows with learning which is related to investment, and thus, learning is made a function of proportionate rate of growth of investment. Arrow (1962), in his model, however, has made learning a function of past gross investments rather than the proportionate rate of growth of investment.

1.1 The Classification of Technological Change

Technological change can be classified into neutral and non-neutral. Some references to this classification can be traced back to Ricardo and Wicksell. Initially, Ricardo thought all technological changes to be neutral, but when he realised that these changes tend to boost up profit and reduce the wage fund, he came to the conclusion that capitalists and workers are differently affected by technological change. Wicksell also held the opinion that an increase in the total output as a result of technical change need not mean that marginal productivities of capital and labour increase at the same rate.[13]

The terms neutral, labour-saving and capital-saving technological changes were introduced by Pigou (1932, p. 674). However, these terms as defined by Hicks (1932), Harrod (1948) and Solow (1963), respectively, are more frequently used in the literature. According to Hicks, neutral technological change is one, in which marginal product of capital and labour increases at the same rate (so that K/L remains constant), whereas a labour saving technological change raises marginal product of capital more than that of labour and *vice versa*. In Harrod's case, technological change is neutral if capital-output ratio remains unchanged at a constant rate of profit. If capital-output ratio increases, a labour saving technological change has occurred and *vice versa*. Harrod's neutral technical change is said to be labour augmenting. Analogously, capital augmenting neutral technical progress has been suggested by Solow. Here labour-output ratio remains constant at a constant wage rate

2. CHANGES IN TECHNOLOGY

The changes in technology itself are brought about by the combination of activities of research, invention (or the knowledge creating activities), development and innovations (or the activities applying knowledge to production process), and the spread of technology depends upon the rate of its adoption and diffusion.

2.1 Research and Development

As already pointed out, research is the knowledge creating activity, whereas development is devoted to the capacity to produce. Research and development can be categorised into three branches: firstly, the basic research, that aims at the original investigations for advancement of scientific knowledge, without any commercial objectives; secondly, applied research that incorporates investigations which are directed towards the discovery of new scientific knowledge having specific commercial objectives with respect to products and processes; and finally, development that is directed towards the technical activities of non-routine nature concerned with translating research findings or other scientific knowledge into products and processes.[14]

Heavy expenditure on research and development is generally incurred by the developed countries, especially in the fields of applied research and development. The impact of research and development activity on growth is difficult to measure, many times failing to create anything new, but when successful, spectacular results are achieved.[15]

2.2 Inventions, Innovations and Diffusion

Inventions may be defined as new ways of attaining given ends. They would, therefore, include, the creation of things previously non-existent, using either new or existing knowledge; and also the creation of the things that have existed all the time, only these have to be discovered. Innovation, on the other hand, is the first commercial application of chosen invention. Early innovators will eventually be followed by the imitators in the same field. This is the third and the most important step of technological change, i.e., the 'diffusion' stage. Schumpeter has made a sharp distinction between invention, innovation and imitation, with the greater emphasis being laid on the innovation and the charismatic figure of the entrepreneur who against all odds takes the bold step to innovate.[16] To him innovation could take the form of a new product or a new process, opening up of new markets, the acquisition of new source of raw material, or a structural reorganisation of an industry.[17] Inventive activity has stood as an exogeneous factor outside his framework. One may trace the cause of this sharp distinction to the discontinuous nature of innovative activity which he emphasised, as the clustering of the innovations were at the heart of his business cycle theory.[18] However, if one looks at technological change as more or less a continuous process, the distinction between these stages becomes rather blurred.

The differences in the rate of technical change between different industries in an economy and between different economies depends upon the speed of initial adoption and the speed of diffusion. The most important hurdles to the use of new techniques are the cost of changing existing techniques, risk, ignorance, institutional factors, such as, patents, and sociological factors leading to a resistance to change.[19]

Enos (1962), Lynn (1962) and Mansfield (1961, 1962) in their empirical investigations found that on an average the time lag between an invention and innovation was 10 to 15 years, with mechanical innovations having the shortest time lag, and the electronic innovations having the longest. Consumer goods have a shorter time lag than the industrial ones. Furthermore, they also came to the conclusion that on an average the time lag between inventions and innovations seems to be shortening.

Diffusion generally is a lengthy process taking about twenty years or more on an average. The rate of imitation also varies to a great extent. In certain cases imitators may take scores of years to copy an innovation, whereas in other cases innovating firm is quickly followed by the imitators, thereby, shortening the diffusion process.[20]

3. TECHNOLOGICAL PROGRESS IN DEVELOPING COUNTRIES

In the context of developing countries, there has been, overtime, a shift in attention from questions like choice of technology, cost of transferring foreign technology, appropriateness of the transferred technology to the dynamic considerations of technological changes occurring within these countries. As already noted, economic literature on technological change has greatly been influenced by major innovations-the discontinuous nature of technological change-mainly advocated by Schumpeter. In the process, the importance of minor changes and improvements in the process of technology-the continuous or incremental kind of technological changes (generally occurring in the Third World countries) has been neglected.[21]

Increasing evidence indicates that technological change is occurring in developing countries in the form of (i) assimilation of technology (i.e. capability of the recipient to reproduce the entire technology); (ii) adaptation of technology (to local conditions, raw-materials, scales and skills, etc.); (iii) improvement of technology; (iv) generation of new technology; and (v) commercial export of locally generated technology.[22] In case of developing countries, technological activities are mainly confined to first three forms as compared tc the fourth one. Thus, the technological change occurring in developing countries tends to be mostly incremental kind rather than Schumpeterian frontier moving type. The cumulative significance of the incremental technological changes, however, should not be underestimated, as the rise of newly-industrialised countries would point out.[23] Therefore, when viewed from the perspective of manufacturing enterprise, technological progress 'covers everything from major innovations in products or processes to the adoption of new techniques innovated elsewhere and the improvement of existing techniques or products, to the raising of productivity of given techniques, by better management, organisation and 'learning by doing'.[24]

Empirical evidence, in case of developing countries, however, indicates that in contrast to the developed countries, technological change makes a smaller contribution to output growth as against the increases in the factor inputs, in majority of cases.[25] Apart from this, some studies on Indian economy[26] show that the contribution of technological change to output growth, compares poorly not only with the developed countries but also some developing countries.

Most of the studies with regard to Indian manufacturing sector paint a dismal picture. The trend is of the declining overall efficiency, constant returns to scale, unitary elasticity of substitution and absence of technical change for the period of 1946-64.[27] Only Hashim and Dadi (1973) in their study bring out a significant shift in the production function along with constant returns to scale for the same time period. However, some studies covering the period of 1946-58, found the evidence of significant economies of scale, high relative efficiency, increased capital deepening, presence of technological change and in some cases low elasticity of substitution.[28] Capital deepening was found to be accompanied by significant increases in labour productivity and a decline in capital productivity.

In the recent years, many studies have taken post-1965 period (it was around this period when a deceleration in industrial growth had taken place) also into consideration. Although a conflicting trend can be observed, majority of studies find deceleration in overall efficiency and the absence of technological change. Mehta (1980) (for the period of 1953-65 and 1965-70) in his study, finds evidence in favour of consant returns to scale, capital deepening and absence of any technical change. The detailed analysis brings out fairly satisfactory performance of industries with diversified product range, like bicycles, glass and glassware, and electrical fans, but there seems to have been a trend of overall decline in traditional industries, like cotton textiles, jute textiles, matches, and sugar.[29] Assumption of unitary elasticity of substitution did not hold for majority of industries studied. Results of similar type have been reported by Ahluwalia (1985), who empirically brought out the main causes of deceleration in industrial sector after 1965. Testing with different measures of total factor productivity, it was found that the average annual growth of TFP ranged from-0.2 percent per annum to-1.3 per cent per annum for the manufacturing sector as a whole. Further, the average annual growth of-0.3 percent and -0.1 percent was noticed for the period of 1959-65 and 1965-78, respectively. As for as the industry-wise analysis is concerned, excepting footwear and furniture and fixtures, the decline in efficiency has been more or less across the board.

Analogously to Hashim and Dadi, Goldar (1986) in his study finds significant technological progress accompanied by constant returns to scale and unitary elasticity of substitution for aggregate manufacturing sector for the period of 1951-65. The average annual growth rate in TFP turned out to be about 1.3 percent. Corresponding estimates for ASI large scale sector for the period of 1959-79 turned out to be almost similar. In contrast to the popular belief, he did not find appreciable decline in the TFP after 1965. A decline in the growth rates of labour productivity and capital intensity and a reversal of the declining trend of capital productivity after 1970, were the important findings of this study. The production function estimates were broadly consistent with the results based on the TFP indices.

That there was not any significant decline in TFP after 1965, was also upheld in the studies of Rajalakshmi (1983) and Alai-Parviz (1987). Parviz finds manufacturing sector to be dominated by the industries having positive TFP index for the period of 1973-79. On the other hand, Rajalakshmi (for the period of 1960-73) finds a decline in TFP index during 1960-66, thereafter showing an increasing tendency (for 1966-73), thereby proving otherwise the decline in overall efficiency in the post-1965 period.

It would clearly be evident from the above review that while much work has been done on measuring the contribution of technological change in the growth process (the macro aspect), little has been done to study the process of technological change itself (i.e., the studies on research and development, invention, innovation and diffusion-or the micro aspect), more so in the context of India, owing mainly to the paucity of data.[30]

To measure the contribution of technological progress to growth, various elements of technological progress need to be estimated empirically. The four elements of technological change are:

(i) *The technical efficiency of production:* Any increases in this leads to reduction in the quantities of all factors used in producing the unit output. In other words, application of better techniques makes possible more output with the help of lesser inputs.

(ii) *The scale of operation of production:* There would be increasing, decreasing and constant returns to scale depending upon whether output increases more, less or in equal proportion to a proportionate change in inputs. These two elements form neutral technological change, i.e., they are independent of the ratio of marginal productivities of the factors.

(iii) *The bias of technological change:* or the change in factor intensity occurs if the new technique leads to greater saving in one input as compared to the other; and

(iv) *The elasticity of substitution:* measures the ease with which the factors can be substituted for each other. The extent of substitutability delineates the range of alternatives that labour abundant (capital scarce) developing countries face in the organisation of production.[31]

The change in one or all of the elements overtime constitutes a technical change. One can measure technological change either through productivity ratios or through production function approach. While TFP indices measure only one element of technological change i.e. the technical efficiency of production, all the elements can be measured directly by estimating the parameters of the production function only. The detailed discussion of the methods of measuring technological change has been carried out separately in the Chapter-III of the study.

References

1. Quoted in A. Heertje (1977), p.11.
2. Quoted in N. Rosenberg (1982), p.9.
3. A. Heertje, (1977), pp. 91-93.
4. B.N. Goldar (1986), p.1.
5. Quoted in A. Heertje (1977), p.99.
6. C. Kennedy and A.P. Thirlwall (1972), p.12.
7. R.M. Solow (1957), reprinted in N. Rosenberg (ed.) (1971), p.345. For a similar definition see V. Ruttan (1956), p.61.
8. For Norway, Finland, and Great Britain see respectively the studies of O. Aukrust and J. Bjerke (1959); O. Niitamo (1958); and W.B. Reddaway and A.D. Smith (1960).

9. E.D. Domar (1961), p.709.
10. A.P. Thirwall (1983), p.69.
11. A. Heerje (1977), p.174.
12. C. Kennedy and A.P. Thirlwall (1972), p.13.
13. A. Heertje (1977), pp.161-62.
14. C. Kennedy and A.P. Thirlwall (1972) p.44.
15. *Ibid.*, p.45.
16. J. Schumpeter (1939), p.103-104; and (1928); reprinted in N. Rosenberg (1971), pp.31-34.
17. J. Schumpeter (1934), p.66.
18. N. Rosenberg (1976), p.67.
19. C. Kennedy and A.P. Thirlwall (1972), p.58.
20. E. Mansfield (1961), reprinted in N. Rosenberg (ed.) (1971), pp.286-87.
21. The importance of incremental technical change is clearly brought out in studies by Usher (1954); Enos (1962); and Hollander (1965).
22. S. Lall (1981), p.134.
23. The changes in the conceptualisation of the process of technical change in the Third World countries have directly been influenced by the changes in theoretical paradigms. More specifically, four factors that combined to produce the change are (i) the decline of dependency theory (ii) the decline of neo-classical theory (iii) the rise of newly-industrialised (or semi-industrial) countries; and (iv) the emergence of new paradigm, emphasising major as well as incremental technical change, aptly labelled neo-Schumpeterian. This approach, however, seems still to be in the pre-paradigmatic stage as much as empirial work on this has not been done. For details see Martin Fransman (1986), pp.59-64.
24. S. Lall (1981), p.134.
25. Some of the important studies are A. Maddison (1970); H. Bruton (1967); S. Robinson (1971); and M.I. Nadiri (1972). For details see A.P. Thirlwall (1983), pp.76-80.
26. For comparison see I.J. Ahluwalia (1985), p.134-135; and (1986), p.7.
27. Raj Krishna and S.S. Mehta (1968); A. Banerji (1975); J.C.H. Fie and G. Ranis (1964); P. Zarembka (1972); D. Gujarati (1966); M.M. Dutta (1955) V.V. Murty and V.K. Sastry (1957); D. Dutta Majumdar (1966); G.V.L. Narasimham and M.Z. Fabrycy (1974); M.G.K. Reddy and S.V. Rao (1962).
28. R.K. Diwan and D. Gujarati (1968); Yeong Her Yeh (1966); R.K. Diwan (1967); U. Sankar (1970); I.L. Sakong and G.V.L. Narasimham (1974).
29. A. Banerji (1975), also finds the sluggish growth rates of traditional industries like cotton and jute textiles, whereas paper, bicycle and sugar showed significant growth for the period 1946-64.
30. Since the technical change process (i.e. changes in the way in which inputs are transformed into outputs) itself is not being measured, the methods measuring technical change indirectly are not able to throw light on the causes of such change. See Martin Fransman (1986), p. 28-31.
31. P.A. Yotopoulos and J.B. Nugent (1976), p. 64.

CHAPTER 3

Data Sources and Methodology

The socio-economic development of an area is influenced by a large number of factors operating in an economy. Some of these factors are tangible while some other are intangible. The choice of these factors is subjected to data availability. Therefore, to fully understand and measure the contribution of individual inputs, and the factors other than the inputs like technical change or better utilisation of existing resources, it is essential to procure data on output and inputs particularly those concerning capital and labour. The data on wages paid to the labour is also needed, besides appropriate price deflators to be used for making the time series data comparable.

The present study covers the period from 1974-75 to 1985-86. Main sources of data are the various issues of 'Annual Survey of Industries' published by the Government of India as well as the Government of Uttar Pradesh. The gross value added at constant prices is selected as a measure of output. The total number of employees (including workers and persons other than workers) is considered as labour input, and value of gross fixed assets at constant prices is used as a measure of capital input.

This chapter is divided into two main sections. The first section describes, in detail, the data sources and definitions of different variables under consideration. Besides, the types of adjustment and changes required to be made in these variables to suit our study have also been discussed in this section. Whereas the second section deals with the methodology followed for conduct of the present study, especially the methods for measuring the technological change.

1. DATA SOURCES AND SELECTED VARIABLES

Although the period of this study starts from 1974-75, the data on fixed capital and depreciation have been procured from 1961 onwards to arrive at a benchmark estimate of capital stock, whereas data on other variables have been taken from 1974-75 onwards.

It is seen that the data on registered factories are being published almost regularly since 1946. Such data from 1946 to 1958 were published in the report entitled 'Census of Manufacturing Industries', conducted under the Industrial Statistics Act, 1942, and the Census of Manufacturing Industries Rules, 1945, framed thereunder.

From 1959 onwards, there has been a continuous flow of data through 'Annual Survey of Industries' (ASI), conducted under the Collection of Statistics Act, 1953, and the Collection of Statistics (Central) Rules, 1959, framed thereunder. It covers all the factories registered under section 2(m) of the Factories Act, 1948. However, the factories under the control of Defence Ministry, oil storage depots and technical training institutes are left out. Section 2(m) of the Factories Act, 1948 is further sub-divided into two parts, i.e., 2(m).1 and 2 (m). 2. Section 2(m). 1 refers to (i) factories employing 50 or more workers with the aid of power, and (ii) factories employing 100 or more workers without the aid of power. Section 2(m). 2 refers to (i) factories employing 10 to 49 workers with the aid of power, and (ii) factories employing 20 to 99 workers without the aid of power. The factories falling under section 2(m). 1 are completely enumerated, forming Census Sector of ASI, and the factories comprising section 2(m). 2 form the Sample Sector of ASI.

However, certain factories left out of the Sample Sector were found to be very important at the State level. To overcome this shortcoming, Economics and Statistics Division of the State Planning Institute, Uttar Pradesh started collecting data on those factories under section 2(m). 2 which did not form the sample factories at the National level. Therefore, from 1961 to 1965 a report entitled 'Census of Industrial Output', was brought out which provided decentralised information collected both at the National level regarding the State and also that collected by the State government on its own.

From 1967 onwards, it was decided that the Directorate of Economics and Statistics, Lucknow be put on the job to collect information for all such factories registered under section 2(m) of the Factories Act, 1948, for which the Government of India is not collecting any data. Hence, From 1967 onwards ASI Reports are being published regularly (except 1972-73) by Economics and Statistics Division, Uttar Pradesh. The information/data of registered factories procured by both the Central and the State governments, are provided for whole of the State and also for different districts.

Overtime, there has been a change in the reference period of these reports. Prior to 1967, the reference period used was a calendar year, except for Sugar where the year ending 30th June was adopted. From 1967 onwards, the reference period changed to an accounting year starting from 1st April to 31st March.

The ASI definitions of different variables relevant for this study are as follows: *Fixed capital* includes factory land and improvements on it and other construction, building, plant and machinery, miscellaneous assets like furniture and fixtures, fittings, transport equipment, tools and other fixed assets having a normal productive age of more than a year and assets under construction/installation. The data on capital are given in terms of book values of capital assets net of cumulative depreciation.

Data regarding the *persons employed* are given in the form of average daily employment. These are divided into workers and persons other than workers. A *worker* is defined as a person employed, directly or through an agency, whether for wages or not, in any manufacturing process or in cleaning any part of machinery or premises used for a manufacturing process, or in any other kind of work, incidental to, or connected with the manufacturing process. *Persons other than workers* include persons holding supervisory and managerial positions, clerks in administrative office, stores and welfare section, watch and ward staff. Apart from workers and persons other than workers, total employees also include unpaid working proprietors (in case of cooperative factory, working members), family workers, etc. (if paid these are included in the categories of workers or persons other than workers).

Remuneration to employees is given under two heads; wages and salaries and total emoluments. Data on both heads are provided for workers as well as total employees (except some years when data on total emoluments are given for total employees only). Besides wages and salaries and bonus, total emoluments include imputed value of benefits in kind, old age benefits, social security and other benefits.

Value added by manufacture is derived by deducting total inputs and depreciation from total output. *Gross ex-factory value of output* comprises value of products and by-products, net value of semi-finished goods, value of industrial or non-industrial services rendered to others and net balance of goods sold in the same condition as purchased, etc. This is net of excise duty paid or sales tax realised (by the factory on behalf of government), transport charges from factory and selling agents commission. *Total input* includes power, fuel and materials consumed, and work done for the factory by other concerns. Inputs are inclusive of transportation charges, agents commission, taxes and duties. *Depreciation* is calculated at the rates allowed by income tax authorities for assessing taxable income. This rate varies according to the type of asset and industry.

Data are available, in detail, for different industry groups which can be aggregated to arrive at two digit industry group-wise classification.[1] The required data have been procured for the period of the study from the various issues of ASI, published by Economics and Statistics Division, U.P., for total manufacturing sector[2] and twenty industry groups at the State level.[3] To get the data of different variables for the manufacturing sector as a whole[4] at the regional level, district-wise data was compiled and aggregates at regional level were worked out.

Apart from the above variables, the data on price indices for deflation purposes were taken from different sources. The Wholesale Price Index of Uttar Pradesh needed to deflate gross value added series was taken from various issues of Statistical Abstracts published by Economics and Statistics Division, State Planning Institute of U.P. Gross fixed capital series was deflated by Price Index of Machinery and Transport Equipment (prepared by the office of the Economic Advisor, Government of India) procured from the Reserve Bank of India Bulletins. To deflate the series of total emoluments, data on Consumer Price Index Number for Industrial Workers in Kanpur,[5] prepared by the Labour Bureau, Government of India were also taken from various issues of Statistical Abstracts.

1.1 Measurement of Output

Output measurement, like other economic aggregates, poses a serious problem due to the extreme heterogeneity of items constituting it. Being valued upon the current market prices, however, simplifies the index number problems associated with output measurement.[6]

As a measure of output, a choice arises between gross output and value added. However, value added figure is generally preferred, as it is felt that gross output varies widely with the changes in the stages of productive process of an industry. Further, for making comparison between firms, industries and even countries, value added figure is found to be more meaningful.[7] It also facilitates aggregation of output across industries. It has also been observed that in case of productivity studies, the choice of gross output will make it necessary to include 'material' as an independent variable in the production function. In such a case, almost all the variation in output in explained by 'material' with labour, capital and technical change having almost little or no role to play.[8]

Once the concept of value added is finally selected, the question of making choice between net value added and gross value added arises. In case of productivity analysis, 'a theoretically more appealing measure of output might be value added by manufacture, which could be net of depreciation'.[9] Denison (1969 p.2) in a similar vein argued in favour of net measure. However, it is very difficult to get a measure of true capital consumption. In case of Indian data, there are further reasons against the use of net measure. Depreciation accounting methods vary between industries and the depreciation figures reported in the data sources are at the rates allowed by income tax authorities being seldom representative of the true deprectiation.[10]

Taking into account the above mentioned arguments, the choice boils down to gross value added as a measure of output.[11] Gross value added is obtained by combining the figures of value added and depreciation as reported in the data sources.

To arrive at the value added measure at constant prices, the yearly figures valued at current prices were deflated by the Wholesale Price Index of relevant commodities.[12] Single deflation was prefered to double deflation,[13] because choice of an appropriate index for 'materials', considering its severe heterogeneity is a difficult task.[14]

The Wholesale Price Indices published by Economics and Statistics Division of the State Planning Institute, Lucknow are based on 1970-71 prices and are available from 1977-78. This required necessary changes to have the time series data for our purposes based on constant prices of 1974-75. To shift the base from 1970-71 to 1974-75, the price index series based on 1970-71 prices was divided every year since 1974-75 with the Wholesale Price Index of 1974-75, such that 1974-75 = 100. Secondly, for obtaining the price index before 1977-78, the index number series was extrapolated backward to cover three years of 1974-75 to 1976-77 on the basis of the industry group-wise Wholesale Price Index of India (See Appendix Table-3.1).

1.2 Measurement of Labour

In comparison to capital, the measurement of labour is less complex due to the existence of physical measures like employment and man-hours. Therefore, the problem of converting values into constant terms does not arise. Besides, the problem of depreciation also does not figure unless one thinks of efficiency deteriorating seriously with age[15].

From various data sources, we get information on manhours, workers, persons other than workers and total employees (including workers and persons other than workers). A choice has to be made among various measures. Denison (1961) disfavours the use of manhours data for assessing the contribution of labour to production. According to him, output per man varies less than ouput per manhour with changes in hours as a result of which the former gets crudely adjusted for one form of quality change-the quality of an hour's work that is due to shortening of hours. There are further reasons for not using the manhours data; the data reported in ASI has been arrived at by simply multiplying the number of workers in a shift by eight and then aggregating the product across industries.[16] In addition, the manhours data for the period considered in the present study have not been reported in ASI for Uttar Pradesh.

Total employees including both workers (i.e. direct labour) and persons others than workers such as supervisors, technicians, managers, clerks, etc. (i.e. indirect labour) have been taken to be a measure of labour input in the present study. The choice of the above measure is justifiable on the ground that indirect labour is as important as the direct labour so far as getting the work done is concerned.[17] However, the choice of above measure is based on the assumption that direct and indirect labour are perfect substitutes. This is a shortcoming of our measure. The chosen measure of labour input has not been corrected for quality changes (due to age, sex, education, etc.) owing to mainly paucity of such data at the State level. Besides, these adjustment are said to embody large and arbitrary elements of choice in them.[18]

1.3 Measurement of Capital

Capital's important role in production and distribution brings it at centre-stage of every sphere of economic activity. Capital, as generally used in economic theory, has two wide interpretations: firstly, as individuals command over resources in the financial sense, and secondly, as a factor of production, being produced by the economic system and itself helping in the production of further goods.[19] In the sense of a factor of production, capital consists of a multitude of heterogeneous capital goods with specific characteristics (due to impermanence, longevity, productive qualities, etc.). Aggregation of heterogeneous capital goods directly poses serious problems. Their values, however, can be aggregated. Capital is, therefore, measured indirectly in terms of its value. Valuation of capital goods being different from the valuation of other economic goods, is more complex.[20] Difference of opinion as far as aggregation of capital is concerned has led to much confusion and controversy in the capital theory. It has been aptly stated by Bliss, 'when economists reach agreement on the theory of capital they will shortly reach agreement on everything else'.[21]

A distinct role of capital in production was recognised from the time of Physiocrats. Classical economists, while recognising the importance of capital in production, did not consider it equal to other factors of production (i.e., land and labour). Capital was used in the sense of money capital, containing capital goods that were needed as an advance to make labour more productive. Therefore, the notion of advances was used as an aggregate, although in a loose manner, with an awareness of the heterogeneity of the capital goods that assisted labour in time consuming production.[22]

A more precise form to the classical theory was given by the development of temporal theory of production by Austrian neo-classical economists. Money capital was required to be invested in time consuming production process. Bohm Bawerk, also did not consider capital, an intermediate factor, to be equal to other factors of production. It was only seen to be embodied in the original factors in the realisation of final product. Although capital itself was not considered to be productive, its use made possible the processes that are productive. Degree of roundaboutness to the Austrian neo-classicals was an indicator of the level of capital intensity of productive processes.

Among the neo-classicals, it was only Wicksell who best understood the problem of working with the value of capital as a factor of production alongwith the physically specified factors of land and labour,[23] because capital and rate of interest enter as a cost in the production of capital goods themselves. He tried to overcome this problem by measuring capital in terms of dated services of original factors.

Wicksell's analytical insight was ignored by his contemporaries as well as his successors of the neo-classical school. The non-Austrian neo-classical economists abandoned the advances view of capital, and some like Clark and Knight completely sacrificed the heterogeneity of capital goods together with time element in production, and developed an atemporal theory of production based on the concept of capital value, or money capital.[24]

This formed the basis of highly microeconomic, static, 20th century neo-classical (also called neo-neo-Classical) growth theory. Whenever the dynamic problems cropped up, they were sorted out with the help of aggregate (macroeconomic) production function which was a logical analogy to the microeconomic production function. As a measure of aggregate capital, recourse was taken to Clark-Knight concept of capital as a homogeneous and amorphous mass. To arrive at a concept of capital as a fairly homogeneous entity which could assume physical form best suited to other variables of production function, highly restrictive assumptions of perfect competition and foresight, independence of quantity of capital from relative prices and distribution of income were made. The necessary conditions required to be satisfied for aggregating variables are (i) the rate of substitution between capital goods for different types be independent of quantity of labour used with them, and (ii) that the marginal rate of substitution between and two types of capital must be constant, i.e., two types of capital are perfect substitutes.[25] These conditions ensure the malleability requirement of capital in aggregate production function. However, if these conditions do not hold and the marginal rate of substitution between two units of the same input change with the change in amount of other factors employed with it and if different types of machines are complementary, as happens quite often in the real World, neo-classical aggregation principle will hardly hold.[26]

Even if one accepts the neo-classical notion of real homogeneous capital, there still remains the problem of establishing a unique link between real value of capital and the quantity of capital in the sense of a productive agent. This is sought to be achieved in the neo-classical scheme through market equilibrium conditions, making for a clear functional relationship between the value and the real magnitude of the factors. The typical cases are the equality of factor prices with their respective marginal products.[27]

It was against the neo-classical concept of aggregate capital that the controversy in capital theory arose, particularly since the publication of Joan Robinson's article in 1953. She alongwith others at the Cambridge School (England), proved that outside the confines of one all-purpose commodity world it is impossible to construct an index of the quantity of capital. In the real world comprising heterogeneous goods, capital is essentially a value concept. It is not, therefore, independent of distribution and relative prices. Current relative prices change with distribution, leading to revaluation of the capital stock (so that the same physical capital represents different values, whereas the different capital goods can have the same value).[28] In his pioneering work Sraffa (1960), conclusively proves the futility of measuring capital in a unit independent of distribution and relative prices.

Further, the neo-classical belief that different production processes can be brought into a continuous ordering in terms of capital intensity along the scale of variation of the rate of interest (i.e. the linearity of the wage-interest frontier) may not always hold true. Joan Robinson (1953-54), Champernowne (1953-54) and, particularly Sraffa (1960), have proved that capital being essentially a value concept, the price frontier may be curvilinear in which there is a possibility of reswitching of techniques so that the same technique of production is profitable at more than one rate of interest.[29] If this is the case, then the possibility of measuring capital in physical units does not hold, making the neo-classical concept of factor intensity and aggregate production function invalid.

The problems outlined above led many economists to measure capital in terms of other factors. Drawing on Wicksell, Joan Robinson (1953-54) measured capital in terms of dated labour time, though this measure itself is not independent of distribution and prices. Solow (1963) by making the rate of return on investment central to the theory of capital, tries to avoid measurement problem and the assumptions linked to it. To provide sounder theoretical basis to the neo-classical production theory, Samuelson (1962) developed surrogate (as if) production function and surrogate capital. On the basis of this function, conclusions similar to those drawn on the basis of certain hetergeneous capital models can be derived. However, this function is based on certain very restrictive assumptions, besides failing to hold in case of curvilinear wage-interest frontier.

These criticisms do limit the usefulness of neo-classical theory, but these are truly speaking only 'theoretical worries, the practical significance of which is minimal. None is so damaging as to suggest the abandonment of the function'.[30]

(i) *Empirical Issues in Capital Measurement:* As already indicated, the only possible measure of capital is in terms of its value. Broadly, two approaches to capital measurement can be followed. Capital can either be measured in terms of its contribution to production (the forward looking concept) or in terms of cost (the backward looking concept).

Mostly used in the studies of embodied technical change, the first method incorporates the increases in the efficiency of capital as a result of technical advance in the measure of capital input.[31] Accurate measurement through this method may be problematic, as separating net contribution of capital to production from various other influences present simultaneously, is a difficult task. By following the second method, increases in the quality of capital are reflected in the technical progress term rather than in the measure of the capital input.[32] Strongly favouring cost method, Joan Robinson argues that 'to treat capital as a quantity of labour time expended in the past is congenial to the production function point of view, for it corresponds to the essential nature of capital regarded as a factor of production'.[33] Denison (1957) also advocates the use of cost method for productivity measurement.

In the cost method, the index of real capital stock is derived by obtaining the value of capital stock in a particular year at some selected base year prices. This measures the amount it would cost in the base year to produce the actual stock of capital goods existing in that particular year. Similarly, gross additions to the capital stock and capital consumption are also valued in terms of base year costs.[34]

However, problems are faced while making use of this method for estimating the capital on account of price changes and technological changes. Construction of an appropriate price index for deflation purposes leads to serious difficulties. The main problem is faced in separating design improvement from the changes in the cost of production as the former have to be excluded from the quantity of capital. Technical change also causes severe index number problems. While it is possible to reproduce today the capital goods of the past, reverse may not hold true due to the lack of necessary technical knowledge, skills, etc. Therefore, the incomparability that arises an account of technological change invalidates the notion that real capital can be measured by what it would cost in the base year to produce a given years stock.[35] However, for the estimation of capital, this method is the only one that is statistically feasible and for which the estimates exist.[36]

Having decided on the approach to be followed, one has to make a choice between the net or gross stock as a measure of capital. Most economists advocate the use of gross stock as it is felt that obsolescence rather than physical deterioration is the major cause of depreciation.[37] Capital goods remain productive even after becoming economically obsolete. The use of net measure is based on the assumption that the depreciation allowance exactly reflect the productivity decline of the assets. A study on the manufacturing sector of U.K. by Tibor Barna (1961) lends support to this view. It was found out that capital goods are maintained in a good condition until a decision is taken to scrap them. Kennedy and Thirlwall (1972; p.30) favouring gross measure, argue that 'the measures of capital which are net at constant prices and which exclude improvements in efficiency, with or without adjustments in capacity utilisation, will tend to underestimate the contribution of capital to growth.'[38] Furthermore, in the cost method, the efficiency improvements are excluded from the measure of capital stock, therefore, there is no logic in carefully taking into account efficiency decline through ageing.[39] In case of underdeveloped countries, the use of gross measure is all the more justified, because, as has been pointed out by Rosen, capital stock is often used at approximately constant level of efficiency for a period far beyond the accounting life measured by normal depreciation until it is eventually discarded or sold for a scrap.[40]

The use of the gross stock of capital is also based on an unrealistic assumption of constant efficiency of capital assets throughout their lifetime. The usual choice is still in favour of the gross stock on account of the fact that correct index of capital services will generally be closer to the gross stock than to the net stock index.[41]

What has so far not been borne in mind is that in the study of technological change it is not the stock of capital but the services that have to be treated as a factor of production. Extreme difficulty in measuring the capital services leaves us only with the choice of 'a less utopian estimate of stock of capital goods in existence'[42] as a proxy. It is however noticeable that 'what belongs to a production function is capital in use, not capital in place.'[43] Therefore, capital stock in existence should be corrected for the degree of utilisation. Solow and some other economists have used the percentage of workforce unemployed as a measure of underutilisation of capital stock. This approach has been criticised, particularly by Kennedy and Thirlwall (1972, p.29) who feel that the percentage of workforce unemployed may not always be repersentative of the underutilisation of capital. Further, it is also felt that 'there is no adequate substitute for a direct measure of unemployed capital'.[44] Kendrick (1973, p.26) does not favour adjustment of capital stock for the rates of utilisation prefering these to be reflected in the changes in productivity ratios because, capital stock, unlike labour force, is available for the productive use always. Denison (1974, p.56) also does not favour such adjustment. Besides, the available estimates of capacity utilisation for Indian manufacturing are not suitable for productivity analysis.[45]

There still remains the problem of whether capital measure should include working capital or not. In other words, should total productive capital or total fixed capital be taken as a measure of capital input. Latter concept has been used in many studies on Indian manufacturing.[46] On this question, Rosen (1959, p.43) is of the view that 'the relation of working capital to industrial output and growth is far less influenced by technological factors (especially the substitutability of labour and capital) than the relationship of fixed investment to output'. Similarly, Sinha and Sawhney (1970 p.19) argued that 'while the importance of working capital to industrial productivity cannot be denied, the inventory and cash holdings are more often determined by supply and market expectations than technological pipeline requirements and have, therefore, far less bearing on productivity than fixed investment.' Apart from these theoretical argument, the peculiar composition of working capital makes it very difficult to arrive at suitable price index for applying price corrections to such data.[47]

(ii) *Available Estimates of Capital Input for Uttar Pradesh:* Total stock of fixed assets at a particular time may be measured either through direct approach[48] or alternatively, through the use of Perpetual Inventory Method (PIM).[49] Considering the feasibility aspect, the use of the latter approach is made in the present context. Two variants of PIM exist, of which the first consists of constructing a fairly long time series of capital formation at base year prices and cumulating the figures year by year. Second variant consists of obtaining the estimates of the bench-mark capital stock at the base period prices and then carrying it backwards or forward on the basis of the estimated capital formation at the base year prices. Therefore, to prepare the series of capital input through PIM, one requires (i) the estimate of bench-mark capital stock at constant prices or fairly long series of capital formation at constant prices on the basis of which bench-mark estimate can be prepared, and (ii) yearly figures of gross fixed capital formation for the period under consideration at the base period prices.

At all India level, estimates of both gross and net capital stock[50] for different points of time, as well as a long series of both gross and net capital formation,[51] is easily available. Problems faced in the estimation of capital formation at the State level is an important cause of shortage of such information. The only approach feasible for measuring gross fixed capital formation at the State level is expenditure approach.[52] However, this approach too is not without difficulties, as it may not always be easy to estimate the State-wise expenditure.[53]

Some attempts have, however, been made to provide estimate of both capital stock and capital formation at the State level including Uttar Pradesh. Net capital stock estimates for registered manufacturing based on ASI data have been provided by R.H. Dholakia (1979) for 1960-61 and 1970-71. Asset-wise (not sector-wise) series of gross capital formation for the State covering the period of 1960-61 to 1972-73 have been prepared by R.N. Lal (1977). Similarly, the estimates of net capital formation have been prepared by the Perspective Planning Division of the State Planning Institute, Uttar Pradesh.[54]

However, it is hardly possible to make use of the above estimates in the present study for several reasons. Net capital stock estimates by Dholakia and net capital formation estimates of the State Planning Institute could not be used, as gross fixed capital has been taken as a measure of capital input in our study. Depreciation, as given in the data sources is not indicative of true capital consumption, but the above studies have relied on the data of depreciation as given in ASI. Lal's estimates have not been used primarily for two reasons; (i) sector-wise information is not available (ii) time period covered is not sufficient to prepare even the estimate of bench-mark capital stock. Besides, these studies provide information for the manufacturing sector at the State level, while this study requires estimates at the disaggregative level also.

(iii) *Methodology for Capital Estimation in the President Study:* Efforts have, therefore, been made here to prepare own estimates of bench-mark capital stock and the fixed capital series based on this, for the total manufacturing sector at the State and regional levels and for twenty industry groups. Gross fixed capital stock at constant prices has been taken as a measure of capital input in the present study. However, what is reported in ASI represents the depreciated book value of capital assets. In other words, ASI fixed capital data for any particular year represents a simple aggregation of expenditure on capital assets, valued at historical prices and adjusted for corresponding annual depreciation charges. Therefore, for any meaningful economic analysis, these figures need to be adjusted simultaneously for both price change as well as arbitrary depreciation charges.[55]

In this case PIM is used to work out estimates of the capital input series. To this end, it was invariably needed to have estimates of the capital stock of the bench-mark year at constant prices and the gross investment series at the constant prices of the base year for the subsequent years. The figures of the fixed capital for 1974-75 pertaining to total manufacturing sector at State and regional levels, as well as for twenty industry groups compiled from ASI give us the depreciated book value of assets at the end of 1974-75. This includes capital goods of different vintages purchased at different points of time. Estimating the replacement value of these assets from their book value requires (i) an estimate of cumulative deprecation to get an estimate of gross fixed assets at purchase prices, and (ii) an idea of the time pattern of the acquisition of these assets for making appropriate price adjustments.[56]

To meet the first requirement, it was essential to know the ratio of gross-net fixed assets for the year 1974-75. Therefore the combined balance-sheet of 1650 public limited companies classified into different industry groups were obtained from the RBI Bulletin. Further, from these, the gross net ratios were compiled. The classification of the industry groups in these balance sheets suited the requirement of the study as it more or less corresponded to ASI two digit level classification. Besides, the ratio of the nearest industry, in the sense of product and process, was applied to the other industry for which the ratio was not available.[57] Here, it is to be noted down that the ratios available from the above source pertain to all-India level and their use without some adjustment would be unjustified.[58] However, as no such information was available at the State level, the gross-net ratios of all-India level were alternatively used, of course, with some crude adjustments.[59] The ratios, thus obtained, were applied to the book value figures for working out estimates of gross fixed assets at purchase prices existing at the end of the year, 1974-75. The ratios of gross-net fixed assets for the total manufacturing sector at the State level were also applied to the total manufacturing sector of all the five economic regions of the state. Further, necessary adjustments were made in these ratios before using them for different industry groups.

Regarding the second problem, it was necessary to know about the time pattern of the acquisition of fixed assets. However, no such information was available at the State level. It is only the report on 'Growth of Factories in Uttar Pradesh' authored by R.C. Pandey (1952), which indicated that mostly traditional industries existed in U.P. prior to independence. In the absence of reliable data base, the actual amount of capital invested in various factories of Uttar Pradesh, for the period prior to independence could not be procured from the said report. However, considering the backwardness of the State, is was safely assumed that the existing assets of the year 1974-75 might have been acquired only after the initiation of the First Five Year Plan, i.e., 1951.[60] This has enabled us to further assume that the existing assets of 1974-75, thus, have a life of 23 Years. Thus, there remains the problem of converting these figures to 1974-75 prices. As in some other studies, the assets acquired before 1974-75 might have been inflated by the average price index of 1951 to 1973-74, but, as pointed out earlier, the book value figure of the Year 1974-75 represented an assortment of capital goods acquired over the past years. Hence applying a blanket price correction to that figure would not have solved the problem.[61] Keeping the availability of data in mind, a two-step procedure was, therefore, applied for the price adjustment of bench-mark capital stock. As mentioned earlier in the section of data sources, the industry-wise data for Uttar Pradesh for the years 1951 to 1960 was available from CMI and thereafter from ASI. Owing to incomparability on account of classification and coverage at the levels of total manufacturing sector, as well as industry groups, the data from CMI were not taken. However, from 1961 to 1974-75, the year-wise data of capital and depreciation was compiled from ASI for total manufacturing sector of U.P. and also for five economic regions and twenty industry groups. From the yearly data, the net additions to capital stock (by subtracting the capital data for the year (t-1) from the capital data of the year (t)) were calculated for 1962 to 1974-75.[62] The depreciation figures of the corresponding years were added to these net additions to obtain gross annual additions. These were, then, inflated by the respective yearly price indices (1974-75=100) to arrive the gross additions at 1974-75 prices. There still remains the problem of price adjustment of gross assets acquired between 1951 to 1961.[63] The year wise data for the above mentioned period were not available since the data source for these years was CMI and the reasons of not procuring data from this source have already been pointed out. In order, therefore, to have the knowledge of the gross value of fixed assets at purchase prices existing in 1961, the cumulative total value of annual gross additions at purchase prices made during the period 1962 to 1974-75 was deducted from the estimated gross stock of assets at purchase prices existing in 1974-75.[64] Again the use of average price index for inflating these assets may not be correct, but the price index from 1952 to 1961 (Appendix Table-3.2) shows that the yearly behaviour of prices indices has remained almost the same with some minor variations in latter three years. As a result, the use of average price index of 1952-61 (base 1974-75) is not expected to yield significantly different estimates from yearly price adjustments. Therefore, pre-1962 assets were inflated by average price index of 1952-1961[65] in order to arrive at the gross value of fixed capital assets acquired before 1962 at 1974-75 prices. Further, to this figure gross investments for 1962 to 1974-75 (at 1974-75 prices) were added so as to arrive at the base year capital stock at current prices for total manufacturing sector at the State and the regional levels and also for twenty industry groups.

For the second step of PIM, it was required to have the estimate of gross investments for subsequent years of the study at the constant/base year prices. As already shown, from the book values of 1974-75 to 1985-86, at first, the net investment figures, by subtracting previous years capital stock from the present years capital stock, were obtained. The depreciation figures of the corresponding years were added to these figures to arrive at gross investment at purchase prices. This series was then deflated by price indices of the relevant years (with 1974-75=100) to get estimates of gross investment at 1974-75 prices.[66] Finally, the series of gross fixed capital stock at 1974-75 prices for the period 1974-75 to 1985-86 were derived by cumulatively adding to the bench-mark capital stock, the gross additions at 1974-75 prices for the subsequent years.

The price index used for deflating capital input series was the Price Index of Machinery and Transport Equipment of India. Obviously, a weighted price index (the weights being the shares of different categories of assets in total fixed assets) has been considered a better index for price adjustment. In contrast to the all-India level, where the category-wise breakup of assets into (a) building and construction (b) plant and machinery, and (c) tools, transport equipment, etc, is available, such break-up is not available in the ASI published at the State level. At attempt to provide such weighted price index at the State level (including U.P.) has been made by Dholakia.[67] But these indices could not be used in the present study, as indices were available only for the period 1960-61 to 1970-71 (based on 1960-61 prices).

2. METHODOLOGY: USE OF ECONOMETRIC MODELS

An investigation into the technological change and development of organised industrial sector has been carried out at the State as well as regional levels through the present study. The State level analysis incorporates manufacturing sector as a whole and twenty two-digit industry groups. Further, for purposes of convenient and meaningful analysis, all the twenty industry groups have been divided into four categories (i.e., highly capital intensive, medium high capital intensive, medium low capital intensive and low capital intensive), in terms of capital-labour ratio slabs in descending order referring to 1985-86, the final year of the time period considered for the study. To explain further; if A, B, C and D denote the lower limits of the intervals in descending order, then A and C were obtained as arithmetical mean values of the capital labour ratios for the industry groups falling respectively above and below the State level arithmetical mean ($\overline{X}$ or B in our case). The value of D was obviously the lowest value of capital-labour ratios across the industry groups. The four categories, thus, arrived at were constituted by the industry groups falling between (i) A and above; (ii) B and A; (iii) C and B; and (iv) D and C (category-wise capital-labour ratios for different industry groups are presented in Appendix Table-3.4). At the regional level, our analysis is confining to whole of the organised manufacturing sector of the five economic regions (namely, Western, Central, Eastern, Uttaranchal and Bundelkhand) only.

Most of the research on technological change aims at isolating a shift in production function with the movement along it. While the latter is termed as 'factor substitution', the former is taken to be an indicator of 'technologcial progress', which enables more output to be produced for unchanged quantities of inputs. Technological progress can be measured through productivity and production function approach, both of which have been used for the empirical analysis in the present study.

2.1 Partial Productivity and Capital Intensity

Partial productivities can be obtained as a ratio of output to input. Most commonly used are productivities of labour and capital, which are computed using the following equation:-

$$PpL=Q/L; PpK=Q/K$$

Where PpL and PpK represent partial productivities of labour and capital respectively. While labour and capital productivities indicate efficiency in the use of these inputs, the changes occurring in these are generated by various economic forces interacting simultaneously.

Besides these, capital labour ratios (K/L) have also been computed to get an idea of capital-deepening over the period and its relationship with capital and labour productivities.

2.2 Total Factor Productivity Index

Total factor productivity index or the index of 'technical progress'[68] as it is often referred to, gives us an idea of overall efficiency in the factor use. This index is the ratio of output to weighted combination of inputs. For empirical purposes, efforts have been made to estimate Kendrick, Solow and Translog indices of total factor productivity.

(i) *Arithmetic Index:* was proposed for the first time by Kendrick (1961). This index is based upon the linear production function of the form:

$$Q = \alpha L + \beta K \qquad ...(1)$$

where Q, K and L represent output, labour and capital respectively and α and β are constants.

Based on the production function of the form (1) and Euler's theorem the productivity index, A can be derived as follows:

$$Q = A\,(woL+roK) \qquad ...(2)$$

or

$$A = Q/(woL+roK) \qquad ...(2a)$$

where wo and ro are the prices of labour and capital in the base year. The productivity index thus derived (i.e. A) compares the output of a particular period with the output that would have been produced by the resources working at their base year efficiency. Being based on Euler's theorem and assuming constant returns to scale, perfect competition and payment to factors according to their marginal products, the productivity index in the base year would be equal to one.

Alternatively, (2a) can be written as:

$$A = Q/Qo/\alpha o\,(L/Lo) + \beta o\,(K/Ko) \qquad ...(3)$$

The above relation shows that if all variables are expressed as index numbers with common base period, the weights can be expressed as factor shares αo and βo.[69]

Inspite of the computational simplicity, this index being based on linear production function implies that the marginal products of inputs are independent of the quantities of inputs and that capital and labour are perfect substitutes in production, which seems hardly tenable.

(ii) *Geometric Index:* An improvement over the arithmetic index was the geometric index put forward by Solow (1957). This index allows prices of inputs, and therefore, their marginal products to vary. Based on the assumption of Hicks-neutral and disembodied technical change, this index is based on the production function of the following form :

$$Q = A(t)\,f\,(K,L) \qquad ...(4)$$

with A(t) measuring cumulative effect of shifts overtime. Differentiating (4) totally with respect to time, we get

$$\frac{\partial Q}{\partial t}=\frac{\partial A}{\partial t}f(K,L)+A\left(\frac{\partial Q}{\partial K}\frac{\partial K}{\partial t}+\frac{\partial f}{\partial L}\frac{\partial L}{\partial t}\right)$$

taking $\partial Q/\partial t = \dot{Q}$ and so on, (5) can be rewritten as:

$$\dot{Q}=\dot{A}\ f(K,L)+A\frac{\partial f}{\partial K}\dot{K}+A\frac{\partial f}{\partial L}\dot{L} \quad \text{...(5a)}$$

and dividing (5a) by Q, we get

$$\frac{\dot{Q}}{Q}=\frac{\dot{A}f(K,L)}{Q}+A\frac{\partial f}{\partial K}\frac{\dot{K}}{Q}+A\frac{\partial f}{\partial L}\frac{\dot{L}}{Q} \quad \text{...(6)}$$

Now assuming that competitive conditions prevail and factors are paid their marginal products, we have $\partial Q/\partial K=r/p$ and $\partial Q/\partial L=w/p$. Since $(\partial Q/\partial K)\ (K/Q)$ is the share of capital, wk and $(\partial Q/\partial L)\ (L/Q)$ is the share of labour, w_L, by substituting these into equation (6) (note that $\partial Q/\partial K = A.\ \partial f/\partial k$ and $\partial Q/\partial L = A.\partial f/\partial L$) we get

$$\frac{\dot{Q}}{Q}+\frac{\dot{A}}{A}+w_K\frac{\dot{K}}{K}+w_L\frac{\dot{L}}{L} \quad \text{....(7)}$$

and $\dot{A}/A$ is obtained as

$$\frac{\dot{A}}{A}=\frac{\dot{Q}}{Q}-w_K\frac{\dot{K}}{K}-w_L\frac{\dot{L}}{L} \quad \text{...(8)}$$

its discrete form being

$$\frac{\Delta A}{A}=\frac{\Delta Q}{Q}-w_K\frac{\Delta K}{K}-w_L\frac{\Delta L}{L} \quad \text{...(8a)}$$

With the help of time series data on output, capital and labour and the shares of capital and labour, one can obtain $\Delta A/A$ as a residual, which gives the index of technological change.

Assuming that constant returns to scale prevail, we have $w_k + w_L=1$ or $w_k=1-w_L$, and dividing equation (8) by L, and letting $Q/L=q$ and $K/L=k$, we obtain

$$\frac{\dot{q}}{q}=\frac{\dot{A}}{A}+w_K\frac{\dot{k}}{k} \quad \text{...(9)}$$

Transposing and writing in discrete form, we have

$$\frac{\Delta A}{A}=\frac{\Delta q}{q}-w_K\frac{\Delta k}{k} \quad \text{...(9a)}$$

From the time series of value added per person, capital per-person and the share of capital in value added, we can estimate $\Delta A / A$ series. Arbitrarily, setting the initial years index as one, the A(t) series can be derived from the following identity:

$$A(t+1) = A(t)\left[1 + \frac{\Delta A}{A}\right] \qquad ...(10)$$

Both Solow and Kendrick indices are based on the homogeneous production function. Under the conditions of competitive equilibrium, the two indices are equivalent for small changes in outputs and inputs.[70]

(iii) *Divisia–Translog Index:* Francois Divisia in 1925-26[71] developed an index number formula that possesses certain very desirable properties. This index satisfies both the time and factor reversal tests.[72] Besides, this index also has the reproductive property, such that a Divisia index of Divisia indices is a Divisia index. As an extension, the Divisia index of technical change was introduced by Solow in 1957. The need for a discrete approximation of continuous Divisia index was met by developing the translog index based on translog production function. This function is characterised by constant returns to scale and variable elasticity of substitution. An added advantage of this function is that it does not require the assumption of Hicks neutrality. While satisfying both the time reversal and factor reversal tests, translog index does not possess the reproductive property of the Divisia index.

For the description of the Divisia index, one has to start with the production function of the form described below characterised by constant returns to scale:

$$Q = f\,(K, L, T) \qquad ...(11)$$

where Q, K, L and T denote output, capital input, labour input and time respectively. Defining output price as p and prices of capital and labour inputs as r and w, respectively, the share of two inputs in the value of output can be defined as:

$$V_K = \frac{rK}{pQ},\ V_L = \frac{wL}{pQ}$$

The conditions for producers equilibrium require that each value share should be equal to elasticity of output with respect to that input, such that

$$V_K = \frac{\partial \ell nQ}{\partial \ell nK}(K, L, T) \qquad .....(12)$$

$$V_L = \frac{\partial \ell nQ}{\partial \ell nL}(K, L, T) \qquad .....(13)$$

and under constant returns to scale the elasticities and value shares sum to unity.

The output and the inputs in the production function are the aggregates that depend on the quantities of individual outputs and inputs. Since the aggregates are considered to be characterised by constant returns to scale, the proportional changes in all components of each aggregate result in the proportional change in the aggregate:

$$Q = Q\,(Q_1, Q_2 \ldots Q_m) \qquad ...(14)$$

$$K = K\,(K_1, K_2 \ldots\ldots Kn) \qquad ...(15)$$

$$L = L\,(L_1, L_2 \ldots\ldots Lp) \qquad ...(16)$$

corresponding to these, there are $(p_1, p_2 \ldots p_m)$ output prices $(r_1, r_2 \ldots r_n)$ capital prices and $(w_1, w_2 \ldots w_p)$ labour prices. Denoting as Q_i, K_j and L_k the set of outputs and set of two inputs and p_i, r_j and w_k as their corresponding prices we can define the share of individual components in corresponding aggregates as:

$$SQ_i = \frac{piQi}{pQ} = \frac{\partial \ell nQ}{\partial \ell nQ_i}(i = 1,2\ldots\ldots m) \qquad ...(17)$$

$$VK_j = \frac{rjKj}{rk} = \frac{\partial \ell nK}{\partial \ell nK_j}(j = 1,2 \ldots n) \qquad ...(18)$$

$$VL_k = \frac{wKLk}{wL} = \frac{\partial \ell nL}{\partial \ell nL_K}(K = 1,2 \ldots p) \qquad ...(19)$$

where SQi, VKj and VLk are the shares of ith, jth and kth component of output, capital and labour in their respective aggregates. Here too, the condition of producers equilibrium requires the equality between the value shares and elasticities of corresponding aggregate with respect to its individual components. Further, under constant returns to scale the elasticities and the value share for each aggregate sum to unity.

Thus, the rate of technical change is defined as the growth of output with respect to time holding capital and labour input constant

$$V_T = \frac{\partial \ell nQ}{\partial T}(K, L, T) \qquad ....(20)$$

By differentiating totally expression (11) with respect to time one can have

$$\frac{d\ell nQ}{dT} = V_K \frac{d\ell nK}{dT} + V_L \frac{d\ell nL}{dT} + V_T \qquad ...(21)$$

Thus, under constant returns to scale, the rate of technical change can be expressed as the rate of growth of output less a weighted average of the rates of growth of capital and labour inputs, with weights being the corresponding value shares. And in this expression, V_T represents the Divisia quantity index of technical change. In the above expression

$$\frac{d\ell nQ}{dT} = \sum SQ_i \frac{d\ell nQi}{dT} \qquad ...(22)$$

$$\frac{d\ell nK}{dT} = \sum VK_j = \frac{d\ell nKj}{dT} \qquad ...(23)$$

$$\frac{d\ell nL}{dT} = \sum VL_K \frac{d\ell nLk}{dT} \qquad ...(24)$$

where the rate of growth of each aggregate is the weighted average of its components; the weights being the corresponding value shares. The above equations (22), (23) and (24) demonstrate the Divisia quantity indices of output, capital and labour respectively.

Further, on the price side, under constant returns to scale, a necessary condition for producers equlibrium requires that the price of output and two inputs are consistent with equality between the value of output and the sum of the values of capital and labour input:

$$pQ = rK + wL \qquad ...(25)$$

Given this equality, price of output can be expressed as a function of the prices of capital and labour inputs and time, such that

$$p=P\,(r, w, T) \qquad ...(26)$$

This is the price function.[73] Similarly, the price of each aggregate can be expressed as a function of the prices of its components. From the point of view of price function, the rate of technical change can be defined as the negative of the growth of price of output with respect to time holding the input prices constant:

$$V_T = -\frac{\partial \ell np}{\partial T}(r, w, T) \qquad ...(27)$$

and

$$\frac{d\ell np}{dT} = V_K \frac{d\ell nr}{dT} + V_L \frac{d\ell nw}{dT} - V_T \qquad ...(28)$$

Equation (28) shows that the rate of technical change can be expressed as the rate of growth of a weighted average of input prices less the rate of growth of price of output, where the weights are given by corresponding value shares. This is the Divisia price index of technical change. It is to be noted again that in the above expression each aggregate price index is a weighted average of its components, so that,

$$\frac{d\ell np}{dT} = \sum SQ_i \frac{d\ell npi}{dT} \qquad ...(29)$$

$$\frac{d\ell nr}{dT} = \sum VK_j \frac{d\ell nrj}{dT} \qquad ...(30)$$

$$\frac{d\ell nw}{dT} = \sum VL_K \frac{d\,\ell n\,wk}{dT} \qquad ...(31)$$

these are referred to as Divisia price indices of output, capital input, and labour input.

For application to the discrete analysis, an approximation of continuous Divisia index known as translog index is used (developed by Tornquist). This index is based on translog production function[74] which naturally accommodates discrete time analysis. This function assumes constant returns to scale but elasticity of substitution is allowed to diverge from unity. The function can be written as follows:

$$\begin{aligned}\ell nQ = \alpha_o + \alpha_L \ell nL + \alpha K\,\ell nK + \alpha_T\,T + 1/2\beta_{KK}(\ell nK) \\ + \beta_{KL}(\ell nK)(\ell nL) + \beta_{KT}T.\ell nK + 1/2\beta_{LL} \\ (\ell nL)^2 + \beta_{LT}\ell nL.T + 1/2\beta_{TT}T^2\end{aligned} \qquad ....(32)$$

constant returns to scale require that

$$\alpha K + \alpha L = 1; \beta KK + \beta KL = 0; \beta KL + \beta LL = 0$$

and the index derived therefrom can be written as

$$\Delta\,\ell nQ = \overline{V}_K(\Delta\ell nK) + \overline{V}_L(\Delta\ell nL) + \overline{V} \qquad ...(33)$$

and by transposing we get

$$\overline{V}_T = \Delta\ell nQ - \left[\overline{V}_K(\Delta\ell nK) + \overline{V}_L(\Delta\ell nL)\right] \qquad ...(33a)$$

where

$$\Delta\ell nQ = \ell nQ(T) - \ell nQ(T-1) \qquad ...(34)$$

$$\Delta\ell nK = \ell nK(T) - \ell nK(T-1) \qquad ...(35)$$

$$\Delta\ell nL = \ell nL(T) - \ell nL(T-1) \qquad ...(36)$$

and

$$\overline{V}_K = 1/2[V_K(T) + V_K(T-1)] \qquad ...(37)$$

$$\overline{V}_L = 1/2[V_L(T) + V_L(T-1)] \qquad ...(38)$$

Thus, the average translog index of technical change, $\overline{V}_T$, can be obtained as the difference between successive logarithms of output less a weighted average of the differences between successive logarithms of capital and labour inputs, with weights being given by average value shares.[75] Similarly, one can extend the methodology to formulate translog indexes of output and inputs as the weighted averages of the rates of growth of their components.[76]

2.3 PRODUCTION FUNCTIONS

Production function is a relation that describes the transformation of a set of inputs into output. Specifically, it shoes how maximum output is obtained from given set of inputs in the existing state of technological knowledge. By estimating the parameters of a production function, one can measure all the elements of technological change such as the efficiency of technology, the economies of scale, the capital intensity of technology and the elasticity of substitution.

The production function is basically a microeconomic concept. Defining for the firm, we may write

$$Q = f(K, L) \qquad \text{...(39)}$$

where Q is output, K and L are capital and labour inputs. Neo-classical theory borrows the same concept and applies it to the economy as a whole. However, here Q, K, and L now become aggregate output, aggregate capital and aggregate labour, respectively. The assumptions inherent here (in the microeconomic as well as macroeconomic models) are: profit maximisation (or cost minimisation) given demand and factor prices; perfect competition in both factor and product markets, so that the industrial units are price takers; free availability of technological knowledge; supply and demand generally is in equilibrium; and factors are paid equal to their marginal products which are used as weights in combining them. At the macro level, some additional assumptions have to be made. It is often assumed that constant returns to scale exist and technical change is neutral.[77]

(i) *Properties of the neo-classical production function:* A well behaved production function must fulfil certain neo-classical criteria. The production function Q = f(K,L) is single valued, continuous and (at least) twice differentiable. The first and the second partial derivates of the independent variables with respect to the dependent variable in the above function can be written as

$$\frac{\partial Q}{\partial K} = f_K \; \frac{\partial Q}{\partial L} = f_L ; \frac{\partial^2 Q}{\partial K^2} = f_{KK} \; \frac{\partial^2 Q}{\partial L^2} = f_{LL}$$

The first condition requires that

$$f_k > 0; f_L > 0; f_{KK} < 0; f_{LL} < 0$$

which ensures that the marginal products of two inputs are positive and decreasing. This means that although the marginal product of a factor is positive, it declines as more of that factor is applied, keeping other factors constant.

Secondly, a production function should exhibit any degree of economies or diseconomies of scale. Consider increasing the independent variables in the above function (i.e. K and L) by some constant, say λ, then the output will increase by λ^n times

$$f(\lambda_K, \lambda_L) = \lambda^n f(K,L) = \lambda^n Q$$

where n gives the degree of homogeneity. If n=1, the production function is said to be homogeneous of degree one or linearly homogeneous. A linearly homogeneous production function exhibits constant returns to scale, the increasing or decreasing returns to scale are indicated depending on whether $n \gtrless 1$. An important property of the homogenous function is given by Euler's theorem, according to which the sum of first partial derivatives weighted by the quantity of the factor is equal to output times the degree of homogeneity, thus

$$f_k K + f_L L = n\,Q$$

and in case of linearly homogeneous function (i.e., n=1), exhibiting constant returns to scale, product gets exhausted if each factor is paid its marginal product (represented by first partial derivative), so that

$$f_k K + f_L L = Q$$

Further, coming to the relation between inputs themselves, there is an isoquant, which expresses one input as a function of another, for a given output. In other words, an isoquant represents the most efficient combinations of factors that give rise to the same level of output. For different levels of output there are different isoquants. Since the equation of isoquants is Q = f (K,L) and since on the same isoquant, output remains unchanged we have f (K,L) = 0. Taking the total derivative of the above gives

$$d\,Q = f_k\,dk + f_L\,dL = 0$$

Since the output does not change as we move along an isoquant, the marginal rate of substitution, R (represented by the slope of isoquant) from above is given by

$$R = -\frac{dK}{dL} = \frac{fL}{fK}$$

This is assumed to decrease as substitution proceeds giving an isoquant that is convex to the origin. Marginal rate of substitution can be applied to estimate a very important parameter i.e. elasticity of substitution (σ), which measures the ease of substitution between factors. Elasticity of substitution can be defined as a percentage change in the factor input ratio as a result of a percentage change in the marginal rate of substitution.

(ii) *Types of Production Functions* : There are atleast four main types of production functions, differing from each other on the basis of the value of elasticity of substitution that they assume. These are Cobb-Douglas production function, Constant Elasticity of Substitution (C.E.S) production function, Leontief or Input-Output production function and Linear Programming production function. Cobb-Douglas production function assumes σ to be equal to one, whereas Leontief production function assumes σ to be equal to zero. On the other hand, σ is assumed to be infinite (∞) in Linear Programming production function. It is only the CES production function, which allows σ to take any constant value from 0 to ∞. Therefore, it can be seen that Cobb-Douglas, Leontief and Linear Programming production functions are all special cases of CES production function. The most widely used are the Cobb-Douglas and the CES production functions.

(a) *Cobb-Douglas Production Function*: This function was introduced by Charles Cobb and Paul Douglas (1928) to test the marginal productivity theory and neo-classical assumptions of constant returns to scale. Tinbergen in 1942 for the first time introduced the exponential time trend in the function to estimate technical progress as a separate item. Due to its computational simplicity, this function came to be widely used to measure technological change in different countries.

The unrestricted Cobb-Douglas production function for two factors may be written as

$$Q = A\,L^{\alpha}\,K^{\beta} \qquad ...(40)$$

where Q is output, L and K are labour and capital inputs, A is the efficiency parameter and α and β represent the elasticity of output with respect to labour and capital respectively. A, α and β represent the constants to be tested empirically. The simplicity of the function is that is becomes linear in its logarithmic form. Thus, the log transformation of (40) becomes

$$\log Q = \log A + \alpha \log L + \beta \log K \qquad ...(41)$$

It can be shown that Cobb-Douglas production function fulfils all the criteria of well behaved neo-classical production function. Homogeneity of the function can be tested by making proportionate change in each input

$$f(\lambda L, \lambda K) = A(\lambda L)^{\alpha}(\lambda K)^{\beta} = A\lambda^{\alpha}L^{\alpha}\lambda^{\beta}K^{\beta}$$
$$= \lambda^{\alpha+\beta}(AL^{\alpha}K^{\beta}) = \lambda^{\alpha+\beta}Q$$

with $\alpha + \beta$ providing the degree of homogeneity. The returns to scale will be increasing, constant and decreasing depending on whether $\alpha + \beta >/< 1$.

Differentiating (40) partially with respect to capital and labour we can obtain their respective marginal products

$$\frac{\partial Q}{\partial L} = \alpha A\ L^{\alpha-1}\ K^{\beta} = \alpha(\frac{Q}{L}),$$
$$\frac{\partial Q}{\partial K} = \beta A\ L^{\alpha}\ K^{\beta-1} = \beta(\frac{Q}{K})$$

and assuming α and β are psitive constants smaller than one, such that $0<\alpha<1$ and $0<\beta<1$ the marginal products of K and L are positive. Taking second derivates of output with respect to K and L in (40) (i.e. differentiating the marginal products of K and L shown above) we get

$$\frac{\partial^2 Q}{\partial L^2} = \alpha(\alpha-1)\,AL^{\alpha-1}K^{\beta} = \alpha(\alpha-1)\left(\frac{Q}{L^2}\right),$$
$$\frac{\partial^2 Q}{\partial K^2} = \beta(\beta-1)\,AL^{\alpha}K^{\beta-2} = \beta(\beta-1)\left(\frac{Q}{K^2}\right)$$

which is negative since $0<\alpha<1$ and $0<\beta<1$. Therefore, Cobb-Douglas function shows marginal products that are positive and decreasing.

The marginal products can be utilised to derive the elasticity of output with respect to K and L. This is given by the percentage change in output with respect to the percentage change in inputs (K,L) so that we have

$$\eta QL = \frac{\partial Q/Q}{\partial L/L} = \frac{\partial Q}{\partial L}.\frac{L}{Q} \text{ and } \eta QK = \frac{\partial Q}{\partial K}.\frac{K}{Q}$$

By substituting

$$\frac{\partial Q}{\partial L} = \alpha\frac{Q}{L} \text{ and } \frac{\partial Q}{\partial K} = \beta\frac{Q}{K},$$

we have

$$\eta QL = \left(\alpha\frac{Q}{L}\right) . \frac{L}{Q} = c$$

and

$$\eta QK = \left(\beta\frac{Q}{L}\right) . \frac{K}{Q} = f$$

Thus, in Cobb-Douglas function α and β represent elasticity of output with respect to labour and capital and the sum of two elasticities is equal to elasticity of scale. (This relationship is known as Wicksell Johnson theorem).[78]

Further, marginal products can also be used to derive the marginal rate of substitution R between two factors.

$$R = \frac{\partial Q}{\partial K} / \frac{\partial Q}{\partial L} = \beta\frac{Q}{K} / \alpha\frac{Q}{L} = \frac{\beta}{\alpha}.\frac{L}{K}$$

This can be used in the derivation of elasticity of substitution that is given by

$$\sigma = \frac{d(K/L)/(K/L)}{dR/R}$$

and from the above we have

$$dR = \left(\frac{L}{K}\right) . \left(\frac{\beta}{\alpha}\right)$$

Substituting dR and R in the equation giving σ we have

$$\sigma = \frac{d(L/K)(K/L)}{d(L/K)(\beta/\alpha)} \left(\frac{\beta}{\alpha}\right)\left(\frac{L}{K}\right) = 1$$

so that in case of Cobb-Douglas function, elasticity of substitution will always be equal to one.

To measure the 'technological progress' an exponential time trend may be incorporated in the function so that equation (40) now becomes

$$Q = A_{oe}{}^{\lambda t} L^{\alpha} K^{\beta} \quad \text{...(42)}$$

where λ is the rate of exponential technological progress. Taking log on both sides of equation (42), we have

$$\log Q = \log A_o + \alpha \log L + \beta \log K + \lambda t \quad \text{...(43)}$$

and its stochastic formulation being

$$\log Q = \log Ao + \alpha \log L + \beta \log K + \lambda t + \mu \quad \text{...(43a)}$$

where μ is the random error term. Equation (43a) can be estimated with the help of technique of ordinary least squares. Technical change may manifest itself by affecting either A, α and β or it might lead to entirely new production function. However, the coefficients of this function may not change always only on account of technological change.[79] The sum of capital and labour coefficients provides an estimate of returns to scale. Thus, we have increasing, constant and decreasing returns to scale depending upon whether $\alpha + \beta \gtrless 1$.

The results derived from above relation may not be precise due to the problem of multicollinearity between the independent variables. The avoid this ratio form of Cobb-Douglas production function[80] under the assumption of constant returns to scale can be estimated

$$\log (Q/L) = \log A + \beta \log (K/L) + \lambda t + \mu \quad \text{...(44)}$$

To allow for variable returns to scale we introduce the coefficient of log (L) in equation(44) so that we have

$$\log (Q/L) = \log A + \beta \log (K/L) + m \log (L) + \lambda t + \mu \quad \text{...(45)}$$

where m provides for returns to scale and its value is equal to $(\alpha + \beta - 1)$. A positive value of m indicates increasing returns to scale and a negative value is indicative of decreasing returns to scale.

The most important shortcoming of Cobb-Douglas production function is that it assumes elasticity of substitution to be equal to one, which may not always be true. The Constant Elasticity of Substitution production function, which is a methodological improvement over Cobb-Douglas production function is subsequently discussed in detail.

(b) *Constant Elasticity of Substitution Production Function*: As already pointed out, Cobb-Douglas production function is based on the restrictive assumption of unitary elasticity of substitution. Elasticity of substitution is a crucial parameter, particularly in case of the underdeveloped countries as it is important not only in determining the pattern of resource allocation and relative distribution of income among other things, it also has important implications for employment generation. High elasticity of substitution is associated with high employment elasticity of output. Besides, differences in elasticity of substitution between different sectors may be associated with the differences in the growth rates of these sectors. For example, an industry with high elasticity of substitution usually will have a higher output rate compared to an industry with low elasticity of substitution.[81] Constant elasticity of substitution (CES) production function, put forward by Arrow, Chenery, Minhas and Solow (SMAC) in 1961, allows elasticity of substitution to take any constant value from 0 to ∞.[82] Working on the international cross section data on twenty four industries for various countries, SMAC tested the following relation

$$\log (Q/L) = a + b \log w + \varepsilon \qquad ...(46)$$

where w is the wage rate and ε is the random stochastic term and b provides an estimate of elasticity of substitution (σ). This relation assumes optimisation behaviour (or cost minimisation), the existence of an aggregate production function with disembodied technical change, the independence of (Q/L) from (K/L) (or capital intensity), no measurement errors in the variables and no adjustment lags between (Q/L) and w.[83] It was found out that for all industries, the value of b was significantly different from zero, thereby rejecting the case of fixed coefficient Leontief production function. Further, in fourteen out of twenty four industries b(i.e., σ) was found to be significantly different from one at 10 percent or higher level of significance.[84] This led them to their path breaking formulation of CES production function

$$Q = \gamma\left[\delta K^{-\rho} + (1-\delta)L^{-\rho}\right]^{-v/\rho} \qquad ...(47)$$

where Q, K and L are output, capital and labour, respectively and γ, δ, v and ρ are efficiency, distribution, homogeneity (or returns to scale) and substitution parameters, with elasticity of substitution being equal to $1/1 + \rho$. In the original SMAC version, v was taken to be equal to one so that constant returns to scale were imposed, but an independent derivation by Brown and deCani (1963) permits v to exhibit any degree of returns to scale. Neutral technical change[85] may be incorporated in the function by putting $\gamma = \gamma_o e^{\lambda t}$, so that(47) now becomes,

$$Q = \gamma_o e^{\lambda t}\left[\delta K^{-\rho} + (1-\delta)L^{-\rho}\right]^{-v/\rho} \qquad ...(48)$$

with λ measuring the rate of exponential technical progress. In its more generalised form, the CES production function fulfils all the properties of well behaved production function.[86]

A major problem with CES production function is that its direct estimation through linear regression analysis is not possible, nor can one transform it into a linear form by taking logarithms, as can be done in case of the Cobb-Douglas production function. Further, the parameters of CES production function are highly sensitive to changes in data and measurement of variables. Indirect approaches to measurement have been suggested. We may use (i) Kmenta's approach, applying least squares to a linear approximation of the CES function (ii) step-wise procedure of estimating, first the ratio of the marginal productivity relations to obtain the estimates of $\hat{\rho}$ and $\hat{\delta}$ in equation 47 and then using these estimates (of ρ and δ) to estimate the remaining parameters i.e. v and γ (iii) Bodkin and Klein's approach of non-linear maximum likelihood procedure; and (iv) Bayesian estimation technique, which combines knowledge about prior distribution of the parameters of the production function, and its stochastic error term, using likelihood function similar to Bodkin and Klein.[87] Alternatively, we may consider the side relation between marginal productivity conditions and labour's share that may be derived from the CES function under the assumption of perfect competition and profit maximization. In case of constant returns to scale (v=1), marginal productivity for labour can be found out by partially differentiating (47) with respect to labour, so that we have

$$\frac{\partial Q}{\partial L} = \left(\frac{1-\delta}{\gamma\rho}\right) \cdot \left(\frac{Q}{L}\right)^{1+\rho} = v$$

which is equal to wage rate under the assumption of perfect competition. This yields the following relation

$$\log (Q/L) = A + \sigma \log w + \mu \qquad \text{...(49)}$$

where $A = \sigma\log(\gamma^{\rho}/1-\delta)$, $\sigma = 1/1+\rho$ giving the estimate of elasticity of substitution and w denotes wage rate. This is the familiar SMAC regression equation referred to above in equation (46). Assuming constant returns to scale and neutral technological progress (λ) to occur, so that $\gamma_t = \gamma_o e^{\lambda t}$ and (v=1), we have the function of the form shown in equation (48). Now, $\gamma_t = \log \gamma_o + \lambda_t$ we can derive

$$\log(Q/L) = A + \sigma \log W + \lambda(1-\sigma)t + \mu \qquad \text{...(50)}$$

where $A = [(1-\sigma)\log\gamma_o - \sigma\log(1-\delta)]$, and $\sigma = 1/1+\rho$

However, suppose that there are non-constant returns to scale (with v≠1) the production function is of the form (47), the marginal product of labour now is

$$\partial Q/\partial L = v^{\partial}(Q/L) . (Q^{\rho/v} . L^{-\rho}$$

and equating it with the wage rate gives

$$(Q/L) = (v\delta)^{-v/v+\rho} . w^{v/v+\rho} . L^{\rho(v-1)}$$

taking log on both sides we have

$$\log\left(\frac{Q}{L}\right) = \left(-\frac{v}{v+\rho}\right)\log(v\delta) + \left(\frac{v}{v+\rho}\right)\log w + \frac{\rho(v-1)}{v+\rho}\log L$$

interpreting this as a stochastic relation we can write the same as

$$\log\left(\frac{Q}{L}\right) = A + \beta_1 \log w + \beta_2 \log L + \mu \qquad \text{...(51)}$$

$$\text{where } A=\left(\frac{-v}{v+\rho}\right)\log(v\delta), \beta_1=\left(\frac{v}{v+\rho}\right) \text{ and } \beta_2=\frac{\rho(v-1)}{v+\rho}$$

The value of β_1 in the above relation gives us an idea of σ and the value of β_2 gives an idea of economies of scale.

Recently many generalisations of the production functions have taken place. For example, the formulation of variable elasticity of substitution production function, where σ varies with relative shares of labour and capital; representation of technology by profit/cost functions on the basis of duality theorems, etc. Indeed, Kaldor[88] has gone as far as rejecting the concept of production function in favour of what he calls 'technical progress function'. Kaldor felt that a distinction between the movement along the production function and a shift in it is arbitrary and artificial, since improved knowledge is embodied in new equipment, the rate of shift of the function will itself depend upon the speed of the movement along it. However, in the absence of intensive explorations of these functions, it is very difficult here to provide justification for their wide usage.

While using any of the above mentioned measures of technological change, one must keep in mind that any misspecification or errors in estimating parameters of the aggregate production function–errors in the measurement of variables or due to ommission of relevant inputs–will spill–over to the measure of total factor productivity and technical change.[89]

Besides measuring technical progress through various measures, effort have also been made to assess the performance, mainly in terms of output and employment growth of total manufacturing sector separately for Uttar Pradesh, five economic regions, twenty industry groups and four identified categories of industry groups. As already stated, all the twenty industry groups have been divided into four categories on the basis of the capital-labour ratio of the final year. This kind of disaggregation is attempted with the hope that is would help in streamlining the analysis of the inter-relationship between technological change and development of the organised industrial sector both at the State and the regional levels.

References

1. As per NIC-1970 classification.
2. Total registered industrial sector excluding industry groups 40 (Electricity), 41 (Gas and Steam), 42 (Water Works and Supply), 74 (Storage and Warehousing), 91 (Sanitary Services) and 96 (Personal Services like laundry, cleaning, dyeing etc.).
3. Under the group 20-21 (manufacturing of Food Products) analysis is carried out separately for Sugar, Khandsari and Gur (206,207) and Edible oil (210,211) owing to their importance in the context of Uttar Pradesh. Further for industry group-wise analysis we have disregarded Repair Services (Group 97) due to non-comparability of time series data.
4. Aggregated data of organised manufacturing sector of all five economic regions do not correspond with the total of manufacturing sector already available at the State level. This is due to the ASI practice of not publishing data of an industry separately unless there are atleast three factories in it in a district, to avoid identification. At the district level, such instances are quite frequently noticed and, therefore, the aggregated data of the region level is not as much exhaustive as we find at the State level.

5. We do not have any Consumer Price Index (CPI) at the State level. And we get the separate index for Kanpur, Saharanpur and Varanasi only. Because of being centrally located, we have, therefore, used the CPI of Kanpur as a proxy for the State.
6. A. Banerji (1975), p.15.
7. George Rosen (1959).
8. Z. Griliches and V. Ringstad (1971).
9. B.F. Massell (1960), p.183.
10. A. Banerji (1975), p.18.
11. The use of value added as a measure is based on the assumptions that either the inputs other than labour and capital are related to output in fixed proportion or that they are substitutable inputs but are instantaneously adapted to changes in prices so as to result in profit maximisation. See L. Johansen (1972).
12. The data pertaining to gross value added of the total manufacturing sector at the State as well as region levels, have been deflated by the Wholesale Price index available for the manufacturing sector at the State level. This assumes that there are no regional variations in prices. However, in the absence of region-wise price index we were left with no other option except to use the State level index. The industry group-wise data have been deflated by the Wholesale Price Index available for respective industry groups.
13. In double deflation method output and input is deflated separately and the difference between the two is taken a measure of value added at constant prices.
14. B.N. Goldar (1986), p.48.
15. C. Kennedy and A.P. Thirlwall (1972), p.37.
16. J.N. Sinha and P.K. Sawhney (1970), p.26.
17. *Ibid.*, p.27.
18. M.I. Nadiri (1970).
19. B.H. Dholakia (1974), p.138.
20. In this context J.R. Hicks remarked, 'capital cannot be measured in the ordinary way as other economic goods–valuation of income goods is characteristically a market valuation, the values of good which enter into capital stock are characteristically imputed values;. See J.R. Hicks (1961), p.19.
21. C.J. Bliss (1975), p.vii
22. K.H. Hennings (1987), p.332.
23. He remarked 'labour and land are measured each in terms of its own technical unit...capital on the other hand,....is reckoned, in common parlance, as a sum of exchange value'. Quoted in Luigi L. Pasinetti and Roberto Scazzieri (1987), p.364.
24. K.H. Hennings (1987), p.332.
25. M.I. Nadiri (1970), p.1144.
26. A. Banerji (1975), p.6.
27. *Ibid.*, p.7.

28. Therefore, it can be shown that rate of interest is generally not equal to marginal productivity of capital. This phenomenon is known as Wicksell effect.

29. This arises because capitalists have an incentive to substitute capital for labour as the price of labour rises, but capital itself is made by labour so that its price also rises when the price of labour rises (and the rate of interest falls). Because of this, given certain critical values, as the price of labour rises a capitalist may find it more profitable to switch to a more labour-intensive technique, rather than a more capital-intensive one and vice-versa.

30. A.P. Thirlwall (1983), p.67.

31. C. Kennedy and A.P. Thrilwall (1972), p.29.

32. *Ibid.*, p.29.

33. This is because; 'the main purpose of the production function is to show how wages and the rate of interest are determined by technical conditions and the factor ratio', On the other hand, in case of forward looking concept we already are aware of the future expected rate of output associated with a capital good as well as the expected future prices and costs and the rate of interest, thereby, defeating the main purpose of the production function. See J. Robinson (1953-54), reprinted in G.C. Harcourt and N.F. Liang (1971), p.48.

34. E.F. Denison (1957), pp.222-223.

35. R. Ruggles and N. Ruggles (1961).

36. E.F. Denison (1957), p.225.

37. C. Kennedy and A.P. Thirlwall (1972), p.30.

38. Along the same lines, Domar argues that, 'working with net investment and net stock of capital in the conventional sense one loses sight of gross investment as a major vehicle of technological progress...' Sec E.D. Domar (1961), p.99.

39. R. Ruggles and N. Ruggles (1961).

40. G. Rosen (1959), p.42.

41. E.F. Denison (1967), pp.140-141.

42. R.M. Solow (1971), p.348.

43. *Ibid.*, p.349.

44. A. Smithies (1962), p.92.

45. B.N. Goldar (1986), pp.63-64.

46. Mainly, G. Rosen (1959); Sinha and Sawhney (1970); A. Banerji (1975); and B.N. Goldar (1986).

47. A. Banerji (1975), p.23, n6.

48. In the direct approach all the fixed assets in use at a given point of time are evaluated.

49. R.W. Goldsmith (1951).

50. See Government of India, Central Statistical Organisation, (1988); and references cited therein.

51. Annually published by C.S.O.

52. At the National level apart from the expenditure approach, two other approaches followed for estimating capital formation are commodity-flow approach and the saving and flow-of-funds approach. The use of latter two approaches is ruled out at the State level on account of

the non-availability of basic data on export and imports of capital goods across the State boundaries, as well as on the net inflow of resources outside the State. See D.N. Chaturvedi (1980), p.23.

53. *Ibid*., p.23-24. See also R.H. Dholakia and P.M. Patel (1980), p.26, for problems faced at regional level while using ASI fixed capital data.

54. S.C. Srivastava and Banwari Lal (1978).

55. B.H. Dholkia (Jan-March 1977), p.337.

56. B.N. Goldar (1986), p.70.

57. S.R. Hashim and M.M. Dadi (1973), p.13.

58. See for example, B.H. Dholakia (January 1977), p.353. Dholakia has applied all-India gross net ratio of iron and steel industry to bench-mark capital stock for Bihar as well as rest of India without any adjustment at these levels.

59. After obtaining the gross-net ratios for total manufacturing sector and different industry groups for 1974-75 from RBI Bulletin, we also procured the data of fixed capital stock (depreciated book value) and depreciation at all-India and at the State level for 1974-75 for the same from ASI. Adding the depreciation figures to book value figure and then dividing the total thus arrived by the book value capital stock, we obtained tentative estimates of gross-net ratios(ASI data) for all-India level and U.P. For obtaining RBI equivalent at the State level, we then used the following formula :

$$\text{RBI equivalent for U.P.} = \frac{\text{RBI (G/N)}}{\text{India (ASI-G/N)}} \times \text{U.P. (ASI-G/N)}$$

Where G/N = gross-net ratio.

60. Even if such assets existed prior to 1951 their proportion to total assets in 1974-75 would be very small to make a major difference.

61. A. Banerji (1975), p.22.

62. However there were certain industries for which ASI data was not available from 1961, though data on these was provided in CMI. For these industry groups year-wise capital and depreciation data was procured from the year it was available.

63. In case of industries mentioned in note 62 the problem of price adjustment was for the period 1951 to the year from which the data for these industry groups was available.

64. See B.H. Dholakia (January–March 1977), Appendix p.352.

65. The index for 1951 was not considered as the Index Number of Machinery and Transport Equipment available was based on 1952-53 prices. The base of this series was shifted to 1974-75 by making necessary adjustments.

66. 'Obviously, application of price correction to such a series is likely to have more meaning because each yearly addition to capital stock is likely to show greater homogeneity as compared with total book value, in terms of quality, vintage and prices. See A. Banerji (1975), p.21.

67. R.H. Dholakia (1979).

68. M.I. Nadiri (1970) p.1138.

69. Compared to factor prices, factor shares are likely to be more stable because of negative correlation between factor prices and rate of growth of inputs. The weights used here can relate to any one period (i.e. the base year) or can be the average over several periods.

70. M.I. Nadiri (1970), p.1139.

71. F. Divisia, 'L' Indice monetaire et la theorie de la monnaie', Revue d' economie politique, 39[e] Annee, No.4, July-August, No.5, September-October, No.6, November-December, 1925 and 'L' indice monetaire et la theorie de la monnaie' Revue d' economic politique, 40[e] Annee, No.1, January-February 1926.

72. The test of a good index number laid down by Fisher. An index number is said to satisfy time reversal test if it is symmetric in different direction of time (i.e. it works both backwards and forwards regardless of whether we take the initial year or the final year as the base) and the factor reversal test is satisfied if the changes in prices multiplied by the changes in quantities are equal to the total change in value. See I. Fisher, 'The Making Of Index Numbers', Houghton Mifflin, Boston, 1922.

73. The price function was introduced by Samuelson, who called this function 'Factor Price Frontier'. See P.A. Samuelson (1953).

74. See L.R. Christensen, D.W. Jorgenson, L.J. Lau (1971) and (1973).

75. The initial year's $\bar{V}_T$ value is arbitrarily fixed at 1.

76. For details of methodology see F.M. Gollop and D.W. Jorgenson (1980).

77. Rod Coombs, Paolo Saviotti and Vivien Walsh (1987).

78. A. Heertje (1977), p.126.

79. *Ibid.*, p.126.

80. See Griliches and Ringstad (1971).

81. M. Brown (1966).

82. The elasticity of substitution is constant in the sense that it does not change with changes in relative prices of factor inputs-its value is determined by the underlying technology and may change with technical progress. See K.F. Wallis (1973), p.52.

83. M.I. Nadiri (1970), p.1151.

84. See Table 2 of the article by Arrow, Chenery, Minhas and Solow (1961), reprinted in Harcourt and Liang (1971), p.137.

85. The three types of neutral technical changes introduced by Hicks, Harrod and Solow (described in Chapter 11) are algebraically equivalent in Cobb Douglas function but in CES function all the three forms are empirically distinguishable. For proof, see D.F. Heathfield (1971), pp.64-67.

86. For detail see K.F. Wallis (1973), pp.52-54.

87. M.I. Nadiri (1970), pp.1154-1156.

88. N. Kaldor (1957).

89. M.I. Nadiri (1970), p.1140.

CHAPTER 4

Investment Pattern and Plan Allocations of Outlays for Industrial Development in Uttar Pradesh

Generally, the developing countries of the world have been striving hard to foster economic development in the shortest possible time. Experiences of the developed countries have adequately demonstrated pivotal role of industrialisation in the process of economic development. As transpires from the literature on development economics, the two have, often, been considered as synonyms. Considering its overwhelming importance, the developing countries, in their development plans, have therefore, laid much stress on rapid industrialisation. While making efforts in this direction, investment is considered to be *sine-qua-non* for economic development *via* industrialisation in these countries including India.

Developing countries usually experience shortage of investible resources. The allocation of resources among competing ends needs to be rational so as to ensure maximum possible advantage in a minimum possible time. Viewing this, the study of investment pattern becomes imperative, particularly in the context of backward areas characterised by the shortage of capital. With this end in view, the present chapter is devoted to study and analyse the investment pattern and plan allocations of outlays for industrial development on all-India level in general, and the State of Uttar Pradesh in particular. The analysis is carried out in two sections; the first attempting to analyse theoretical issues underlying investment pattern and the second concerning observed investment pattern of the industrial sector in U.P. *vis-a-vis* all India level.

1. PATTERN OF INVESTMENT: THEORETICAL ISSUES

The pivotal role of investment in development has been recognised by the classical as well as the modern economists. While the classicals emphasised the capacity creating aspect of investment, Keynes was primarily concerned with the demand and income generating effect of investment. A reconciliation between the two was sought to be achieved through Harrod-Domar growth model, which involved a simultaneous consideration of both the capacity creating and income generating aspects of investment.

Similarly, the modern economists also over emphasised the crucial role of investment in the process of economic growth. For example, Rostow's 'take-off' into self-sustained growth requires an increase in the rate of productive investment from 5 per cent or less to over 10 percent of the National Income.[1] Arthur Lewis holds the similar view.[2] In his 'big-push' hypothesis Rosenstein-Rodan (1961, p.57) suggests that 'there is a minimum level of resources that must be devoted to...a development programme if it is to have any chance of success'. Stressing the importance of investment in a new perspective, Hirschman (1960, p.4) recognised investment to be a pace setter for further investment.

Investment, which enhances scope for greater capital accumulation, is considered to be the main vehicle for introduction of technical progress in the eco-system, particularly in case of the developing economies facing acute shortages of capital. The very act of capital deeepening in such economies might result in greater increases in productivity and consequently in per capita incomes.[3] Importance of capital accumulation to growth in developing countries is also demonstrated by the production function studies concerning India.[4]

1.1 Investment Pattern: Importance of Need-Based Allocation of Resources

Allocation decisions shaping the investment pattern have direct impact not only on productivity, output and employment but also on other factors, like income distribution, regional balance, external balance, technological change, supply and distribution of the labour force, growth and quality of population, social and cultural conditions and generally on prospects of growth.[5] In case of developing countries, however, free market forces cannot be relied upon to help in achieving the need based investment allocation as the markets are beset with imperfections, externalities and disequilibrium prices. Solution has to be sought out of the market mechanism through some sort of conscious investment planning. An important aspect of investment planning is the choice of appropriate investment criteria depending upon the conditions prevailing in a particular country and the objectives to be fulfilled.

Economists, form time to time, have put forward different investment criteria as a guide to optimal allocation of resources. Thus, 'the rate of turnover criterion' or 'minimum capital-output ratio criterion' propounded by Polak (1943) and Buchanan (1945) advocates the selection of quick yielding labour intensive projects that release resources quickly for reinvestment. Maximisation of social marginal productivity of investment by the capital scarce economies was suggested by Kahn (1951) and Chenery (1953) in their 'social marginal productivity criterion'. On the other hand, Galenson and Leibenstein (1955) in their 'marginal per capita reinvestment quotient criterion' are in favour of using capital intensive techniques even by capital scarce economies as these techniques permit a large reinvestible surplus. While deciding on allocation of resources, the 'tradeoff' between present and future welfare is to be taken into consideration. An investment criterion should, therefore, reflect both the immediate contribution of projects to consumer welfare and the future welfare made possible by additions to the capital stock from savings generated by the current investment. One solution to the problem of the relative valuation of present and future consumption, and hence the choice of projects, is to fix a socially acceptable time horizon, within which future welfare gains must offset welfare losses in the present.[6]

The 'time series criterion' suggested by Sen (1957) involves comparing and evaluating the time series of income streams associated with the alternative techniques over the relevant time horizon. If the stipulated time horizon exceeds the actual length of time it takes for welfare gains to match welfare losses (or the 'period of recovery' as termed by Sen), relatively capital intensive projects must be chosen with some sacrifice of present consumption, and *vice versa*.

Owing to obvious reasons, application of these criteria as such is the remotest possibility in developing countries. In spite, they seem to have been quite helpful in planning for better allocations of investible capital in developing countries particularly India.

1.2 Investment Allocation: The Broad Policy Choices

Apart from deciding on how much to invest and what criterion to choose, investment planning is concerned with the question of 'optimal allocation' from the point of view of achieving the chosen objectives. Four aspects of the problem can be distinguished– (i) Sectoral, (ii) Regional, (iii) Temporal, and (iv) Technological.[7]

(i) *Sectoral Allocation of Investment*: The historical pattern of development has been such that with the development of a nation's economy and a consequent increase in per capita incomes, resources first shift from agriculture to industry and with further progress and increases in per capita incomes to the tertiary sector. This is simple Fisher-Clark theory of development. This is the reason why the developed countries are generally engaged with highly industrialised and service production and the developing countries with primary production.

As a result, predominantly agrarian developing countries lay greater emphasis on economic development *via* industrialisation in their National Plans. Further, it is also argued that industrial development increases the productivity and stimulates the growth of all sectors of the economy. But, considering the agrarian nature of most of the developing economies, some economists emphasise that agriculture should be developed first, and the choice next to it be given to industry. However, the two sectors are complementary to each other, having strong backward and forward linkages. Both influence each other. On the demand side, increased industrial incomes create additional demand for agricultural goods and thereby, stimulate the otherwise stagnant agriculture.

On the supply side, important raw materials, tools and implements for the modernisation of agriculture are provided by the industrial sector. Transfer of surplus labour from agriculture to industry results in the increased National product. Conversely, agriculture also provides raw materials to industry and with increased agricultural production and productivity and consequently incomes, the demand for industrial goods also increases. Poor agricultural growth may greatly hamper the industrial growth. Commenting on the inter-relationship between the two sectors Baran (1962) says 'it would seem that what we are faced with is a vicious circle. There can be no modernisation of agriculture without industrialisation and there can be no industrialisation without an increase in agricultural output and surplus.' Taking into account the complementary of the two sectors, modern economists hold the view of striking the balance between industry and agriculture. However, for agriculture to play a constructive role, it should attain a certain minimum level of development, where it emerges from stagnatory and subsistence level. This transformation of agriculture is a pre-condition to the stage of 'take-off' into self-sustained growth.[8]

On the other hand, for the consistent development of a sector and consequently the whole economy, investment planning has to be undertaken properly by streamlining the intra-sectoral priorities also. Modernisation of agriculture must be accompanied by the development of allied activities, such as, animal husbandry, forestry and fisheries to supplement the agricultural income. Apart from the development of agriculture, increased agricultural income may prove to be stimulant to the growth of other sectors as well.

The pattern of investment in the industrial sector would largely depend upon the pattern of industrialisation, which a particular country aims at. A country may like to pursue path of industrialisation by emphasising the development of consumer goods industries and/or the capital goods industries. As shown by a number of studies carried out in the context of developed countries, in early phases consumer goods industries predominate, and after a stage rapidly growing capital goods industries leave consumer goods industries far behind.[9] A departure from the historical pattern is a pattern primarily evolved from the views of Fel 'dman/Domar[10] and Mahalanobis (1963) who advocate the development of capital goods industries first so that the long term growth of consumer goods industries is maximised. Besides, many economists[11] stress the importance of capital goods industries on the basis of the historical evidence pointing to these industries being major channels of technological progress. It is, therefore, pointed out that if developing countries have to develop technologies suited to their needs, the presence of capital goods industries in these countries is absolutely necessary.[12]

Moreover, the investment pattern is also guided by the intra-sectoral priorities in terms of developing large scale or small scale industries. Local conditions of both the demand and potential would be the decisive factors in such choices.

Similarly, a well developed infrastructural base is necessary for all round development of the economy. Investment pattern is to be evolved in such a manner that the consistent development of both social and economic infrastructure is ensured.

(ii) *Regional Aspect of Investment*: Persistence of regional imbalances, particularly in the developing countries is a matter of great concern. There is a great difference in the problem of regional inequality between developed and developing countries. In case of the former, a study by Willamson (1965) indicates that regional disparities tend to widen in the early stages of development, narrowing down eventually. On the other hand, in case of the developing countries, regional disparities have a tendency to persist. The cumulative causation theory by Myrdal (1957) proves that in under-developed countries strong backwash (or negative) effects against weak spread (or positive) effects are the causes of these continuing disparities. Hirschman (1960) also feels that resources have the tendency to be attracted towards the favoured regions, enhancing the polarisation effect. However, he envisages a later corrective stage of counterbalances which help in restoring equilibrium.

Developing countries require a deliberate regional planning to overcome the problem of regional disparities. Greater outlays would have to be earmarked for the development of backward areas. One serious cause of concern in developing countries is the pace at which urbanisation, through migration of people from country-side, is increasing. This means greater social costs in terms of providing urban infrastructure and social services for greater numbers. Development of rural areas and making these areas attractive might weaken the aspiration of people to move to big cities thereby checking the increase of regional imbalances. In short, regional planning and consequently investment pattern should aim at: (i) balanced regional development, (ii) provision of minimum level of subsistence to masses living in backward areas, and (iii) proper urban and rural planning.

The proper distribution of investible resources between primary, secondary and tertiary sectors at the regional level is essentially required for a harmonious and self-sustaining regional development. Sectoral planning, being highly aggregative, without spatial integration leads to serious human and social problems, such as environmental pollution, social disintegration, mass poverty amidst plenty and serious sectoral and spatial imbalances.[13] In this context, Hermansen argues that 'the order in the process of development is not...confined to functional sub-system; it is equally profound in the spatial incidence and spread of economic development and manifests itself in the formation of spatial sub-systems and regions'.[14]

Integration should be such that sectoral development emanates from consistent spatial plan. Sectoral and sub-sectoral requirements are different at every spatial level, therefore, an in-depth study of sectoral/spatial relationship is required for the identification of sectors or mix of sectors important at different territorial levels in varying situations. Resource plan should be drawn by taking into account these considerations.

(iii) *Temporal Aspect of Investment*: Time influences the rate of investment to a great extent. Requirements of resources differ from one stage of development to another. Therefore, phasing of investment needs to be integrated with growth performance of the country. Many economists like Marshall, Stanley and Gopal are of the view that the demand for investment increases at an increasing rate in the early stages of development, remains constant for sometimes thereafter, and finally stabilises at a rate lower than required at the initial stage of development.[15]

Regional and sectoral investment requirements are also influenced by time. The importance of different sectors may differ with progress and with the aims and objectives of different countries and investment pattern would be affected accordingly. Similarly, regions backward at one point of time may not demand the same amount of attention after achieving a certain level of development, thereby affecting quantum requirement of resources at different points of time.

(iv) *Technological Aspect of Investment*: One of the important problems facing developing countries is related to choice of techniques–whether techniques should be capital intensive or labour intensive. It has been suggested that these countries must adopt techniques suited to their factor endowments. For the labour abundant developing countries, the choice naturally boils down to quick yielding, high employment generating labour intensive techniques. It has been suggested by Nurkse (1980, p.45) that 'the same capital intensity as in the economically advanced countries should be neither desired nor permitted.' As against this, is the view of Galenson and Leibenstein (1955) who feel that the 'successful economic development...particularly in the face of gross backwardness hinges largely upon the introduction of modern technology upon as large a scale as possible'. Capital intensive techniques are also associated with greater saving and reinvestment potential. It is also felt that productivity improvements and the production of 'high quality low cost products' are possible only by the use of capital intensive techniques.

Whatever arguments may be forwarded in favour of both techniques, developing countries in reality may have no choice for certain reasons, such as, (i) for certain commodities large scale capital intensive setting may be absolutely necessary to capture economies of scale. (ii) labour may not be necessarily cheap due to the low skill and low productivity and also due to the government policies resulting in artificially high wages in these countries, (iii) technologies are mainly imported from developed countries, which are capital intensive in nature. One way out of the dilemma may be the use of abandoned techniques of developed countries. However, these techniques may neither be cost-effective nor suitable to present day conditions of developing countries. On the other hand,

Schumacher (1977, p.167) favoured adoption of intermediate (appropriate) technology which lies somewhere between primitive traditional method and costly sophisticated techniques of the west.

The final choice depends upon the 'trade-off' between present and future welfare; between raising the present level of output and employement or future growth and welfare. Investment pattern of every country will be guided by the valuation of present versus future welfare.

2. PLAN ALLOCATIONS OF OUTLAYS FOR DEVELOPMENT OF INDUSTRIAL SECTOR

At the time of Independence, Indian economy was characterised by deep rooted stagnation, large agricultural sector using outmoded production methods and industrial sector mainly comprising small scale and consumer goods industries. Deliberate efforts had to be made to gear up the economy and to move it on the path of rapid economic progress. The process of planning was an outcome of the desire to achieve definite targets and objectives, such as, increasing the rate of economic growth, achieving full employment, reducing inequalities of income and wealth, modernisation of the economy, attainment of self-reliance and promotion of social justice within a specified period of time and the requirement of channelising resources in the right direction.

Basic strategy of development throughout the planning period has been the achievement of economic progress through accelerated industrial development, particularly the development of heavy capital goods industries. Industrial growth was to be attained within the broad framework of the industrial policy resolutions and the Five Year Plans. Summingly, the various industrial policy resolutions laid down from time to time, aim at (i) maximising production and achieving higher productivity especially in priority sectors, (ii) regionally balanced industrial development, especially by giving preferential treatment to backward areas, (iii) encouraging small scale industries for employment generation and fostering of entrepreneurial talents, (iv) reducing concentration of economic power in private hands, (v) reducing the role of private foreign capital in industrial development, (vi) promotion of self-reliance through export promotion and import substitution, (vii) setting up of mixed economy where public sector plays a central role with private sector playing a complementary role in the process of development,[16] and (viii) strengthening agricultural base by giving preferential treatment to agro-based industries. These objectives were to be achieved by channelising resources of the private sector to desired directions through numerous rules, regulations and measures, such as, Industries Development and Regulation Act, 1951, MRTP Act, 1969, price and distribution controls, import licensing, trade policy measures, and regulation on import of foreign technology and capital, etc. Though the system of control and regulation of industries has theoretical advantages, yet the manner of implementation in India proved to be highly defective. Efforts have, therefore, been made since the Fourth Five Year Plan to make improvements in the licensing policy to improve its soundness and efficacy as control device. A major policy package announced in 1988 aimed at further liberalisation of industrial licensing system and also to provide incentives to give a stimulus to industrialisation of backward areas. It was hoped that these measures would give a boost to the investment climate and lead to rapid industrial growth, particularly of backward areas.

The objectives of various industrial policy resolutions formed the basis of the priorities of industrial development laid down in different Five Year Plans. The First Five Year Plan, based on Harrod-Domar type of exercise, did not have any clear-cut strategy of industrialisation. It aimed at correcting disequilibrium and imbalances caused by the Second World War and partition through overall balanced development.

The Second Five Year Plan, based on Mahalanobis strategy, was conceived in a period of economic stability. It was felt that the country could reach 'take-off' stage through rapid industrialisation, particularly the development of heavy industries. Major objectives for industrial development were as follows: (i) increased production of heavy industries, such as iron and steel, heavy chemicals, heavy engineering and machine building, (ii) expansion of capacity in respect of other development commodities and producer goods such as aluminium, cement, etc., (iii) modernisation of traditional industries, such as, jute, cotton textiles and sugar, (iv) fuller capacity utilisation, and (v) expansion of capacity for consumer goods to meet the consumer demands.[17]

The Third Five Year Plan, based on sophisticated multi-sector model, continued with the policy of according high priority to capital goods industries. The objectives for industrial sector in the Third Plan were: (i) completion of on-going projects, (ii) expansion and diversification of heavy industries and stepping up production of fertilizers and petroleum products, (iii) increasing production of basic raw materials and producer goods, and (iv) increased production from domestic industries to meet essential needs.[18]

Due to various stresses and strains caused in the country due to succession of droughts, wars, foreign exchange shortages, inflationary pressures, etc., the period 1966—1969 was declared as Plan Holiday and the Fourth Plan commenced from April 1969. The objectives guiding the investment pattern of the industrial sector were: (i) completing investments where commitments have already been made, (ii) increasing existing capacities to meet increasing demand for essentials and to meet the demands of import substitution and export promotion, and (iii) taking advantage of internal development or availabilities to build new industries or new bases for industries.[19]

The Fifth Five Year Plan, based on a mix of Harrod-Domar macro-economic model and Leontief inter-industry model, aimed at achieving the twin objectives of self-reliance and growth. The priorities laid down for investment in the industrial sector were: (i) rapid growth of core sector industries, (ii) development of industries leading to diversification and export promotion, (iii) increasing production of industries providing mass consumption goods, (iv) restraint on production of non-essential goods, except for exports, and (v) development of small industries as well as of ancillary industries as the feeder units to large scale industries.[20]

The Sixth Five Year Plan was formulated in a period of crises arising out of the failure of the Fifth Plan to achieve its targets and the political instability. Broadly, the plan aimed at alleviation of poverty, increasing employment opportunities and strengthening infrastructure for rapid development of all sectors of the economy. Modernisation and technological self-reliance were the guiding objectives of the plan. For industrial development the plan included the following: (i) enhancement of manufacturing capacities in public/private sector for providing not only consumer durables and non-durables but also intermediate and capital goods for agricultural and industrial growth, (ii) emphasis on capital goods industry in general and electronics industry in particular, (iii) increase in the exports of engineering goods and industrial products to meet foreign exchange requirements, (iv) a judicious blend of the import of contemporary technology and promoting development of indigenous know-how through domestic R & D, and (v) devising new strategies for development of backward areas to prevent the concentration of industries in already developed areas.[21]

The Seventh Five Year Plan Commenced at a time when most of the plan targets of the Sixth Plan were achieved. Overall objective of the Seventh Plan was growth with social justice and improvement in the productivity of all sectors. The objectives for development of industrial sector incorporated in the Plan were: (i) ensuring adequate supply of wage goods and low cost/better quality consumer articles of mass consumption, (ii) fuller utilisation of existing capacity through restructuring, improved productivity and upgradation of technology, (iii) concentrating on development of industries with large domestic market and high export potential, (iv) encouragement of sunrise industries with high growth potential for higher productivity through use of the latest technology, (v) evolving an integral policy towards self-reliance in strategic fields and opening up of avenues of employment for skilled and trained personnel.[22] These objectives were to be achieved in a general industrial climate of liberal industrial policies and regulations. Seventh Plan also aimed at removing infrastructural bottlenecks, modernising traditional industries, productivity upgradation, export promotion, location of industries in zero industry districts, etc.

2.1 National Level Scenario

Prioritisation in various Five Year Plans, both at the National and the State levels, has been *inter-alia* one of the crucial factors in determining the shape of investment pattern. A higher level of investment leading to faster growth seems to have been the guiding principle of planning strategy in India. As a result, the public sector outlays in India's successive Five Year Plans have continuously increased with the Seventh Plan outlay being almost 92 times the First Plan outlay, as would be evident from Table 4.1.

It would be clear from the table that India's First Five Year Plan accorded the highest priority to agriculture and irrigation, receiving about 31 per cent of the total Plan outlay. The priority was also given to development of transport and communication and social services, visualising the crucial role that these sectors have to play in development. Unfortunately, the industrial sector received the lowest priority with only 5 per cent allocation of the total plan outlay.

The Table 4.1 further reveals that the industrial sector, since the Second Five Year Plan onwards, has been treated as one of the priority sectors. As deciphers from the Table, approximately 16 per cent of the total resources were allocated for industrial development during the planned development period (1951-1990) in India. It was about 20 per cent and above in almost all the Plans excepting the Sixth and the Seventh Plans during which the allocations of outlays for industrial development were only 16 per cent and 12 per cent respectively.

Table-4.1 : Plan wise Outlay by Heads of Development (India)

(Rs. in Crore)

	Head of Development	First Plan (1951-56) Actual	Second Plan (1956-61) Actual	Third Plan (1961-66) Actual	Annual Plans (1966-69) Actual	Fourth Plan (1969-74) Actual	Fifth Plan (1974-79) Actual	Annual Plan (1979-80) Actual	Sixth Plan (1980-85) Actual	Seventh Plan (1985-90) Outlay	Total (First to Seventh Plan)
	1	2	3	4	5	6	7	8	9	10	11
1.	Agriculture and Allied Sectors	290 (14.8)	549 (11.8)	1,089 (12.7)	1,107 (16.7)	2,320 (14.7)	4,865 (12.3)	1,997 (16.2)	13,620* (12.2)	19,429* (10.8)	45,266 (12.0)
2.	Irrigation and Flood Control	314 (16.0)	430 (9.2)	665 (7.8)	471 (7.1)	1,354 (8.6)	3,877 (9.8)	1,288 (10.6)	10,930 (10.0)	16,979 (9.4)	36,308 (9.6)
3.	Energy	269 (13.7)	452 (9.7)	1,252 (14.6)	1,213 (18.3)	2,932 (18.6)	7,400 (18.8)	2,241 (18.4)	30,752 (28.1)	55,129 (30.6)	1,01,640 (26.9)
4.	Industry and Minerals	97 (5.0)	1,125 (24.1)	1,967 (22.9)	1,636 (24.7)	3,107 (19.7)	9,582 (24.3)	2,640 (21.7)	16,948 (15.5)	22,108 (12.3)	59,210 (15.6)
4.1	Large and Medium Industries	55 (2.8)	938 (20.1)	1,726 (20.1)	1,510 (22.8)	2,864 (18.2)	8,989 (22.8)	2,384 (19.6)	15,002 (13.7)	19,355 (10.8)	52,823 (14.0)
4.2	Village and Small Industries	42 (2.1)	187 (4.0)	241 (2.8)	126 (1.9)	243 (1.5)	593 (1.5)	256 (2.1)	1,945 (1.8)	2,753 (1.5)	6,386 (1.7)
5.	Transport and Communication	518 (26.4)	1,261 (27.0)	2,112 (24.6)	1,222 (18.4)	3,080 (19.5)	6,870 (17.4)	2,045 (16.8)	17,678 (16.2)	27,119 (15.1)	61,905 (16.4)
6.	Social Services	472 (24.1)	855 (18.3)	1,492 (17.4)	976 (14.7)	2,985 (18.9)	6,834 (17.3)	1,968 (16.2)	15,917 (14.6)	31,545 (17.5)	63,044 (16.7)
7.	Miscellaneous	- -	- -	- -	- -	- -	- -	- -	3,448 (3.2)	7,690 (4.3)	11,138 (2.9)
	Total	1,960 (100.0)	4,672 (100.0)	8,577 (100.0)	6,626 (100.0)	15,779 (100.0)	39,426 (100.0)	12,177 (100.0)	1,09,292 (100.0)	1,80,000 (100.0)	3,78,509 (100.0)

Source: Cols. 2&3 'Kothari's Year Book on Business and Industry, 1988', p.14 and the remaining cols. from 'Economic Survey–1988-89', Government of India, pp.S 40-S 43.

Notes :
1. Figures in parentheses are respective percentages to the totals.
2. Upto 6th Plan energy includes only power, thereafter also including non-conventional energy.
3. * Includes Rural Development also.

A further break-up of the outlays allocated for industrial development points out that its lion share was received by the sub-sector of large and medium industries and hardly about 2 per cent of this could be allocated for the development of the village and small industries sector. This shows that relatively low priority in terms of allocation of outlays was accorded to development of village and small industries during the period of planned development programme in India.

2.2. Scenario of Uttar Pradesh

The objectives and priorities of the State reflect the wider National objectives, and the State of Uttar Pradesh also has tried to give concrete shape to the social philosophy and economic objectives adopted by the country. Broadly, the economic policy of the Centre as well as the State aims at accelerating the rate of economic growth and overall development of the economy, reduction of regional disparities and ensuring social justice, creation of employment opportunities, removal of poverty and raising standard of living of the weaker section of the society.

Directions for industrial development are set taking into account the broad framwork of the objectives. Therefore, the Second Plan of the State, following the Centre, aimed at accelerated development of industrial sector, particularly heavy industries. The next two Five Year Plans also broadly followed the objectives of industrial development as laid down in the National Plans. The Fifth Plan of the State aimed at fuller utilisation of existing capacities, setting up of new units and increasing the production of textiles and sugar to attain a growth rate of 8-10 per cent. To achieve the growth target of about 10 per cent in the industrial sector, the Sixth Plan aimed at augmenting the level of investment in the State, establishing the Joint Sector Projects and giving priority to such industries which have greater potential of employment. The industrial policy of the State formulated within the framework of the National policy aimed at[23]:

(i) Establishment of certain major industrial projects in the Central Sector.

(ii) Creation of industrial environment to attract investment from private sector and heavy and medium projects suitably supplemented by public and joint ventures.

(iii) Promotion of small scale, khadi and village industries through suitable policies and by providing requisite assistance including development of infrastructure.

(iv) Special attention to handicrafts for benefiting artisans and economically weaker sections of the society.

(v) Development of agro/food-based industries to utilise the surplus of agricultural products.

(vi) Accelerated development of electronics industry, particularly in areas not open to other industries.

(vii) Providing requisite infrastructure facilities for industrial development, like, land, power, water and telecommunications.

(viii) Arrangement for satisfactory supply of required raw materials and marketing of products.

(ix) To provide for technical counselling to entrepreneurs including special programmes for entrepreneurial development.

(x) Modernisation of traditional industries like sugar and textiles and proper treatment of sick industries.

(xi) Development of backward areas and special concession/incentives for attracting investment in industrial ventures, particularly in backward areas.

It was envisaged that rapid growth in the State would be achieved by giving due priority to both heavy and light industries. Heavy industries would act as nucleus of industrial growth and small scale industries would result in greater employment generation. Regional disparities were sought to be reduced by industrial development of the backward areas.

The sector-wise Plan allocations of outlays for U.P. during the period (1951-1990) are shown in Table 4.2. A close examination of the Table indicates that agriculture, irrigation and flood control, energy and social services were treated as priority sectors in the First Five Year Plan. In its support, we notice that nearly 85 per cent of the total outlay was allocated for the development of these sectors. The industrial sector was assigned the lowest priority; only about 4 per cent of the total plan resources could be allocated for development of this sector.

In subsequent Five Year Plans, we notice that the percentage allocation of Plan resources for development of this sector was extremely low as compared to the corresponding percentage on all-India level. In case of U.P., the proportion of outlays earmarked for the development of industrial sector for whole of the period (1951-1990) is found to be only 6 per cent for whole of the country. Only fortunate part is that the sharing of the outlays of industrial sector between large and medium industries and village and small industries was not as much biased to the former in U.P. as against what we observed at the National level. In other words, while allocating funds, much more congnizance seems to have been given to development of village and small industries in U.P.

Comparing the outlays of industral sector it would be noticed that the objective of accelerated industrial development was backed by increased outlays at the National level, but the situation in the context of U.P. was altogether different. On an average, only 6 per cent of the total plan outlay has been spent on industrial development upto the Seventh Plan in the State as against 16 per cent on all-India level. However, a decline in the percentage outlay of industrial sector on all-India level is observed since the Sixth Plan. But there has been a significant increase in outlay of industrial sector in the State since the Fifth Plan onwards.

Thus, it becomes clear that there has been a significant gap in allocation of plan outlays for development of industrial sector between the State and the Centre; the former was far behind the latter. Apart from this, the kind of effective cooperation that the State needed was not extended by the Centre. Inspite of the development of large and heavy industries in the State being the responsibility of the Centre, not even a single Central Sector industrial project was established in U.P. during the first two plans. A beginning was made only in the Third Plan when a provision of Rs. 72.1 crore (against the total investment of Rs. 1144.2 crore in the country) was made for establishing industries under Central Sector in the State. This was hardly 6.3 per cent of the total investment under this sector in the country. Upto the middle of the Sixth Plan, the Central Sector investment in

Table-4.2 : Plan wise Outlay by Heads of Development (U.P)

(Rs. in lakhs)

	Head of Development	First Plan (1951-56) Actual	Second Plan (1956-61) Actual	Third Plan (1961-66) Actual	Annual Plans (1966-69) Actual	Fourth Plan (1969-74) Actual	Fifth Plan (1974-79) Actual	Annual Plan (1979-80) Actual	Sixth Plan (1980-85) Actual	Seventh Plan (1985-90) Outlay	Total (First to Seventh Plan)
	1	2	3	4	5	6	7	8	9	10	11
1.	Agriculture and Allied Sectors	2,356 (15.4)	2,411 (10.3)	4,983 (8.9)	3,025 (6.6)	7,794 (6.7)	13,127 (4.5)	4,176 (5.0)	36,081 (5.5)	76,737 (6.8)	1,50,690 (6.2)
2.	Cooperation	131 (0.9)	414 (1.8)	806 (1.4)	199 (0.4)	2,127 (1.8)	3,227 (1.1)	1,072 (1.3)	8,226 (1.2)	8,412 (0.7)	24,614 (1.0)
3.	Rural Development	851 (5.5)	2,764 (11.8)	4,876 (8.7)	2,251 (4.9)	3,367 (2.9)	10,927 (3.8)	4,273 (5.1)	45,800 (6.9)	62,585 (5.5)	1,37,694 (5.7)
4.	Irrigation and Flood control	3,871 (25.2)	4,110 (17.6)	11,917 (21.3)	13,095 (28.8)	29,381 (25.2)	71,522 (24.6)	22,672 (27.2)	1,39,582 (21.2)	2,18,450 (19.3)	5,14,600 (21.2)
5.	Energy	2,331 (15.2)	5,675 (24.3)	15,701 (28.0)	17,536 (38.5)	44,651 (38.3)	1,12,023 (38.5)	25,047 (30.0)	1,86,217 (28.2)	3,46,050 (30.6)	7,55,231 (31.2)
6.	Industry and Minerals	637 (4.2)	1,292 (5.5)	2,084 (3.7)	1,824 (4.0)	4,177 (3.6)	17,899 (6.2)	4,201 (5.0)	43,077 (6.5)	73,748 (6.5)	1,48,939 (6.1)
6.1	Large and Medium Industries	345 (2.3)	376 (1.6)	715 (1.3)	1,396 (3.1)	2,691 (2.3)	13,639 (4.7)	2,575 (3.1)	29,488 (4.5)	51,938 (4.6)	1,03,163 (4.3)
6.2	Village and Small Industries	292 (1.9)	910 (3.9)	1,344 (2.4)	393 (0.9)	1,337 (1.2)	3,517 (1.2)	1,478 (1.8)	11,976 (1.8)	18,650 (1.6)	39,897 (1.6)
6.3	Mining	- -	6 (0.03)	25 (0.04)	35 (0.1)	149 (0.1)	743 (0.3)	148 (0.2)	1,613 (0.2)	3,160 (0.3)	5,879 (0.2)
7.	Transport and Communications	686 (4.5)	1,537 (6.6)	2,814 (5.0)	1,689 (3.7)	7,796 (6.7)	24,666 (8.5)	8,568 (10.3)	67,790 (10.3)	1,15,849 (10.2)	2,31,395 (9.6)
8.	Social and Community Services	4,474 (29.2)	4,601 (19.7)	10,294 (18.4)	4,915 (10.8)	14,825 (12.7)	36,731 (12.6)	12,112 (14.5)	1,25,871 (19.1)	1,78,588 (15.8)	3,92,411 (16.2)
9.	Miscellaneous	- -	532 (2.3)	2,588 (4.6)	998 (2.2)	2,436 (2.1)	800 (0.3)	1,233 (1.5)	6,785 (1.0)	50,936 (4.5)	66,308 (2.7)
	Total	15,337 (100.0)	23,336 (100.0)	56,063 (100.0)	45,532 (100.0)	1,16,557 (100.0)	2,90,923 (100.0)	83,354 (100.0)	6,59,429 (100.0)	11,31,355 (100.0)	24,21,886 (100.0)

Source : State Plan Documents.

Note: Till the Fifth Plan energy incorporates only power, thereafter including non-conventional energy as well.

the State averaged only 4.4 per cent of the total investment made under this sector in the country. The inadequacy of this amount is clearly brought out when we compare it to the total population of the State, which represents nearly 16 per cent of the total population of the country.[24]

A lower order of funds made available for development of industrial sector in U.P. seems to have been caused by the significant gap in per capita plan outlays/central assistance between U.P. and all-States during various plans, as would be evident from the following Table :

Table 4.3 : Per Capita Plan Outlay/Central Assistance (Rs.)

Plan	*Plan Outlay*		*Central Assistance*	
	U.P.	*All States*	*U.P.*	*All States*
1	*2*	*3*	*4*	*5*
First Plan (1951-56)	25	38	13	23
Second Plan (1956-61)	32	51	17	25
Third Plan (1961-66)	72	92	46	55
Annual Plans (1966-69)	53	61	32	36
Fourth Plan (1969-74)	132	142	61	65
Fifth Plan (1974-79)	322	365	123	128
Annual Plan (1979-80)	78	106	38	39
Sixth Plan (1980-85)	559	694	174	203
Seventh Plan (1985-90)	992	1,165	284	352

Source: Till Sixth Plan, Draft Seventh Five Year Plan and Annual Plan 1985-86 and for Seventh Plan, State of the Economy, Government of Uttar Pradesh.

Finally, it may be remarked that while the importance of increased investment to growth cannot be denied, equally important factor of economic development having all pervading effect is the technical change or innovation which involves use of resources in a manner that leads to increased efficiency. In this context, Schumpeter has rightly remarked that the slow and continuous increase in time of the national supply of productive means and of saving is obviously an important factor in explaining the course of economic history through the centuries, but it is completely overshadowed by the fact that development consists primarily in employing existing resources in a different way, in doing new things with them, irrespective of whether those resources increase of not.[25] Therefore, the subsequent chapters of our study are exclusively devoted to analyse, in detail,technological change and development of organised industries in U.P. both at the State and the sub-State levels.

References

1. W.W. Rostow (1971), p.20
2. Lewis considers process of development to be one where a country is transformed from being a 5 percent saver and investor to 12 percent saver and investor (particularly referring the Indian case). See W.A. Lewis (1978), p.208.

3. A.P. Thirlwall (1983), p.119.
4. See section 1.4 of chapter-V of the present book.
5. A.P. Srinivasamurthy (1981), p.21
6. A.P. Thirlwall (1983), p.199
7. A.P. Srinivasamurthy (1981), p.23.
8. W.W. Rostow (1971), p.21-24.
9. W.G. Hoffman (1960).
10. G.A. Fel'dman (1928). This article was popularised in West by E.D. Domar (1957).
11. N. Rosenberg (1963); and H.J. Habakkuk (1962).
12. F. Stewart (1976), p.132.
13. R.P. Mishra, K.V. Sundaram and V.L.S. Prakash Rao (1974), p.8.
14. Quoted in *Ibid.*, p.8
15. For details see A.P. Srinivasmurthy (1981), pp.35-36.
16. I.J. Ahluwalia (1987), p.389.
17. Government of India, *The Second Five Year Plan*, 1956-61, Planning Commission, New Delhi, pp.393,394.
18. Government of India, *The Third Five Year Plan*, 1961-66, Planning Commission, New Delhi, p.459.
19. Government of India, *The Fourth Five Year Plan*, 1969-74, Planning Commission, New Delhi, pp.304.
20. Government of India, *Draft Fifth Five Year Plan*, 1974-79, vol. II, Planning Commission, New Delhi, p.133.
21. Government of India, *The Sixth Five Year Plan*, 1980-85, Planning Commission, New Delhi, p.261.
22. Government of India, *The Seventh Five Year Plan*, 1985-90, Planning Commission, New Delhi, p.170.
23. Government of Uttar Pradesh, *Draft Annual Plan*, 1987-88, Vol. II, Planning Department, p.138.
24. See V.S. Singh, 'Measuring Inter-State Development: Multiple Indicators Approach', in R.T. Tewari and A. Joshi (eds.) (1988).
25. Quoted in I.R. Bidkar (1988), p.48.

CHAPTER 5

//Technological Change and Development of Organised Industries in U.P. : State–Level Analysis

Uttar Pradesh is the most populous state of India and generally suffers from industrial backwardness. No doubt, since dawn of the Seventies, there has been a gradual improvement in the situation.[1] This is mainly due to an increase in the investment effort accompanied by expansion of promotional and protective measures, effecting a favourable environment for growth. But, because of being a poor State characterised by the shortage of capital, it would be imperative to ensure maximum possible utilisation of the scarce resources with optimum efficiency.

Giving due weightage to the above state of art, the present chapter aims at measuring and analysing the relationship between technological change and development of organised industries in U.P. during the period: 1974–1986. The chapter is divided into three sections. The first section deals with the measurement of technological change in the organised manufacturing sector of U.P., twenty industry groups and also four categories of these industry groups delineated on the basis of capital intensity or capital-labour ratio. In the second section, we have analysed the performance of organised industries, mainly in terms of output and employment growth. Finally, the last section is devoted to analyse inter-relationship between technological change and development of organised industries in U.P. during the reference period.

1. MEASUREMENT OF TECHNOLOGICAL CHANGE: 1974-75 TO 1985-86

1.1 Trends in Partial and Total Factor Productivity in Organised Manufacturing Sector

To begin with, it is aimed at analysing the trends in partial productivities and capital intensity of the organised manufacturing sector in U.P. Increase in the partial productivity ratio signifies efficiency in the use of a particular input overtime. During the pariod under study, it is seen that labour productivity increased at the trend growth rate of 4.1 percent while capital productivity showed a decreasing trend of 0.13 percent (statistically insignificant), as would be evident from Table-5.1. Moreover, during the same period, capital intensity registered a trend growth rate of 4.24 percent.[2] Since there have been yearly fluctuations in the indices of all the three ratios, the entire period is divided into two sub-periods and the trend growth rates have been worked out separately for each of the sub-periods so as to analyse the inter temporal differences. Sharp differences in the trend growth rates of all three types of ratios can be observed between the two sub-periods. During the first sub-period (1974-80), all the three ratios, i.e. labour productivity, capital producitvity and capital intensity registered a positive but insignificant trend growth rates. Contrary to this, a sudden spurt in the trend growth rates of all the three ratios can be observed in sub-period II: 1980-86. And these are found to be significant in respect of all the three ratios. The trend growth rate of labour productivity (16.77 percent) exceeded the trend growth rate of capital intensity (11.50 percent) and also the trend growth of capital productivity (4.73 percent). Thus, during the second sub-period the organised industrial sector of the State is characterised by significant improvements in efficiency, particularly in the use of labour input.

Table-5.1 : Indices of Partial Productivity Ratios and Capital Intensity for Organised Manufacturing Sector in Uttar Pradesh: 1974-75 to 1985-86

Year	*Labour Productivity*	*Capital Productivity*	*Capital Intensity*
1	2	3	4
1974-75	100.00	100.00	100.00
1975-76	92.91	91.81	101.20
1976-77	96.46	97.92	98.51
1977-78	101.15	105.77	95.63
1978-79	107.45	105.99	101.38
1979-80	101.91	98.49	103.47
1980-81	80.54	84.02	95.85
1981-82	82.39	78.47	105.00
1982-83	116.06	102.68	113.03
1983-84	137.08	99.90	137.22
1984-85	139.67	93.05	150.10
1985-86	168.03	105.37	159.47
Trend Growth Rate:			
1974-75 to 1979-80	**1.666**	**1.242**	**0.419**
	(1.588)	**(0.949)**	**(0.599)**
1980-81 to 1985-86	**16.772***	**4.725*****	**11.504***
	(7.611)	**(2.150)**	**(12.954)**
1974-75 to 1985-86	**4.101****	**-0.130**	**4.236***
	(2.770)	**(0.158)**	**(4.625)**

Notes: Figures in parentheses are t value of estimates.

* Significant at 1 percent level.

** Significant at 5 percent level.

*** Significant at 10 percent level.

Generally, most of the earlier studies on the aforesaid subject observed increases in labour productivity accompanied by still greater increases in capital intensity and a considerable fall in capital productivity. It is asserted that most of the increases in labour productivity were due to capital deepening and the greater use of capital was not accompanied by significant technical progress, which might have prevented capital productivity from falling.[3] A study on Punjab manufacturing by L. Singh (1987) also found the similar movements in the three ratios, but in contrast to the above, the study identified increased wage rage as one of the major factors of increased labour productivity. The results of our study do not show similarities with the above studies, but like Goldar (1986, p.78) this study also finds that the trend growth rate of capital intensity is not much above the trend growth rate of labour productivity. This is accompanied by only slight (insignificant) fall in capital productivity. Our correlation results also go in favour of this finding. While a highly significant coefficient of correlation of 0.94 is found between labour productivity and capital intensity, a slightly weak but significant correlation of 0.53 is also observed between the two partial productivities, pointing towards efficiency in input use in the organised industrial sector.[4] The reason being that during sub-period II: 1980-86, the highly significant trend of growth rate of labour productivity exceeded that of the capital intensity. This accompanied by low but significant trend growth rate of capital productivity exhibited a phenomenal improvement in technological progress of the State manufacturing during the period 1980-86.

Besides, there are also certain studies, where both capital and labour productivities have similar movements.[5] A study of the manufacturing sector in Karnataka for the period of 1968-77 by S.S. Dhillon (1983), found a decline in the two productivity ratios accompanied by significant increase in capital intensity. On the other hand, a study by D. Gupta (1985) in case of Maharastra manufacturing found an increase in capital productivity accompanied by a decline in both labour productivity and capital intensity during 1969-76. However the results of the present study are somewhat different from the results of these studies.

An examination of cost ratios (Appendix Table-5.1) indicates that a significant trend growth of wage rate is accompanied by an insignificant decrease in rate of return (which simply measures surplus obtained after deducting wage bill from value added, per unit of capital). High wage rate in the organised manufacturing sector might be one of the important reasons for increased capital intensity during the period of the study.

It would be evident from various studies cited above that no general conclusion on overall efficiency can be drawn on the basis of partial productivities. Therefore, the estimates of total factor productivity (TFP) indices have also been worked out for the organised manufacturing sector of the State. The estimates of Kendrick, Solow and translog indices of TFP[6] are given in Table-5.2. The trend growth rates of these indices are found to be 1.7, 2.42 and 1.27 percent respectively during the period of 1974-86. However, only Solow index is found to be significant at 10 percent level. The trend growth rate of gross value added during the same period is noticed to be 6.56 percent. Therefore, according to the three TFP indices, the contribution of technical change to output growth lies in the range of 20-36 percent.

Table-5.2 : Indices of Total Factor Productivity for Organised Manufacturing Sector in Uttar Pradesh: 1974-75 to 1985-86.

Year	*Kendrick Index*	*Solow Index*	*Translog Index*
1	2	3	4
1974-75	1.000	1.000	1.000
1975-76	0.923	0.923	0.921
1976-77	0.972	0.969	0.967
1977-78	1.035	1.029	1.027
1978-79	1.067	1.060	1.058
1979-80	1.001	0.994	0.991
1980-81	0.823	0.816	0.787
1981-82	0.803	0.809	0.780
1982-83	1.088	1.119	1.025
1983-84	1.151	1.214	1.104
1984-85	1.111	1.183	1.078
1985-86	1.287	1.388	1.244
Trend Growth Rate:			
1974-75 to 1979-80	**1.447**	**1.280**	**1.239**
	(1.267)	**(1.143)**	**(1.091)**
1980-81 to 1985-86	**9.780****	**11.716***	**9.995***
	(4.461)	**(5.141)**	**(5.237)**
1974-75 to 1985-86	**1.702**	**2.419*****	**1.266**
	(1.609)	**(2.065)**	**(1.150)**

Source: Based on ASI Reports: Various Issues

Notes : Figures in parentheses are t values of the estimates.

* Significant at 1 percent level of significance.

*** Significant at 5 percent level of significance.

*** Significant at 10 percent level of significance.

Comparing the trend growth rates of these indices for the two sub-periods, it is further noticed that there was a positive but insignificant trend rate of growth in all the three indices in the first sub-period: 1974-80. However, in the second sub-period (1980-86), there was an unprecedented increase in the trend growth rates of all the three indices with the highest growth rate in Solow index (11.76 percent) being followed by those in translog (9.99 percent) and Kendrick (9.78 percent) indices. This along with high growth rates in both capital and labour productivity during this sub-period seems to be *inter-alia* an outcome of the favourable impact of the on-going public policies.

Comparing our results with those of other studies, it is observed that some of the earlier studies in the context of Indian manufacturing found a sluggish growth rate in TFP.[7] Against these, a steady decline in TFP is observed in studies of Raj Krishna and Mehta (1968) and also of Banerji (1975) for the time period of 1946-64 and that of Reddy and Rao

(1962) for the period of (1946-57). In her study, Ahluwalia (1985) noticed a significant decline in both Solow and translog indices of TFP for Indian manufacturing during the period of 1959-80. Besides these, many studies[8] on the manufacturing sector of different States have also found the similar trend in TFP.

As against these studies, Hashim and Dadi (1973) in their study observed an increase of 2.8 percent in Solow index with technical progress contributing about 50 percent to output growth during 1946-64. Similarly, Goldar (1986) in his study covering the period 1951-65 witnessed positive growth rates in Kendrick, Solow and translog indices, although the contribution of TFP to output growth (21-24 percent) was much less as compared to the previous studies. In this study also the contribution of TFP to output growth was positive and approximately 36 percent (on the basis of Solow index).

1.2 Trends in Partial and Total Factor Prductivty: Inter-Category/Inter-Industry Analysis

For an indepth analysis, partial and TFP indices for twenty industry groups and the four categories delineated following the capital-labour ratios, have been estimated. The industry groups are arranged category-wise in the descending order of capital intensity. The category-I includes highly capital intensive, category-II, medium-high capital intenstive, category-III medium-low capital intensive and category-IV low capital intensive industry groups respectively. The trend growth rates of partial productivity ratios, capital intensity, and TFP indices of Kendrick, Solow and Translog are given in Table-5.3 (year-wise indices for the period of 1974-86 are provided in Appendix-Table 5.2).

Excepting category-I, significant trend growth of labour productivity is observed in the remaining categories. The highest trend growth rate of 8.5 percent in labour productivity is observed in category-II, whereas the corresponding trend growth rate is found to be the lowest in category-I. The categories IV and III with the respective trend growth rates of 5.5 percent and 3.5 percent in labour productivity occupy the second and the third place in ranking. The trend growth rate of labour productivity for the total organised manufacturing sector is estimated at 4.1 percent, which is slightly greater than that of category-III.

Out of twenty industry groups, significant growth rate of labour productivity is found in thirteen industry groups. The highest trend growth rate of 8.6 percent (significant at 10 percent level) is observed in rubber, plastic, petroleum and coal products followed by the trend growth rate of 8.5 percent (significant at 1 percent level) in electrical machinery, apparatus, appliances and supplies and parts. The higher trend growth rates of labour productivity found in three out of four industry groups constituting category-II have contributed significantly to the highest growth rate of labour productivity in this category. The labour productivity recorded the lowest and insignificant trend growth rate of 1.4 percent in chemicals and chemical products.

Insignificant trend growth rates of capital productivity are observed in three out of the four categories. This seems to have depressed the trend growth rates of capital productivity (which again is insignificant) for total manufacturing sector at the State level. In case of category-II, however, a highly significant trend growth rate of 7.6 percent in capital productivity can be observed. This accompanied by the highly significant trend growth rate of labour productivity suggests that there has been efficient use of inputs in the industry groups constituting this category.

Table-5.3 : Category/Industry Group-wise Trend Growth Rates in Partial Productivities, Capital Intensity and Total Factor Productivity in U.P.: 1974-75 to 1985-86

	Category/Industry Group	*Labour Productivity*	*Capital Productivity*	*Capital Intensity*	Total Factor Productivity Index *Kendrick*	*Solow*	*Translog*
	1	*2*	*3*	*4*	*5*	*6*	*7*
1.	Manufacture of chemicals & chemical products (except products of petrol and coal)	1.361 (0.753)	-1.402 (0.907)	2.802* (3.893)	-0.724 (0.458)	-0.405 (0.247)	-2.863*** (1.928)
2.	Basic metals and alloys industries	3.881** (2.574)	3.147*** (2.185)	0.712*** (1.939)	3.591** (2.439)	3.622** (2.468)	1.967 (1.331)
3.	Manufacture of wool, silk and synthetic fibre textiles	3.312 (1.655)	-1.222 (0.630)	4.590** (2.741)	0.509 (0.295)	-1.616 (0.734)	-4.281** (2.523)
	Category I	**2.359** **(1.668)**	**0.074** **(0.064)**	**2.283*** **(3.639)**	**0.861** **(0.707)**	**1.293** **(0.996)**	**-0.092** **(0.075)**
4.	Manufacture of electric machinery, apparatus, appliances & supplies & parts	8.526* (4.477)	9.621* (5.311)	-0.999*** (2.188)	8.749* (4.657)	9.256* (5.107)	7.338* (5.021)
5.	Manufacture of rubber, plastic, petroleum & coal products	8.600*** (2.020)	0.823 (0.192)	7.711* (3.919)	2.398 (0.565)	-2.311 (0.488)	-4.576 (1.270)
6.	Manufacture of edible oil and vanaspati ghee	5.544*** (1.941)	-2.068 (0.869)	7.773* (8.318)	0.838 (0.332)	-0.536 (0.216)	-3.729 (1.432)
7.	Other manufacturing industries	4.989 (1.234)	-3.015 (0.781)	8.253* (4.610)	0.936 (0.936)	-9.957*** (1.905)	– –
	Category II	**8.528*** **(5.477)**	**7.615*** **(4.886)**	**0.848***** **(2.129)**	**8.242*** **(5.334)**	**7.983*** **(5.117)**	**6.477*** **(5.320)**
8.	Manufacture of paper, paper products & printing, publishing & allied industries	1.744 (1.463)	-6.342* (6.700)	8.633* (12.197)	-2.812** (2.962)	-1.596 (1.340)	-1.811 (1.625)
9.	Manufacture of alcohol, beverages, tobacco & tobacco products	4.715** (2.911)	0.633 (0.376)	4.056* (4.556)	2.409 (1.497)	1.671 (0.985)	-0.396 (0.236)

Table 5.3 (Contd...)

1	2	3	4	5	6	7
10. Manufacture of machinery, machine tools and parts (except electrical)	5.409* (3.223)	3.033*** (2.041)	2.305* (5.430)	4.200** (2.671)	4.527** (2.868)	1.523 (0.980)
11. Manufacture of cotton textiles	1.974 (1.501)	-0.743 (0.475)	2.737* (4.859)	1.247 (0.912)	1.052 (0.782)	-0.092 (0.069)
12. Manufacture of food products (except sugar, khandsari & gur)	5.571* (5.910)	3.890* (5.955)	1.618** (2.764)	4.506* (6.276)	4.721* (6.562)	3.279* (0.696)
13. Manufacture of textile products (including wearing apparel other than footwear)	3.400 (1.012)	-6.875** (2.352)	11.034* (5.583)	-4.750 (1.642)	-4.320 (1.250)	-9.046** (2.488)
Category III	**3.516*** **(4.869)**	**-0.095** **(0.104)**	**3.615*** **(8.410)**	**1.917**** **(2.411)**	**1.861**** **(2.347)**	**1.515***** **(2.024)**
14. Manufacture of metal products and parts (except machinery & transport equipment)	4.978* (5.224)	-0.043 (0.038)	5.023* (11.470)	1.961*** (1.890)	2.214*** (2.143)	1.700 (1.633)
15. Manufacture of non-mettalic mineral products	2.623*** (2.142)	-1.627 (1.684)	4.320* (3.809)	1.976 (1.749)	1.772 (1.535)	0.537 (0.484)
16. Manufacture of jute, hemp and mesta textiles	7.399* (5.448)	0.365 (0.110)	7.009** (2.385)	7.184* (5.249)	1.822 (0.834)	2.020 (1.087)
17. Manufacture of sugar, khandsari & gur	6.705** (2.670)	-2.146 (1.153)	9.046* (5.246)	4.612*** (2.070)	2.276 (0.911)	0.504 (0.221)
18. Manufacture of transport equipment and parts	1.641 (1.044)	4.906** (2.463)	-3.112 (1.625)	2.516 (1.724)	2.387 (1.595)	0.375 (0.300)
19. Manufacture of wood & wood products, furniture & fixtures	3.536*** (2.010)	-0.211 (0.181)	3.754*** (2.085)	3.206*** (1.958)	4.309** (2.991)	-0.741 (0.469)
20. Manufacture of leather and leather & fur products (except rapair)	4.798** (2.384)	-0.021 (0.010)	4.820* (4.073)	1.949 (0.986)	2.280 (0.823)	0.589 (0.238)
Category IV	**5.524*** **(3.685)**	**-0.578** **(0.750)**	**6.137*** **(4.530)**	**3.603**** **(3.124)**	**3.480**** **(2.669)**	**2.667**** **(2.312)**

Table 5.3 (Contd...)

1	2	3	4	5	6	7
Total Manufacturing	**4.101****	**-0.130**	**4.236***	**1.702**	**2.419*****	**1.266**
	(2.770)	**(0.158)**	**(4.625)**	**(1.609)**	**(2.065)**	**(1.150)**

Source: Appendix Table-5.2.

Notes: Figures in parentheses are t values of the estimates.

* Significant at 1 percent level of significance.

** Significant of 5 percent level of significance.

*** Significant at 10 percent level of significance.

Positive trend growth rates of capital productivity are observed in eight industry groups, out of which five experienced significant trend growth rates. These groups are: basic metals and alloys; electrical machinery apparatus, appliances and supplies and parts; machinery, machine tools and parts (except electrical); food products; and transport equipment and parts. The highest trend growth rate of 9.6 percent in capital productivity is noticed in electrical machinery, apparatus, appliances and supplies and parts. A significant trend rate of decline of capital productivity was observed in paper and paper products, printing, publishing and allied industries; and textile products.

Significant trend growth rates of capital intensity can be seen in all the four categories. The growth rates of category-IV (6.14 percent) and category-III (3.62 percent) have exceeded those of category-I (2.28 percent) and category-II (0.85 percent). As already indicated, categories-I and II are relatively more capital intensive as compared to the categories-III and IV. The latter two are characterised by significant capital deepening during the period 1974-86 as the index of capital-labour ratio has increased from 100 to 201 in category-IV and from 100 to 154 in category-III. Further, in category-I, the index has risen from 100 to 135 only, with its lowest increase from 100 to 107 seen in category-II (see Appendix Table-5.2.). Summingly, the growth rate of capital intensity is found to be highly significant for whole of the organised manufacturing sector at the State level.

There has been a significant capital deepening in eighteen out of total twenty industry groups. The highest trend growth rate of 11.03 percent is witnessed in textile products followed by the trend growth rate of 9.05 percent in sugar, khandsari and gur. A significant trend rate of decline of capital intensity (-0.99 percent) in electrical machinery, apparatus, appliances and supplies and parts has effected a comparatively lower trend growth rate of capital intensity in category-II.

So far these ratios have been discussed in isolation of each other. However, to arrive at some meaningful conclusions, inter-relationship between these ratios is also needed to be analysed. Significant trend growth rates of labour productivity, capital productivity and capital intensity are observed in category-II. A modest trend growth rate of 0.8 percent in capital labour ratio is accompanied by significantly high growth rates of 7.6 percent in capital productivity and 8.5 percent in labour productivity. Capital intensity seems to be accompanied by increases in both the productivity ratios. A positive coefficient of correlation of 0.99 between the two partial productivity indices confirms this. Further, a positive correlation of 0.66 (significant at five percent level) is also observed between capital intensity and labour productivity but it seems that other factors like 'technical progress' and 'economies of scale' have also played an important role in the increased output per person. Besides, correlating labour productivity to wages, the coefficient of 0.85 also shows a significant role of latter in the former.[9] The trend growth rate of wages (4.2 percent) is just half of the trend growth of labour productivity implying a fall in the cost of labour per unit of output.[10] Further, it is observed that rate of return on capital has witnessed a highly significant trend growth of 11.53 percent. High growth of capital productivity associated with high rate of return signifies increasing returns to capital in this category (Appendix-Table 5.1).

In categories-III and-IV, it is seen that increased capital intensity is accompanied by a high growth rate of labour productivity and a negative though insignificant growth rate of capital productivity. Significant positive correlation of 0.72 and 0.96 (significant at 1 percent level) is observed between capital-labour and value added-labour ratio in categories-

III and IV respectively. It seems that capital substitution has been the major source of growth in these categories. Looking to the cost ratios (Appendix Table 5.1), we observe high trend growth rates of wages in categories-III and IV. High correlation between labour productivity and wages per person is observed in category-III (r=0.81) and category-IV (r=0.93), meaning thereby both have mutually influenced each other. However, in case of category-IV, contribution of capital deepening to growth of labour productivity outweights that of wage rage.[11]

Further, in case of highly capital intensive category (i.e., category-I), there has been a significant growth in capital-labour ratio accompanied by insignificant trend growth rates of both capital and labour productivity indices. It seems that increased capital intensity in the industry groups of this category has not been conducive to productivity improvements. Excess capacity may be one of the factors responsible for its. A significantly high trend growth of wage rate as compared to that of labour productivity points towards the increased labour cost per unit of output. This might have led entrepreneurs to decide in favour of substituting capital for labour in category-I. However, increases in remuneration also have not resulted in a positive impact on the growth of labour productivity. Further, insignificant trend growth of the rate of return on capital indicates poor reinvestment potential of the industry groups constituting this category.

Out of twenty industry groups, positive significant trend growth rates of both labour and capital productivities are seen in four industry groups, namely, electrical machinery, apparatus, appliances and supplies and parts; basic metals and alloys; food products; and machinery, machine tools and parts (except electrical). This is accompanied by a significant trend rate of decline in capital intensity in the first industry group, whereas the latter three industry groups have experienced significant capital deepening (the trend growth rates being lower than those of the two partial productivity ratios). Coefficient of correlation between the two productivity ratios is found to be highly significant, being 0.99, 0.97, 0.95 and 0.97 in all the four industry groups respectively. Technological change and economies of scale seem to be the major factors of growth of these industry groups. A fall in labour cost per unit of output in electrical machinery, apparatus, appliances and supplies and parts; food products and machinery, machine tools and parts (except electrical) is witnessed by the lower trend growth rate of wage rate than that of labour productivity. A significantly high trend growth of rate of return in the first two industry groups (i.e., electrical machinery, apparatus, appliances and supplies and parts; and food products) shows a wider scope for reinvestment.

In four industry groups, namely, chemicals and chemical products, wool, silk and synthetic fibre textiles; other manufacturing industries; and cotton textiles; a significant capital deepening is accompanied by insignificant labour and capital productivities, whereas in paper and paper products, printing, publishing and allied industries; and textile products; the decline in capital productivity is found to be significant. The input proportion used in these industry groups seems to have resulted in the inefficient use of both capital and labour. Highly significant trend growth of wage rate for these industry groups again indicates increased per unit labour cost. Further, in paper and paper products, printing, publishing and allied industries; and textile products; a significant negative trend growth of the rate of return accompanied by a significant decrease of capital productivity seems to indicate diminishing returns to capital in these industry groups.

In case of nine industry groups, namely, rubber, plastic, petroleum and coal products; edible oil and vanaspati ghee; alcohol, beverages, tobacco and tobacco products; metal products (except machinery and transport equipment); non-metallic mineral products; jute, hemp and mesta textiles; sugar, khandsari and gur; wood and wood products, furnitures and fixtures; and leather and leather and fur products; significant trend growth rates of capital intensity and labour productivity are accompanied by insignificant trend growth rate of capital productivity. A higher output per unit of labour appears to have resulted from greater use of capital.

Only in respect of transport equipment and parts, there has been a significant trend growth rate of capital productivity accompanied by insignificant trend growth rate of labour productivity and capital intensity. Therefore, a greater use of capital might prove to be effective in augmenting the productivity level in this industry group.

The partial productivity indices, as discussed above, are not very helpful in drawing specific conclusions regarding the increase / decrease in overall efficiency, particularly when the ratios show divergent movements. Therefore, alternatively we have worked out estimates of Kendrick, Solow and translog indices of TFP. The trend growth rates of these TFP indices are given in Table-5.3 (See also Appendix Table-5.2). Significant trend growth rates in respect of all the three indices are observed in all the categories excepting the category-I. The highest trend growth rates of 8.2 percent, 7.9 percent and 6.5 percent in Kendrick, Solow and translog indices respectively are experienced in the category-II. As shown earlier, this is supported by the significant growth rates of partial productivity ratios also. A significantly high positive coefficient of correlation of 0.99 between Solow index and partial productivities of both labour and capital also goes in favour of this finding. Industry groups constituting this category contributed 30.8 percent to total gross value added of the organised manufacturing sector in 1985-86 (Appendix Table -5.3).

The categories-IV and III occupied the second and the third place respectively so far as the trend growth rates of all the three TFP indices are concerned. As stated previously, significant trend growth rate of labour productivity was accompanied by insignificant trend growth rate of capital productivity in both these categories. In the category-III, the coefficient of correlation of Solow index with both capital and labour productivities (r=0.78 and 0.98 respectively) indicates the positive association of the former with the latter two indices. Whereas in the category-IV, the coefficient of correlation is found to be highly significant (r=0.98) between Solow index and labour productivity only.

In case of individual industry groups, as many as ten industry groups have positive trend growth rates in respect of these indices, out of which these are found to be significant only in two industry groups, namely, electrical machinery, apparatus, appliances and supplies and parts; and food products. These two industry groups have also experienced high growth rates of both capital and labour productivities. These two industry groups together have contributed about 25 percent to the gross value added of the manufacturing sector in 1985-86.

Significant trend growth rates in Kendrick and Solow indices of TFP can be observed in basic metals and alloys; machinery, machine tools and parts (except electrical); metal products; and wood and wood products, furtniture and fixtures, which have contributed 11.6 percent to the gross value added of the organised industrial sector in U.P during 1985-86. In the first two industry groups, there have been significant increases in labour and capital productivity ratios. Whereas, in case of the latter two industry groups, a significant trend growth rate of labour productivity is noticed with insignificant trend rate of decline in capital productivity.

In two industry groups, namely, jute, hemp and mesta textiles; and sugar, khandsari and gur; a significant trend growth rate is observed in respect of Kendrick index only. In these industry groups, a significant growth rate of labour productivity is accompanied by significant capital deepening.

The trend rate of a simultaneous decline in respect of all the the three indices of TFP is not found significant in any industry group. However, there has been a significant decline in one index or the other in five industry groups (i.e., chemicals and chemical products; wool, silk and synthetic fibre textiles; other manufacturing industries; paper and paper products; and printing, publishing and allied industries; and textile products). Insignificant trend growth rates of partial productivities accompanied by significant capital deepening are witnessed in the first three industry groups, whereas a significant trend rate of decline in capital productivity is observed in the latter two industry groups. Thus, the contribution of factor inputs to output growth predominates in these industry groups.

As far as ranking of industries on the basis of efficiency is concerned, no general conclusions could be drawn from the earlier studies. Some studies have found new industries to be more efficient, while some others have identified traditional industries qualifying for higher efficiency. There are some studies, which have attempted to measure TFP of individual industries on all India level, and a few are found to have dealt with certain industries at the State-level. In case of the former, Sinha and Sawhney (1970) observed increased efficiency during the period of 1950-63 in respect of five industries, namely cotton textiles, jute textiles, sugar, cement, and paper and paper board.

In his study of five industries (for the period of 1946-64) Banerji (1975) does not find appreciable increases in the overall efficiency of any of them. However, the performance of sugar and bicycles is found to be better than that of cotton, jute, and paper industries (so far as Solow index and partial productivities are concerned). The technical progress and economies of scale are identified as factors responsible for the better performance of the first two industries. Further, Mehta (1980) studied twenty seven comparable ASI and CMI industries for the period of 1953-65. Based on the analysis, he found that there was an over all decline in efficiency. However, in certain industries like biscuit making, vegetable oils, tanning, glass and glassware he noticed an increase in the TFP. A significant decline was observed in sugar, cement, paper and paper board, matches, iron and steel, cotton textiles and ceramics. On the whole, traditional industries have shown a decline in efficiency, most of the growth being attributed to capital deepening. An overall decline in efficiency was found in most of the industries studied by Ahluwalia (1985) for the time period of 1959-80. A significant decline was found in rubber products, miscellaneous industries, food manufacturing, wood and cork, metal products, leather and fur products, chemicals, and non-metallic mineral products. Two industries, namely footwear, and furniture and fixtures experienced significant growth in the TFP (Solow and translog indices).

Goldar (1986) in his study for the period 1960-70 noticed a significant trend growth rate in Kendrick index in tobacco manufacture, paper and paper products, and leather and fur. On the other hand, a significant decline was experienced in respect of food products, rubber products, petroleum products and basic metals. Industries with productivity losses outweigh the industries with productivity gains. Further, on the basis of regression analysis, it was concluded that growth rate of new industries tends to be lower than that of traditional industries, probably due to large scale nature of new industries (requiring a larger gestation period) and relatively higher cost of manufacture resulting from inefficient use of resources in the initial stages.

Covering a similar time period (1961-70), a study by Kumar (1983) observed a decline in both partial productivity and TFP in three out of four industries, namely, cotton, jute, iron & steel, excepting the increase in sugar industry. However, a significant capital deepening is observed in all the four industries.

Inter-State analysis of individual industries has been carried out by Subramaniyan (1979) and Rajalakshmi (1983). Subramaniyan analysed the trends of TFP in sugar industry in selected States of U.P., Bihar, Maharashtra, Tamil Nadu and Andhra Pradesh for the period 1953-69. Labour productivity showed a significant increase in all the States, whereas capital productivity experienced a decline. Much increases in labour productivity were attributed to significant capital deepening experienced by this industry in almost all the States analysed. Excepting Tamil Nadu, the TFP (Kendrick and CES index) showed a general decline. The study of Rajalakshmi found significant growth of TFP (Divisia index) in electrical machinery in Karnataka and Maharashtra, while the index experienced the decline in West Bengal.

Based on these studies it is very difficult to sum up and draw any precise and meaningful conclusion regarding the overall development of the industrial sector. However, increased use of capital seems to have been a major source of industrial growth. Besides, in our case, based on the previous analysis it is noticed that as compared to highly capital intensive category, greater productivity increases were observed in less capital intensive categories, particularly the medium-capital intensive one (i.e., category-II). The organised industrial sector of the State experienced a positivie though sluggish TFP growth, with a substantial acceleration in the growth of both partial and TFP indices especially during the period 1980 onwards. The sluggish growth in TFP for the entire period may be due to the fact that only eight out of twenty industry groups experienced significant increases in TFP. Whereas in remaining twelve industry groups overall efficiency has either remained constant or has shown a significant decline.

1.3 Sources of Growth of Output: Decomposition Based on Growth Rates

Based on linear homogeneous production function and the trend growth rates of gross value added, labour, capital and the average relative shares of the latter two in value added, it has been tried to estimate contributions of various factors to output growth. Labour and capital contributions are obtained by multiplying the trend growth rates by the respective average relative share of these inputs. The contribtion of TFP is obtained as a residual.[12]

The absolute and relative contributions of various factors to the output growth of the organised manufacturing sector are presented in Table-5.4. During the entire period, the total factor inputs played a significant role in the growth of value added, with capital contributing about 47 percent which is much greater than that of labour (about 19 percent). The contribution of TFP to output growth was about 34 percent.[13] Marked variations in the contributions of different factors can be seen between the two sub-periods. During the first sub-period (1974-80), the contribution of factor inputs to the growth of value added in the

Table-5.4 : Sources of Growth of Output in Organised Manufacturing Sector in U.P.: 1974-75 to 1985-86

(in percentage points) (percent)

Year	*Average Relative Share of Labour and Capital in Value Added*		*Absolute contribution of*			*Growth of Gross Value Added*	*Relative Contribution of*			
	Share of Labour	Share of Capital	Labour	Capital	TFP		Labour	Capital	TFP	Total
1	2	3	4	5	6	7	8	9	10	11
1974-75 to1979-80	0.52	0.48	2.69	2.70	1.55	6.94**	38.76	38.90	22.33	100.0
1980-81 to 1985-86	0.57	0.43	-1.87	3.37	11.44	12.94*	-14.45	26.04	88.41	100.0
1974-75 to 1985-86	0.54	0.46	1.28	3.06	2.22	6.56*	19.51	46.65	33.84	100.0

Source: Table 5.14

* Significant at 1 percent level of significance.

** Significant at 5 percent level of significance.

organised industrial sector was as high as 78 percent. Contrary to this, a marked reversal in the trend is noticeable during the second sub-period (1980-86); the share of factor inputs considerably reduced to 12 percent, with the result, the share of TFP appreciably increased from 22 percent in the first sub-period to about 88 percent in the second sub-period. Thus, the latter period seems to have demonstrated much higher efficiency in the use of factor inputs. The fall in the contribution of labour input [14] is found to be mainly responsible for a considerable shortfall in the contribution of factor inputs.

Based on decomposition results, Dholakià (Jan. 1977), Goldar (1986), and Ahluwalia (1985) have identified capital as a major source of output growth in Indian manufacturing sector. Almost similar results for twenty-two developing countries (for the period of 1950-65), are brought out in a study by Maddison (1970) (see Appendix Table-5.4). The contributions of labour and capital to average measured growth were 35 percent and 55 percent respectively. Besides, the residual 10 percent was attributable to increased efficiency in resource allocation. One of the most striking points emerging from the present study is that TFP has played a significant role in growth of value added of organised manufacturing sector of U.P. during the second sub-period (1980-86).

Category/industry group-wise average and relative contributions of different inputs to the growth during the reference period are shown in Table-5.5. Factor inputs are found to be major source of growth in the Category-I (79 percent) followed by the Category-III (70 percent). Increased efficiency plays a greater role in the category-II (61 percent) followed the category IV (51 percent). In almost all the cases, the contribution of capital has oustripped that of labour, while in case of category-I and III, it outstrips the contribution of TFP as well. Thus, the accelerated growth of capital seems to have been the major source of growth in these two categories.

Importance of capital is also brough out by industry group-wise analysis. There are only four industry groups (cotton textiles; non-metallic mineral products; transport equipment and parts; and leather and leather and fur products), which have demonstrated higher contribution of labour than that of capital. The contribution of TFP is greater that than of total factor input in basic metals and alloys; electrical machinery, apparatus, appliances and supplies and parts; metal products and parts; jute, hemp and mesta textiles; sugar, khandsari and gur; and wood and wood products showing increased efficiency in input use. Negative contribution of the residual is seen in chemical and chemical products; paper and paper products, printing, publishing and allied industries; and textile products. The contribution of labour is found to be negative in edible oil and vanaspati ghee; metal products and parts; and jute, hemp and mesta textiles. Thus, the latter three industry groups have experienced a negative growth of employment during the period 1974-86. Inspite of these inter-category/inter-industry variations, it is observed that the increased level of investment has contributed significantly to the growth of value added in the organised industrial sector of U.P. during the reference period.

1.4 Production Function Estimates

So far the arnalysis has been carried out with the help of different TFP indices. These indices are based on the restrictive assumptions of perfect competition and constant returns to scale. Further, only one element of technological progress (i.e. efficiency of technology) can be measured through these indices. The estimation of the unrestricted Cobb-Douglas production function relaxes these assumptions and therefore with its application apart from the neutral shifts in production function, returns to scale can also be estimated.

Table 5.5 : Category/Industry Group-wise Sources of Growth of Output in U.P.: 1974-75 to 1985-86

(in percentage points)

(percent)

	Category/Industry Grouup	*Average Relative Share of Labour and Capitals in Gross Value Added*		*Absolute contribution of*			*Growth of Gross Value Added*	*Relative Contribution of*			*Total*
		Share of Labour	Share of Capital	Labour	Capital	TFP		Labour	Capital	TFP	
	1	2	3	4	5	6	7	8	9	10	11
1.	Manufacture of chemical and chemical products (except products of petroleum and coal)	0.353	0.647	1.089	3.865	-0.467	4.487**	24.27	86.14	-10.41	100.0
2.	Basic metals & alloys industries	0.573	0.427	1.501	1.430	3.671	6.602*	22.74	21.66	55.60	100.0
3.	Manufacture of wool, silk & synthetic fibre textiles	0.518	0.482	0.977	3.164	1.121	5.262***	18.57	60.13	21.30	100.0
	Category I	**0.433**	**0.567**	**1.165**	**2.855**	**1.093**	**5.113***	**22.79**	**55.84**	**21.38**	**100.0**
4.	Manufacture of electrical machinery, apparatus, appliances & supplies and parts	0.423	0.577	2.313	2.547	9.601	14.461*	15.99	17.61	66.39	100.0
5.	Manufacture of rubber, plastic, petroleum & coal products	0.373	0.627	3.103	10.453	4.076	17.632**	17.60	59.28	23.12	100.0
6.	Manufacture of edible oil & vanaspati ghee	0.308	0.692	-0.720	3.635	0.162	3.077	-23.39	118.13	5.26	100.0
7.	Other manufacturing industries	0.507	0.493	1.797	5.960	0.952	8.709***	20.63	68.43	10.95	100.0
	Category II	**0.399**	**0.601**	**1.927**	**3.437**	**8.405**	**13.769***	**14.00**	**24.96**	**61.04**	**100.0**
8.	Manufacture of paper & paper products & printing, publishing and allied industries	0.637	0.363	1.936	4.332	-1.432	4.836*	40.03	89.58	-29.61	100.0
9.	Manufacture of alcohol, beverages, tobacco & tobacco products	0.423	0.577	1.108	3.785	2.431	7.234*	14.07	52.32	33.61	100.0
10.	Manufacture of machinery, machine tools and parts (except electrical machinery)	0.473	0.527	1.709	3.163	4.345	9.217*	18.54	34.32	47.14	100.0
11.	Manufacture of cotton textiles	0.812	0.188	2.325	1.067	1.501	4.893**	47.52	21.81	30.68	100.0
12.	Manufacture of food products (except sugar, khandsari and gur)	0.324	0.676	1.474	4.218	4.68	10.372*	14.21	40.67	45.12	100.0
13.	Manufacture of textile products (including wearing apparel other than footwear)	0.404	0.596	2.843	11.232	-3.4	10.675**	26.63	105.22	-31.85	100.0
	Category III	**0.592**	**0.408**	**1.949**	**2.866**	**2.108**	**6.923***	**28.15**	**41.40**	**30.45**	**100.0**
14.	Manufacture of metal products and parts (except machinery and transport equipment)	0.482	0.518	-0.676	1.839	2.342	3.505***	-19.29	52.47	66.82	100.0

Table-5.5 (Contd...)

	1	2	3	4	5	6	7	8	9	10	11
15.	Manufacture of non-metallic mineral products	0.834	0.166	2.904	1.320	1.972	6.196*	46.87	21.30	31.83	100.0
16.	Manufacture of jute, hemp & mesta textiles	0.701	0.299	-0.715	1.769	5.250	6.304***	-11.34	28.06	83.28	100.0
17.	Manufacture of sugar, khandsari and gur	0.742	0.258	0.367	2.473	4.393	7.233*	5.07	34.19	60.74	100.0
18.	Manufacture of transport equipment & parts	0.832	0.168	9.501	1.336	2.41	13.247*	71.72	10.09	18.19	100.0
19.	Manufacture of wood & wood products, furniture & fixtures	0.731	0.269	0.162	1.072	2.531	3.765*	4.30	28.47	67.22	100.0
20.	Manufacture of leather & leather & fur products (except repair)	0.732	0.268	5.124	3.528	3.751	12.133*	42.23	26.85	30.92	100.0
	Category IV	**0.731**	**0.269**	**1.537**	**2.251**	**3.954**	**7.742***	**19.85**	**29.08**	51.07	100.0
	Total Manufacturing	**0.543**	**0.457**	**1.283**	**3.061**	**2.216**	**6.560***	**19.56**	**46.66**	**33.78**	**100.0**

Source : Table 5.16.

* Significant at 1 percent level of significance.

** Significant at 5 percent level of significance.

*** Significant at 10 percent level of significance.

However, one shortcoming of the Cobb-Douglas production function is that is assumes elasticity of substitution (σ) to be equal to one. We have, therefore, estimated side relations derived from the CES production function under the conditions of perfect competition. The CES production function allows σ to take any constant value from 0 to $\propto$.

(i) Estimates of the Cobb-Douglas Production Function in Organised Manufacturing Sector: Different estimates of the Cobb-Douglas production function for manufacturing sector of Uttar Pradesh are given in Table-5.6.

The unrestricted Cobb-Douglas production function without time trend[15] (Model I) yielded a very high and statistically significant estimate of capital coefficent. The corresponding estimate of labour coefficient turned out to be negativie (insignificant), thereby indicating a negligible role of labour in output growth and the capital being the major source of growth. This fact has clearly been brought out by the analysis of previous sections also. Returns to scale (given by the sum of labour and capital coefficients)[16] is not significantly different from one indicating that constant returns to scale have operated in the organised manufacturing sector of the State during the reference period.

Table-5.6 : Estimates of the Cobb-Douglas Production Function for Organised Manufacturing Sector in U.P.: 1974-75 to 1985-86

No. of observations: 12 — Dependent variable : Model-I & II: Log V; Model-III: Log V/L

	Model-I	Model-II	Model-III
1	2	3	4
Log L	-0.393	-0.222	–
	(-1.326)	(-0.630)	
Log K	1.132*	2.258	-
	(7.358)	(1.838)	
Log (K/L)	–	–	1.101*
			(7.161)
t	–	-0.078	–
		(-0.925)	
Returns to scale	0.739	2.036	–
	(-1.145)	(0.775)	
R^2	0.883	0.893	0.823
$\bar{R}^2$	0.871	0.869	0.823
SE	0.087	0.083	0.092
F Value	33.727*	21.968*	46.618*
D.W.	1.820	1.749	1.470

Source : Based on ASI Reports: Various Issues.

Note : Figures in parentheses are t values of the estimates.

V : value added; L : labour; K : capital; and t : time.

* : Significant at 1 percent level of significance.

Incorporation of the time trend in the Cobb-Douglas production function[17] (Model-II) lead to rather implausible results. Numerical value of capital coefficient has increased but it has turned out to be insignificant even at 10 percent probability level. Coefficient of labour is still found to be negative and insignificant. Similarly, the time trend has also turned out to be negative but insignificant. Returns to scale are again not found to be significantly different from one, substantiating the evidence of constant returns to scale observed in Model-I. The inflated standard errors due to multicollinearity have resulted in insignificant estimates of the independent variables in this model. The high coefficient of correlation (0.99) between log (K) and t also confirms this.[18]

Since the estimates point towards the existence of constant returns to scale in the organised industrial sector of the State, we have alternatively estimated the ratio form of the constrained Cobb-Douglas production function without time trend[19] (Model-III). High $\bar{R}^2$ in all three equations indicates a good fit. Durbin-Watson (D.W.) test indicates absence of significant auto-correlation of the error terms. However, the insignificant estimates of independent variables indicate that model-II is not of much interpretative value.

The general conclusions emerging with the help of these three Models of Cobb-Douglas function are as follows: capital alone has been the major source of output growth. Besides, the production function has not been subject to significant neutral shifts, and constant returns to scale prevail in the organised industrial sector of the State.

(ii) *Cobb-Douglas Production Function: Category/Industry Group-wise Estimates*: The estimates for four categories and twenty industry groups are provided in Tables-5.7, 5.8 and 5.9. The estimates of Model-I are provided in Table 5.7. Positive coefficients of capital and labour are observed in all the categories, excepting category-I. Significant estimates of capital coefficient exist in the categories-I, II and IV, while estimate of labour coefficient is significant in category-III only. Thus, capital seems to be a major source of output growth in the three out of the four categories. Moreover, increasing returns to scale have operated in categories-II and III and constant returns to scale in the remaining two categories (i.e.,-I and IV).

Regarding the individual industry groups, positive coefficients of both capital and labour can be seen in fourteen out of the twenty industry groups. Both capital and labour coefficients are found to be significant in four industry groups, i.e., wool, silk and synthetic fibre textiles; metal products; jute, hemp and mesta textiles; and transport equipment and parts. Output seems to be responsive to variations in input uses of labour as well as capital in these industry groups. Moreover, significant capital coefficient is seen in another six industry groups, namely, basic metals and alloys; alcohol, beverages, tobacco and tobacco products; food products, non-metallic mineral products; sugar, khandsari and gur; and wood and wood products, furnitures and fixtures. Capital seems to be major source of output growth in these industry groups. In the remaining four industry groups, the coefficients of both labour and capital are found to be positive but not significant.

Besides these fourteen industry groups, in the rest six industry groups positive significant coefficient of capital is seen in electrical machinery, apparatus, applicances and supplies and parts; and machinery, machine tools and parts (except electrical). Analogousaly, coefficient of labour is found to be positive and significant in rubber, plastic, petroleum and coal products; and cotton textiles. On the whole, we observe significant coefficients of capital in twelve industry groups as against those of labour in six industry groups only.

Table-5.7 : Category/Industry Group-wise Estimates of the Cobb-Douglas production Function in U.P.: 1974-75 to 1985-86- Model I

No. of observations: 12

Dependent Variable: log V

	Category/Industry Group	*Constant*	*Log L*	*Log K*	*Returns to Scale (3+4)*	*R^2*	*$\overline{R}^{-2}$*	*SE*	*F Value*	*D.W.*
	1	2	3	4	5	6	7	8	9	10
1.	Manufacture of chemicals & chemical products (except products of petroleum & coal)	0.160	-0.132 (-0.124)	0.924 (1.642)	0.792 (-0.335)	0.519	0.471	0.182	4.864**	2.676
2.	Basic metals & alloys industries	-14.190	0.082 (0.077)	2.043*** (2.192)	2.125++ (2.606)	0.760	0.736	0.144	14.242*	0.998
3.	Manufacture of wool, silk & synthetic fibre textiles	-5.453	0.616*** (2.191)	0.791** (2.934)	1.407 (1.468)	0.723	0.695	0.186	11.757	2.570
	Category I	**-2.306**	**-0.123 (-0.180)**	**1.138** (2.733)**	**1.016 (0.039)**	**0.688**	**0.657**	**0.131**	**9.884***	**1.444**
4.	Manufacture of electrical machinery, apparatus, appliances & supplies & parts	-24.285	-0.095 (-0.082)	3.232*** (2.201)	3.137+ (4.497)	0.858	0.843	0.198	27.241*	0.454
5.	Manufacture of rubber, plastic, petroleum and coal products	-15.379	2.968** (2.774)	-0.453 (-0.799)	2.515++ (2.706)	0.809	0.790	0.367	19.116*	1.852
6.	Manufacture of edible oil & vanaspati ghee	15.954	-1.085 (-1.682)	0.021 (0.044)	-1.064+++ (-2.095)	0.295	0.225	0.234	1.886	1.746
7.	Other manufacturing industries	0.609	0.085 (0.071)	0.653 (1.427)	0.738 (-0.287)	0.337	0.271	0.436	2.291	2.352
	Category II	**-17.595**	**0.757 (0.728)**	**1.728*** (1.895)**	**2.485+ (5.304)**	**0.913**	**0.905**	**0.149**	**47.246***	**1.069**
8.	Manufacture of paper products & printing publishing & allied industries	1.818	0.217 (0.184)	0.392 (1.201)	0.609 (-0.449)	0.696	0.665	0.124	10.293*	0.984
9.	Manufacture of alcohol, beverages, tobacco & tobacco products	-3.219	0.386 (0.625)	0.849** (2.448)	1.235 (0.510)	0.607	0.568	0.189	8.962**	1.678
10.	Manufacture of machinery, machine tools & parts (except electrical)	-6.73	-0.073 (-0.073)	1.664** (2.564)	1.591 (1.346)	0.848	0.832	0.147	25.065*	1.700
11.	Manufacture of cotton textiles	-10.805	1.794** (2.471)	-0.055 (-0.128)	1.739 (1.754)	0.675	0.643	0.141	9.337*	0.914
12.	Manufacture of food products (except sugar, khandsari & gur)	-6.942	0.047 (0.134)	1.602* (5.919)	1.649+ (4.603)	0.965	0.961	0.069	122.611*	2.831
13.	Manufacture of textile products (including wearing apparel other than footwar)	-3.391	0.889 (1.511)	0.336 (1.151)	1.225 (0.588)	0.674	0.641	0.344	9.307*	0.771
	Category III	**-13.173**	**1.801** (3.124)**	**0.130 (0.453)**	**1.931++ (2.904)**	**0.918**	**0.910**	**0.074**	**51.891***	**1.585**

Table-5.7 (Contd...)

	1	2	3	4	5	6	7	8	9	10
14.	Manufacture of metal products and parts (except machinery & transport equipment)	-13.765	0.970**	1.366*	2.336++	0.719	0.690	0.102	11.452*	0.978
			(2.426)	(5.026)	(2.357)					
15.	Manufacture of non-metallic mineral products	-3.045	0.419	0.637*	1.056	0.834	0.817	0.105	22.559*	1.493
			(1.265)	(3.607)	(0.244)					
16.	Manufacture of jute, hemp & mesta textiles	-6.924	0.867*	0.809**	1.676+++	0.735	0.709	0.225	12.490*	1.097
			(4.251)	(2.704)	(1.953)					
17.	Manufacure of sugar, khandsari & gur	1.066	0.018	0.735*	0.753	0.576	0.533	0.211	6.108**	1.171
			(0.058)	(3.618)	(-0.724)					
18.	Manufacure of transport equipment & parts	-5.989	0.649*	0.800**	1.449++	0.938	0.932	0.134	68.149*	1.316
			(3.547)	(2.880)	(2.970)					
19.	Manufacure of wood & wood products, furniture & fixtures	-1,856	0.176	0.800**	0.976	0.508	0.459	0.125	4.648**	4.664
			(0.923)	(2.952)	(-0.077)					
20.	Manufacture of leather and leather & fur products (except repair)	-4.498	0.713	0.588	1.301	0.804	0.784	0.219	18.403*	0.966
			(1.496)	(1.735)	(1.227)					
	Category IV	**-1.137**	**0.054**	**0.913***	**0.967**	**0.904**	**0.895**	**0.088**	**42.447***	**1.431**
			(0.289)	**(8.548)**	**(-0.196)**					
	Total Manufacturing	**1.955**	**-0.393**	**1.132***	**0.739**	**0.883**	**0.871**	**0.087**	**33.727***	**1.820**
			(-1.326)	**(7.358)**	**(-1.145)**					

Source: Based on ASI Reports: Various issues.

Note: Figures in parentheses are t values of the estimates.

V : value added; L: labour; K: capital; and t: time.

*, **, *** : Significant at 1, 5 and 10 percent level of significance.

+, ++, +++ : Significantly different from unity at 1,5 and 10 percent level of significance.

Diminishing returns to scale (significantly less than unity at 10 percent probability level) are found to operate in edible oil and vanaspati ghee, whereas increasing returns to scale are experienced by basic metals and alloys; electrical machinery apparatus, appliances and supplies and parts; rubber, plastic, petroleum and coal products; food products; metal products; jute, hemp and mesta textilels; and transport equipment and parts. The remaining twelve industry groups are operating under constant returns to scale as the sum of labour and capital coefficients is not found to be significantly different from one. Excepting for a few cases, high $\bar{R}^2$ indicates a good overall fit. D.W. test indicates that the errors terms are not auto-correlated in all industry groups excepting seven.

Estimates of Cobb-Douglas production function with time trend (Model-II) are presented in Table 5.8. Due to increased standard errors, insignificant coefficients of both labour and capital are observed in category-IV. The picture remains almost the same in regard to other three categories with capital coefficient being significant in categories-I and II and labour coefficient in category-III. Only category-II is seen to be operating under increasing returns to scale. Remaining three categories witness constant returns to scale. Excepting category-II, time trend is found to be insignificant. The category-II witnesses significant but negative time trend, showing signs of a decline in overall efficiency. This finding goes against our earlier findings based on partial and TFP indices, which have indicated increased efficiency in input use as far as this category is concerned.

Industry group-wise analysis shows implausible estimates through the application of Model-II. Negative coefficients of either labour of capital (or both) are found in ten industry groups but in none of the cases these are found to be significant. Positive significant coefficients of both labour and capital are seen only in one industry group, i.e., transport equipment and parts. Capital coefficient is found to be significant in chemicals and chemical products; basic metals and alloys; wool, silk and synthetic fibre textiles; paper and paper products, printing, publishing and allied industries; machinery, machine tools and parts (except electrical); food products; textiles products; non-metallic mineral products; and transport equipment and parts. Output seems to be more responsive to quantitative change in capital. Analogously, significant coefficient of labour its noticed in rubber, plastic, petroleum and coal products; cotton textiles; jute, hemp and mesta textiles; and transport equipment and parts. This way, the increased employment is identified as major source of output growth in these industry groups.

Decreasing returns to scale are observed in the industry groups of edible oils and vanaspati ghee; alcohol, beverages, tobacco and tobacco products; and wood and wood products. On the other hand, increasing returns to scale are seen in basic metals and alloys; wook, silk and synthetic fibre textiles; rubber, plastic, petroleum and coal products; machinery, machine tools and parts (except electrical); manufacture of textile products; and manufacture of transport equipment and parts. The remaining industry groups are found to be operating under constant returns to scale.

The time trend being positive in nine industry groups is found to be significant only in respect of alcohol, beverages, tobacco and tobacco products; jute, hemp and mesta textiles; and wood and wood products. These industry groups have experienced neutral technological change during the reference period. Negative and significant estimates of time trend are observed in three industry groups, i.e., (i) wool, silk and synthetic fibre textiles; (ii) basic metals and alloys; and (iii) machinery, machine tools and parts (except electrical). The productivity estimates substantiate the results of the first industry group,

Table-5.8 : Category/Industry Group-wise Estimates of the Cobb-Douglas Production Function in U.P.: 1974-75 to 1985-86-Model II

No. of observation:12

Dependent Variable: Log V

	Category/Industry Group	Constant	Log L	Log K	t	Returns to Scale (3+4)	R^2	$\bar{R}^2$	SE	F Value	D.W.
	1	2	3	4	5	6	7	8	9	10	11
1.	Manufacture of chemicals & chemical products (except products of petroleum & coal)	-28.771	1.581 (1.190)	2.047** (2.590)	-0.123 (-1.846)	3.628 (1.674)	0.651	0.574	0.155	4.992**	2.388
2.	Basic metals & alloys industries	-60.141	-0.454 (-0.591)	7.032* (4.284)	-0.156** (-3.314)	6.578+ (4.194)	0.890	0.865	0.096	24.249*	2.129
3.	Manufacture of wool, silk & synthetic fibre textiles	-13.461	0.325 (1.175)	2.056** (3.251)	-0.085*** (-2.149)	2.381++ (2.906)	0.817	0.776	0.151	11.900*	2.964
	Category I	**-23.103**	**0.332 (0.454)**	**2.553** (2.338)**	**-0.084 (-1.392)**	**2.885 (1.408)**	**0.743**	**0.686**	**0.119**	**7.658****	**1.169**
4.	Manufacture of electrical machinery, apparatus, appliances & supplies & parts	-0.085	-0.326 (-0.243)	1.113 (0.202)	0.104 (0.400)	0.787 (-0.038)	0.860	0.829	0.197	16.411*	0.428
5.	Manufacture of rubber, plastic, petroleum & coal products	-16.181	3.014** (2.656)	-0.393 (-0.621)	-0.018 (-0.280)	2.621++ (2.443)	0.811	0.769	0.365	11.450*	1.949
6.	Manufacture of edible oil & vanaspati ghee	25.742	-0.793 (-1.086)	-1.646 (-0.853)	0.096 (0.891)	-2.439+++ (-1.973)	0.352	0.208	0.224	1.452	1.989
7.	Other manufacturing industries	2.436	0.019 (0.015)	0.451 (0.593)	0.031 (0.342)	0.470 (-0.451)	0.346	0.201	0.433	1.410	2.478
	Category II	**-65.598**	**0.674 (0.799)**	**6.408** (3.251)**	**-0.259** (-2.561)**	**7.082+ (3.565)**	**0.951**	**0.940**	**0.114**	**49.225***	**1.552**
8.	Manufacure of paper & paper products & printing, publishing & allied industries	-2.811	0.222 (0.199)	0.957*** (1.958)	-0.067 (-1.489)	1.179 (0.201)	0.753	0.701	0.111	8.265*	1.454
9.	Manufacture of alcohol, beverages, tobacco & tobacco products	16.490	0.448 (0.907)	-1.818 (-1.701)	0.175** (2.583)	-1.370++ (-2.350)	0.774	0.724	0.143	9.167*	2.733
10.	Manufacture of machinery, machine tools and parts (except electrical)	-26.260	-0.411 (-0.580)	4.293* (4.700)	-0.147** (-3.327)	3.882+ (4.038)	0.932	0.916	0.099	36.403*	1.882
11.	Manufacture of cotton textiles	-6.117	1.771*** (2.280)	-0.508 (-0.180)	0.026 (0.163)	1.263 (0.090)	0.676	0.605	0.141	5.562**	1.047
12.	Manufacure of food products (including khandsari & gur)	-13.586	0.226 (0.499)	2.193** (2.344)	-0.044 (-0.661)	2.419 (1.285)	0.966	0.958	0.067	76.207*	2.742
13.	Manufacture of textile products (including wearing apparel other than footwear	-6.658	0.733 (1.355)	1.105*** (2.181)	-0.139 (1.780)	1.838+++ (1.946)	0.759	0.705	0.296	8.396*	1.078

Table-5.8 (Contd...)

	1	2	3	4	5	6	7	8	9	10	11
	Category III	**-18.312**	**1.925**** (2.771)**	**0.485 (0.461)**	**-0.028 (-0.352)**	**2.41 (1.068)**	**0.919**	**0.901**	**0.073**	**31.634***	**1.323**
14.	Manufacture of metal products and parts (except machinery & transport equipment)	-9.194	1.335 (1.539)	0.386 (0.187)	0.040 (0.480)	1.721 (0.540)	0.726	0.665	0.100	7.044**	0.676
15.	Manufacture of non-metallic mineral products	-9.998	0.646 (1.825)	1.171** (2.833)	-0.052 (-1.414)	1.817 (1.497)	0.864	0.834	0.095	16.951*	1.296
16.	Manufacture of jute, hemp & mesta textiles	0.805	1.079* (8.053)	-0.662 (-1.687)	0.110* (4.232)	0.417 (-1.701)	0.911	0.892	0.130	27.451*	1.459
17.	Manufacture of sugar, khadsari & gur	20.387	0.364 (0.913)	-1.703 (-0.921)	0.224 (1.326)	-1.339 (-1.628)	0.645	0.566	0.193	4.85**	1.233
18.	Manufacture of transport equipment & parts	-10.062	0.738* (4.163)	1.186* (3.420)	-0.046 (-1.655)	1.924++ (3.152)	0.953	0.942	0.117	53.458*	1.339
19.	Manufacture of wood and wood products, furniture & fixtures	6,627	0.259 (1.484)	-0.769 (-0.907)	0.066*** (1.930)	-0.510+++ (-1.924)	0.652	0.575	0.105	4.998**	4.484
20.	Manufacture of leater & leather & fur products	-10.218	0.448 (0.682)	1.812 (0.891)	-0.124 (-0.611)	2.26 (0.916)	0.811	0.769	0.214	11.467*	0.851
	Category IV	**1.658**	**0.052 (0.264)**	**0.646 (0.348)**	**0.022 (0.144)**	**0.698 (-0.176)**	**0.904**	**0.883**	**0.088**	**25.227***	**1.401**
	Total Manufacturing	**-13.886**	**-0.222 (-0.630)**	**2.258 (1.838)**	**-0.078 (-0.925)**	**2.036 (0.775)**	**0.893**	**0.869**	**0.083**	**21.968***	**1.749**

Source : Based on ASI Reports : Various Issues.

Notes : Figures in parentheses are t values of the estimates.

V : value added; L: labour; K: capital; and t: time.

*, **, *** Significant at 1, 5 and 10 percent level of significance.

+, ++, +++ Significantly different from unity at 1, 5 and 10 percent level of significance.

whereas significant increases in both partial productivities and TFP are observed in the latter two industry groups. The time trend is found to be insignificant in fourteen out of twenty industry groups. Thus, the organised industrial sector of the State did not experience significant technological progress during the reference period.

The implausible estimates yielded by the application of Model-II were probably due to multicollinearity between independent variables. To avoid this, the ratio form of unconstrained Cobb-Douglas with time trend [20] has also been estimated. The results are provided in Appendix Table-5.5. Comparing the results of Table-5.8 and Appendix Table-5.5, there does not appear to be any substantial difference in the estimates. Here too, multicollinearity between log (K/L) and 't' might have affected our results.

Besides, efforts have also been made to work out estimates of the ratio form of constrained Cobb-Douglas production function without time trend (Model-III) for whole of the organised manufacturing sector of the State, Categories-I and IV and twelve industry groups, which are found to be operating under constant returns to scale on the basis of Model-I. The estimates are provided in Table-5.9.

Significant coefficients of capital are seen in the State level organised industrial sector, the two categories and the nine out of twelve industry groups. Comparing the results of Table-5.7 (Model-I) with those of Table-5.9, it is observed that capital coefficients, which were insignificant in the three industry groups (chemicals and chemical products; paper and paper products, printing publishing and allied industries; and leather and leather and fur products) in the former, have emerged significant according to the latter. This is probably due to the fact that multicollinearity, which has influenced the result in case of the former, has been largely overcome by the transformation in the functional form, bringing improvement in the estimates.[21]

Main conclusions emerging from the foregoing analysis are as follows: capital seems to have been playing a major role in output growth of the organised industrial sector. This is because coefficient of capital is found to be significant in greater number of categories and industry groups as compared to that of labour. Further, the organised industrial sector of U.P. is dominated by industries experiencing constant returns to scale. It is supported by the fact that constant returns to scale are operative in two categories (I and IV) and twelve out of twenty industry groups according to Model-I and in three categories (I, III and IV) and eleven out of twenty industry groups according to Model-II. Besides, the insignificant coefficient of time trend (being positive and significant in only three cases) leads us to the conclusion that neutral technological progress has not contributed much to output growth during the period of study.

(iii) *Estimates of the Constant Elasticity of Substitution (CES) Production Function in Organised Manufacturing Sector*: Elasticity of subsitution (σ) reflecting responsiveness of factor proportions to a change in the relative factor prices, is a crucial parameter, particularly in case of underdeveloped countries. It has important policy implications for economic growth, resource allocation and relative income distribution.[22] High elasticity of substitution (or easy substitutability) has a favourable impact on the levels of both output and employment. It has been pointed out that the conflict between high employment and high output (the dilemma faced by most of the under developed economies) essentially arises from low substitutability of the production structure.[23] Apart from these, estimate of elasticity of substitution is necessary to make choice of the form of production function to be applied

Table-5.9 : Category/Industry Group-wise Estimates of the Cobb-Douglas Production Function in U.P.: 1974-75 to 1985-86- Model III

No. of observations:12

Dependent Variable: Log (V/L)

	Category/Industry Group	*Constant*	*Log (K/L)*	R^2	$\bar{R}^2$	*SE*	*F Value*	*D.W.*
	1	2	3	4	5	6	7	8
1.	Manufacture of chemicals & chemical products (except products of petroleum & coal)	0.309	0.809*** (1.883)	0.244	0.244	0.183	3.224	3.805
2.	Manufacture of wool, silk and synthetic fibre textiles	2.806	0.604** (2.416)	0.347	0.347	0.205	5.308**	2.902
	Category I	**-3.782**	**1.143** (3.109)**	**0.467**	**0.467**	**0.131**	**8.787****	**1.456**
3.	Other manufacturing industries	3.089	0.588 (1.545)	0.178	0.178	0.438	2.170	2.281
	Category II X	-	-	-	-	-	-	-
4.	Manufacture of paper and paper products, printing publishing & allied industries	6.375	0.257** (2.095)	0.285	0.285	0.125	3.990	0.994
5.	Manufacture of alcohol, beverages, tobacco & tobacco products	0.329	0.876** (2.645)	0.389	0.389	0.192	6.362**	1.772
6.	Manufacture of machinery, machine tools and parts (except electrical)	-14.824	2.233* (4.389)	0.637	0.637	0.160	17.512*	2.136
7.	Manufacture of cotton textiles	5.960	0.286 (0.685)	0.041	0.041	0.161	0.427	1.194
8.	Manufacture of textile products (including wearing appearel other than footwear	5.244	0.424 (1.740)	0.216	0.216	0.350	2.753	0.791
	Category III X	-	-	-	-	-	-	-
9.	Manufacture of non metallic mineral products	1.576	0.651* (4.072)	0.601	0.601	0.105	15.075*	1.581
10.	Manufacture of sugar, khandsari & gur	0.505	0.799* (4.467)	0.645	0.645	0.216	18.142*	1.069
11.	Manufacture of wood & wood products, furniture and fixtures	0.101	0.816* (5.214)	0.712	0.712	0.125	24.715*	4.469

Table-5.9 (Contd...)

1	2	3	4	5	6	7	8
12.Manufacture of leather & fur products	1.733	0.718*** (2.184)	0.302	0.302	0.234	4.335	1.350
Category IV	**-0.578**	**0.916* (9.062)**	**0.882**	**0.882**	**0.088**	**74.657***	**1.380**
Total Manufacturing	**-2.699**	**1.101* (7.161)**	**0.823**	**0.823**	**0.092**	**46.618***	**1.470**

Source: Based on ASI Reports: Various Issues.

Notes 1 : X not computed.

2 : Figures in parentheses are t values of the estimates.

v : value added ; L: labour; and K: capital.

* : Significant at 1 percent level of significance.

** : Significant at 5 percent level of significance.

*** : Significant at 10 percent level of significance.

for empirical analysis, as a wrong assumption regarding this will lead to specification error leading to biased estimates.[24]

Keeping these facts in mind, estimates of σ for the organised industrial sector of U.P. have been arrived at by applying side relations derived from the CES production function under the assumption of perfect competition and profit maximisation.[25] The results are provided in Table-5.10.

Model-I is the original SMAC formulation relating the log of (V/L) to the log of wage rate. The coefficient of wage rate (giving estimate of σ) is found to be significant at 1 percent level. However, it was not found to be significantly different from unity. Incorporation of time trend (Model-II) resulted in an improvement in overall fit and D.W. test indicates the absence of significant serial correlation of the error terms. Despite the higher numerical value of σ, it is not found to be significantly different from unity. The time trend though negative is not significant. Neutral technical progress has not played any significant role in the growth of organised industrial sector of U.P. during the reference period. Inclusion of labour variable (Model-III) has given the best fit as far as the three models are concerned. The estimate of σ is significant but again it is found not to be significantly differnt from unity. Insignificant labour coefficient implies constant returns to scale for organised manufacturing sector. This corroborates the results derived through the application of Cobb-Douglas production function.

Table-5.10 : Estimates of the CES Production Function for Organised Manufacturing Sector in U.P.: 1974-75 to 1985-86.

No. of Observation:12 — Dependent Variable: Log (V/L)

	Model-I	*Model-II*	*Model-III*
Log w	1.073*	1.511**	1.216*
	(0.220)	(0.485)	(0.210)
Log L	–	–	–0.567
			(0.292)
t	–	–0.023	–
		(0.022)	
R^2	0.684	0.713	0.771
$\bar{R}^2$	0.684	0.685	0.748
SE	0.124	0.118	0.105
FValue	21.588*	11.175*	15.067*
D.W.	0.803	1.094	1.442

Source: Based on ASI Reports: Various Issues

Note : Figures in parantheses are standard errors of the estimates.

V : value added; L: labour; W: wage rate; and t: time.

* Significant at 1 percent level of significance.

** Significant at 5 percent level of significance.

The assumption of unitary elasticity of substitution is upheld on the basis of all the three models. As has already been pointed out, σ has important implications with respect to income distribution also. In case of σ being equal to one; factor shares will remain constant even if capital substitutes for labour overtime as a result of change in the factor intensity of technology and/or of changes in relative factor prices.[26] Keeping in view the limitations of capital data and the fact that capital share includes many non-capital items, opposite movements of the pure capital share and the non-capital items might be the real reason of the constancy observed.[27] Owing to this fact, we rely on the observations of labour share only and derive inference therefrom. Negligible growth of labour share in value added (Appendix Table-5.1) indicates that it has remained more or less constant during the reference period, supporting thereby the assumption of unitary σ in U.P. manufacturing. This finding seems to carry greater importance and as a result it is expected that a proportionate increase in factor prices would result in an equi-proportionate change in the factor ratio.

On the whole, the broad conclusions emerging for the organised indsutrial sector at the State level based on different models of the CES function are as follows: there has not been any significant 'technical progress' and 'economies of scale' for the manufacturing sector during the reference period. Further, estimates of σ being equal to one indicates the responsiveness of the production structure to changes in factor price ratio, besides justifying the use of Cobb-Douglas production function.

(iv) *CES Production Function: Category/Industry Group-wise Estimates*: Inter-Industry variations in output and employment growth may be *inter-alia* due to inter-industry differences in σ. To examine this in greater detail, we have estimated the side relations based on marginal productivity conditions derived from CES function (already mentioned above). The results of Model-I are provided in Table-5.11. Coefficient of wage rate (or σ) is significantly different from zero in three categories (II, III and IV). It is greater than unity (at 10 percent level) in category-II, whereas in categories-III and IV, σ is not significantly different from one. The data fit is good for all categories, excepting the category-I.

Moreover, in case of sixteen out of twenty industry groups, the value of σ is found to be significantly different from zero. In two industry groups, namely, electrical macinery, apparatus, appliances and supplies & parts; and metal products; the value of σ is found to be significantly greater than unity (at 5 percent and 10 percent levels respectively). In the remaining fourteen industry groups (namely basic metals and alloys; wool, silk and synthetic fibre textiles; rubber, plastic, petroleum and coal products; edible oil and vanaspati ghee; alcohol, beverages and tobacco and tobacco products; machinery, machine tools and parts (except electrical); cotton textiles; food products; textile products; non-mettalic mineral products; jute, hemp and mesta textiles; sugar, khandsari & gur; transport equipment and parts; and wood and wood products, furniture and fixtures); estimate of σ is not significantly different from unity.

Incorporation of time trend (Model-II) leads to rather implausible results as would be evident from Table-5.12. The significant coefficient of wage rate σ can be seen only in category-IV, which again is not significantly different from unity. While time trend is positive in all the four categories, significant technical progress is observed only in case of category-II. Standard errors have shown an increase possibly due to multicollinearity among the independent variables. This is confirmed by significantly high coefficient of correlation existing between log (w) and 't' in cases of category-I (0.96), category-II (0.96) and category-III (0.91) respectively.

Table-5.11 : Category/Industry Group-wise Estimates of the CES Production Function in U.P.: 1974-75 to 1985-86- Model I

No. of Observations : 12 — Dependent Variable : Log (V/L)

	Category/Industry Group	*Constant*	*Log w*	$\overline{R}^2$	R^2	*SE*	*F Value*	*D.W.*
	1	2	3	4	5	6	7	8
1.	Manufacture of chemicals & chemical products (except products of petroleum and coal)	6.485	0.406 (0.344)	0.112	0.112	0.198	1.266	1.764
2.	basic metals & alloys industries	2.885	0.736** (0.299)	0.355	0.355	0.175	5.515**	0.971
3.	Manufacture of wool, silk & synthetic fibre textiles	1.546	0.902*** (0.494)	0.233	0.233	0.222	3.035	1.959
	Category I	**5.281**	**0.504** **(0.304)**	**0.200**	**0.200**	**0.161**	**2.496**	**0.987**
4.	Manufacture of electrical machinery, apparatus, appliances & supplies & parts.	-10.728	2.271* (0.524)	0.630	0.630	0.219	17.082*	0.539
5.	Manufacture of rubber, plastic, petroleum & coal products	-0.718	1.199* (0.221)	0.727	0.727	0.288	26.674*	2.048
6.	Manufacture of edible oil & vanaspati ghee	2.489	0.853*** (0.423)	0.270	0.270	0.318	3.704	0.875
7.	Other manufacturing industries	-2.182	1.347 (0.933)	0.159	0.159	0.443	1.899	2.038
	Category II	**-6.317**	**1.806*** **(0.391)**	**0.659**	**0.659**	**0.199**	**19.368***	**0.495**
8.	Manufacture of paper & paper products & printing publishing & allied industries	5.995	0.358 (0.337)	0.093	0.093	0.141	1.027	1.011
9.	Manufacture of alcohol, beverages tobacco & tobacco products	1.330	0.948* (0.267)	0.535	0.535	0.167	11.489*	2.583

Table-5.11 (Contd...)

1	2	3	4	5	6	7	8
10. Manufacture of machinery, machine tools and parts (except electrical)	-0.805	1.180* (0.246)	0.677	0.677	0.151	20.936*	1.793
11. Manufacture of cotton textiles	3.964	0.573** (0.257)	0.312	0.312	0.136	4.527*	1.276
12. Manufacture of food products (except sugar, khandsari & gur)	-12.619	2.669** (0.978)	0.403	0.403	0.171	6.765**	0.630
13. Manufacture of textile products (including wearing apparel other than footwear)	-3.160	1.476** (0.538)	0.407	0.407	0.305	6.852**	1.158
Category III	**1.668**	**0.868* (0.188)**	**0.658**	**0.658**	**0.087**	**19.293***	**2.092**
14. Manufacture of metal products and parts (except machinery & transport equipment)	-4.877	1.674* (0.312)	0.724	0.724	0.108	26.159*	1.565
15. Manufacture of non-metallic mineral products	-0.560	1.093* (0.319)	0.515	0.515	0.116	10.617*	1.434
16. Manufacture of jute, hemp & mesta textiles	1.037	0.924* (0.276)	0.504	0.504	0.210	10.168*	1.766
17. Manufacture of sugar, khandsari & gur	-0.456	1.098* (0.209)	0.715	0.715	0.194	25.050*	2.040
18. Manufacture of transport equipment & parts	1.474	0.856* (0.117)	0.831	0.831	0.077	49.115*	1.992
19. Manufacture of wood & wood products, furniture & fixtures	-0.332	1.083** (0.448)	0.347	0.347	0.189	5.314**	3.090
20. Manufacture of leather and leather & fur products (except repair)	2.301	0.765 (0.563)	0.144	0.144	0.260	1.682	0.789
Category IV	**0.260**	**1.007 (0.151)**	**0.801**	**0.801**	**0.114**	**40.337***	**1.643**

Table-5.11 (Contd...)

1	2	3	4	5	6	7	8
Total Manufacturing	**(-0.002)**	**1.073*** **(0.220)**	**0.684**	**0.684**	**0.124**	**21.588***	**0.803**

Source : Based on ASI Reports : Various Issues.

Note : Figures in parentheses are standard errors of the estimates.

V : value added; L: labour; and W: wage rate.

* Significant at 1 percent level of significance.

** Significant at 5 percent level of significance.

*** Significant at 10 percent level of significance.

A similar trend can be observed in case of individual industry groups. Coefficient of wage rate is significant in only seven industry groups (namely, rubber, plastic, petroleum and coal products; machinery, machine tools and parts (except electrical); food products; textile products; non-metallic mineral products; sugar, khandsari and gur; transport equipment and parts). However, in none of these industry groups are the estimates of σ found to be significantly different from unity. Time trend is positive in thirteen out of twenty industry groups. However, the significant estimates are confined to three industry group only (namely, food products; jute, hemp and mesta textiles; and leather and leather and fur products). These industry groups seem to be experiencing signficant shifts in the production function.

Inclusion of labour variable in Model-I to provide for non-constant returns to scale gives us Model-III. The results are provided in Table-5.13. The estimate of σ is significantly different from zero but not from unity in category-IV. The remaining categories have again witnessed insignificant estimates of σ probably due to multicollinearity between the independent variables. This is confirmed by the significantly positive coefficient of correlation between log(w) and 't' in category-I (0.87), category-II (0.89) and category-III (0.88). Significant estimates of labour variable in categories-II and III indicate significant economies of scale, whereas in the remaining two categories (I and IV) constant returns to scale prevail. One fact that stands out here is that in case of total manufacturing sector, we observe negative and significant (however at 10 percent level only) coefficient of labour, leading to the conclusion that diseconomies have set in. However, this conclusion cannot be accepted readily because on the basis of Cobb-Douglas production function (Model-I & II), the evidence in favour of constant returns to scale has been categorical.

Thus, there seems to be a slight improvement in the estimates of Model-III as compared to those of the Model-II. This is witnessed by the significant coefficient of wage rate, observed in respect of eleven industry groups (namely wool, silk and synthetic fibre textiles; rubber, plastic, petroleum and coal products; alcohol, beverages, tobacco and tobacco products, machinery, machine tools and parts (except electrical); food products; textile products; metal products; non-metallic mineral products; jute, hemp and mesta textiles; sugar, khandsari and gur; and transport equipment and parts). In metal products, σ is found to be greater than unity (at 10 percent level), while in other industry groups, the value of σ is not significantly different from one.

Significant economies of scale are observed in the industry group of food products. Diseconomies are observed in cases of edible oil and vanaspati ghee; and wood and wood products, furniture and fixtures. The remaining industry groups are not experiencing significant economies of scale (i.e. constant returns to scale prevail). As compared to Models-I and II, data fit is good in greater number of cases. However, like previous models, industry groups constituting category-I witness low $\bar{R}^2$ here also.

Finally efforts have been made to draw general inferences regarding the organised manufacturing sector of U.P. based on estimates of all the three models. In category-IV, the hypothesis of σ =0 implying fixed coefficients is rejected conclusively. The estimatte is, however, not found to be significantly different from unity. In seven industry groups (i.e., rubber, plastic, petroleum and coal products; machinery, machine tools and parts (except electrical); food products; textile products; non-metallic mineral products; sugar, khandsari gur; and transport equipment and parts) also the estimates of σ are not significantly different from unity on the basis of all the three models. Analogously, on the basis of Model-I and

Table-5.12 : Category/Industry Group-wise Estimates of the CES Production Function in U.P.: 1974-75 to 1985-86- Model II

No. of Observations : 12

Dependent Variable : Log (V/L)

	Category/Industry Group	*Constant*	*Log w*	*t*	R^2	$\bar{R}^2$	*SE*	*F Value*	*D.W.*
	1	2	3	4	5	6	7	8	9
1.	Manufacture of chemicals & chemical products (except products of petroleum and coal)	-3.202	1.508 (1.132)	-0.056 (0.055)	0.196	0.116	0.189	1.099	2.430
2.	Basic metals & alloys industries	8.288	0.092 (0.807)	0.034 (0.039)	0.399	0.399	0.169	2.993	0.902
3.	Manufacture of wool, silk & synthetic fibre textiles	4.275	0.582 (0.689)	0.018 (0.026)	0.267	0.194	0.217	1.642	2.051
	Category I	**10.230**	**-0.070 (1.228)**	**0.026 (0.054)**	**0.218**	**0.140**	**0.159**	**1.255**	**1.014**
4.	Manufacture of electrical machinery, apparatus, appliances & supplies & parts.	3.025	0.726 (1.402)	0.058 (0.049)	0.676	0.643	0.206	9.381*	0.513
5.	Manufacture of rubber, plastic, petroleum & coal products	-0.897	1.233* (0.305)	-0.004 (0.034)	0.728	0.700	0.288	12.026*	1.543
6.	Manufacture of edible oil & vanaspati ghee	5.629	0.464 (0.709)	0.031 (0.045)	0.303	0.234	0.310	1.960	0.883
7.	Other manufacturing industries	0.219	1.052 (1.733)	0.014 (0.068)	0.163	0.079	0.442	0.876	2.035
	Category II	**14.213**	**-0.547 (1.243)**	**0.104*** (0.053)**	**0.755**	**0.730**	**0.169**	**13.853***	**0.911**
8.	Manufacture of paper & paper products & printing publishing & allied industries	11.761	-0.332 (0.699)	0.028 (0.250)	0.195	0.114	0.133	1.086	1.146
9.	Manufacture of alcohol, beverages tobacco & tobacco products	1.192	0.964 (0.754)	-0.001 (0.044)	0.535	0.488	0.167	5.170**	2.339
10.	Manufacture of machinery, machine tools and parts (except electrical)	-5.611	1.759** (0.697)	-0.032 (0.036)	0.700	0.671	0.146	10.523*	2.009
11.	Manufacture of cotton textiles	3.046	0.682 (0.489)	-0.006 (0.023)	0.316	0.248	0.136	2.084	1.308

Table 5.12 (Contd...)

	1	2	3	4	5	6	7	8	9
12.	Manufacture of food products (except sugar, khandsari & gur)	-3.153	1.485** (0.487)	0.046* (0.007)	0.885	0.873	0.075	34.621*	1.779
13.	Manufacture of textile products (including wearing apparel other than footwear)	-11.761	2.518** (0.841)	-0.062 (0.040)	0.522	0.474	0.274	4.909**	1.756
	Category III	**6.420**	**0.303** **(0.432)**	**0.024** **(0.017)**	**0.717**	**0.689**	**0.079**	**11.418***	**1.853**
14.	Manufacture of metal products and parts (except machinery & transport equipment)	1.611	0.874 (0.550)	0.027 (0.016)	0.786	0.765	0.095	16.521*	1.017
15.	Manufacture of non-metallic mineral products	0.406	0.968*** (0.465)	0.005 (0.013)	0.522	0.474	0.115	4.914*	1.388
16.	Manufacture of jute, hemp & mesta textiles	7.740	0.106 (0.332)	0.066** (0.021)	0.750	0.726	0.149	13.541*	1.717
17.	Manufacture of sugar, khandsari & gur	0.511	0.962* (0.289)	0.016 (0.022)	0.729	0.702	0.189	12.116*	1.491
18.	Manufacture of transport equipment & parts	0.803	0.938* (0.130)	-0.009 (0.007)	0.854	0.840	0.071	26.455*	2.196
19.	Manufacture of wood & wood products, furniture & fixtures	1.894	0.786 (0.510)	0.021 (0.018)	0.424	0.367	0.177	3.316	2.926
20.	Manufacture of leather and leather & fur products (except repair)	14.484	-0.748 (0.872)	0.071*** (0.034)	0.406	0.347	0.216	3.076	1.423
	Category IV	**1.270**	**0.874*** **(0.249)**	**0.011** **(0.016)**	**0.810**	**0.791**	**0.111**	**19.202***	**1.284**
	Total Manufacturing	**-3.598**	**1.511**** **(0.485)**	**-0.023** **(0.023)**	**0.713**	**0.685**	**0.118**	**11.175***	**1.094**

Source : Based on ASI Reports : Various Issues.

Note : Figures in parentheses are standard errors of the estimates.

V : value added; L: labour; and W: wage rate and t: time.

* Significant at 1 percent level of significance.

** Significant at 5 percent level of significance.

*** Significant at 10 percent level of significance.

Table-5.13 : Category/Industry Group-wise Estimates of the CES Production Function in U.P.: 1974-75 to 1985-86- Model III

No. of Observations : 12

Dependent Variable : Log (V/L)

	Category/Industry Group	*Constant*	*Log W*	*Log L*	R^2	$\bar{R}^2$	*SE*	*F Value*	*D.W.*
	1	2	3	4	5	6	7	8	9
1.	Manufacture of chemical & chemical products (except products of petroleum and coal)	8.243	10.601 (0.663)	-0.346 (0.989)	0.123	0.036	0.197	0.632	2.047
2.	Basic metals & alloys industries	-0.748	0.398 (0.668)	0.634 (1.114)	0.376	0.313	0.172	2.707	0.910
3.	Manufacture of wook, silk & synthetic fibre textiles	1.434	1.379** (0.599)	-0.446 (0.338)	0.347	0.281	0.205	2.387	2.352
	Category I	**9.891**	**0.979 (0.614)**	**-0.793 (0.888)**	**0.259**	**0.185**	**0.155**	**1.571**	**1.210**
4.	Manufacture of electrical machinery, apparatus, appliances & supplies & parts.	-9.937	1.659 (1.008)	0.460 (0.642)	0.648	0.613	0.214	8.307*	0.565
5.	Manufacture of rubber, plastic, petroleum & coal products	-0.436	1.304** (0.482)	-0.135 (0.544)	0.729	0.702	0.289	12.105*	1.897
6.	Manufacture of edible oil & vanastpati ghee	33.368	-0.290 (0.498)	-2.466** (0.820)	0.617	0.579	0.230	7.250**	2.116
7.	Other manufacturing industries	-2.114	1.353 (1.046)	-0.015 (0.882)	0.159	0.075	0.443	0.854	2.010
	Category II	**-8.360**	**0.468 (0.768)**	**1.300*** (0.666)**	**0.753**	**0.729**	**0.169**	**13.736***	**1.052**
8.	Manufacture of paper & paper products & printing, publishing & allied industries	3.459	-0.096 (0.508)	0.653 (0.559)	0.202	0.122	0.133	1.140	0.911
9.	Manufacture of alcohol, beverages tobacco & tobacco products	2.799	1.019* (0.306)	-0.234 (0.442)	0.547	0.502	0.165	5.442**	1.869
10.	Manufacture of machinery, machine tools annd parts (except electrical)	0.707	1.452** (0.584)	-0.399 (0.772)	0.685	0.654	0.149	9.787*	1.766
11.	Manufacture of cotton textiles	1.609	0.397 (0.357)	0.350 (0.485)	0.346	0.280	0.133	2.377	1.057

Table 5.13 (Cont....)

	1	2	3	4	5	6	7	8	9
12.	Manufacture of food products (except sugar, khandsari & gur)	-15.2	2.002** (0.645)	0.831* (0.202)	0.778	0.756	0.104	15.866*	1.196
13.	Manufacture of textile products (including wearing apparel other than footwear)	-3.264	1.535*** (0.724)	-0.049 (0.374)	0.408	0.348	0.304	3.096	1.180
	Category III	**-2.455**	**0.246 (0.343)**	**0.808*** (0.389)**	**0.761**	**0.737**	**0.073**	**14.372***	**1.877**
14.	Manufacture of metal products and parts (except machinery & transport equipment)	-7.121	1.745* (0.373)	0.172 (0.441)	0.728	0.701	0.107	12.014*	1.629
15.	Manufacture of non-metallic mineral products	-1.566	1.046** (0.342)	0.132 (0.244)	0.528	0.481	0.114	5.046**	1.341
16.	Manufacture of jute, hemp & mesta textiles	2.265	0.980* (0.279)	-0.199 (0.182)	0.557	0.513	0.198	5.661**	0.972
17.	Manufacture of sugar, khandsari & gur	-2.865	1.171* (0.277)	0.151 (0.357)	0.720	0.692	0.192	11.556*	1.645
18.	Manufacture of transport equipment & parts	1.545	0.940* (0.124)	-0.081 (0.054)	0.862	0.848	0.070	28.119*	2.403
19.	Manufacture of wood & wood products, furniture & fixtures	7.759	0.612 (0.453)	-0.573*** (0.275)	0.544	0.499	0.158	5.373**	2.345
20.	Manufacture of leather and leather & fur Products (except repair)	6.255	-0.340 (1.278)	0.578 (0.601)	0.216	0.138	0.248	1.243	1.008
	Category IV	**1.453**	**1.000* (0.158)**	**-0.091 (0.217)**	**0.805**	**0.785**	**0.113**	**18.554***	**1.734**
	Total Manufacturing	**6.289**	**1.216* (0.210)**	**-0.567*** (0.292)**	**0.771**	**0.748**	**0.105**	**15.067***	**1 . 4 4 2**

Source : Based on ASI Reports : Various Issues.

Note : Figures in parentheses are standard errors of the estimates.

V : value added; L: labour; and W: wage rate.

* Significant at 1 percent level of significance.

** Significant at 5 percent level of significance.

*** Significant at 10 percent level of significance.

III, the estimates of σ are not significantly different from unity in three industry groups of wool, silk and synthetic fibre textiles; alcohol, beverages, tobacco and tobacco products and jute, hemp and mesta textiles. For the category-IV and ten industry groups, where estimates of σ were closer to unity, we tested for constancy of factor shares. While labours share remained more or less contant in the category-IV and four out of ten industry groups it showed considerable variations in the remaining industry groups.

As far as the remaining industry groups are concerned, estimates of σ are found to be significantly exceeding unity in metal products on the basis of Models-I and III. Thus, a proportionate change in factor price ratio would lead to more than proportionate change in factor ratio, indicating a highly flexible production structure in this industry group.

The estimates of σ are are found to be significant only through application of Model-I in categories-II and III and five industry groups. The estimates are found to be significantly greater than unity in category-II and electrical machinery, apparatus, appliances and supplies and parts, whereas in category-III and basic metals and alloys; edible oil and vanaspati ghee; cotton textiles; and wood and wood products; the value of σ is not found to be significantly different from unity. In the remaining two models, estimates of σ are found to be insignificant in the above mentioned categories and industry groups. The reason probably being that the movement from simple to multiple regression has led to increased standard errors due to the presence of multicollinearity between the independent variables, resulting in less precise estimates.

Insignificant estimates of σ on the basis of all the three models are found in category-I and four industry groups, i.e., chemicals and chemical products; other manufacturing industries; paper and paper products and printing, publishing and allied industries; and leather and leather and fur products. Of these, technology can be used only in fixed proportions as the input ratio would not be responsive to changes in factor price ratio. In general, the estimate of σ is found to be equal to zero in highly capital intensive category-I and industry groups (excepting leather and leather and fur products). This is in accordance with the general observation that elasticity of substitution goes on declining with a successive replacement of traditional technology by the modern one.[28]

The technical progress on the basis of the CES production function (Model-II) is found to be significant only in category-II and the three industry groups (i.e. food products; jute, hemp and mesta textiles; and leather and leather and fur products). Besides these, neutral technical progress has not played any significant role in development of organised manufacturing sector of U.P. during the reference period. Futher, The organised manufacturing sector is dominated by industry groups exhibiting constant returns to scale. Economies of scale are observed in only two categorieis (II and III) and one industry group (i.e. food products), while diseconomies are found to be operating in edible oil and vanaspati ghee; and wood and wood products, furniture and fixtures.

Significant differences in the findings of earlier production fucntion studies in the context of the organised industrial sector at all India and State levels are explained through succeeding paragraphs. So far as the estimates of σ are concerned, no general conclusions can be drawn on the basis of existing studies. Diwan and Gujarati (1968) on the basis of time series data of 1946-58 find σ to be significantly less than unity in twenty-six out of twenty-eight industries studied. Bhasin and Seth (1980) for the period of 1950-65 also find less than unity estimates of σ in most of the industries studied. Similar results regarding jute industry (1958-78), Karnataka manufacturing (1968-78), and Punjab manufacturing (1967-80) are brough out in the respective studies of Verma (1985), Dhillon (1983) and Singh (1987). On the other hand, estimates of σ are not found to be significantly different from unity in twenty one out of twenty eight industries studied by Venkataswami (1968). Similarly, Banerji (1975) finds estimates of σ not significantly different from unity with regard to Indian manufacturing sector (1946-64) and five industries (i.e., cotton textiles, jute textiles (1946-64), sugar (1946-63), paper and bicycles (1946-58)). Similar estimates of σ are found in an inter-state study on sugar industry by Subramaniyan (1979). Gupta (1985) also finds evidence in favour of unitary σ in Maharastra manufacturing for the period of 1969-77. Large inter-industry variations in the estimates of σ are found in a study by Mehta (1980) for 1953-65. In general, on the basis of various models derived from CES production function estimates of σ are not found to be significantly different from zero in seven industries, and not significantly different from one in ten industries. On the other hand, in ten industries, estimates of are found to be significantly different from one. Similar trends are found in an earlier study by Sankar (1970), which is based on application of Bayesian technique to fifteen Indian industries for the period 1946-58. Estimate of σ is not found to be significantly different from unity in 50 percent cases, being insignificant in one, while in the remaining industries σ is significantly different from unity. In his study, Goldar (1986) finds σ to be quite close to unity for aggregate CMI (1951-65) and large scale sector (ASI census sector) for 1959-79. However, in respect of small scale sector (ASI sample sector) for 1960-78, estimate of σ is found to be less than unity.

Conflicting evidences are also available regarding the returns to scale. Findings of earlier studies have mostly gone in favour of constant returns to scale. Dutta (1955) on the basis of cross-section data of 1946 and 1947, Murty and Sastry (1957) on the basis of cross-section data of 1951, Dutta Mazumdar (1966) on the basis of time series data of 1951 to 1961 and Narasimham and Fabrycy (1974) on the basis of pooled cross-section time series data of 1946-58 have shown evidences in favour of constant returns to scale. Banerji (1975) in his study finds constant returns operating in Indian manufacturing, jute textile industry and cotton textile industry. However, contrary to this, the remaining three industries (namely sugar, paper and bicycles) have experienced increasing returns to scale. Mehta (1980) has found evidence in favour of constant returns to scale in twenty three out of twenty seven industries studied. On the basis of Tintner test, hypothesis of constant returns is rejected in the case of only five industries. Conversely, Bhasin and Seth (1980) for almost similar time period (1950-65) find the same industries operating under constant returns to scale. Hashim and Dadi (1973) find Indian manufacturing sector experiencing increasing returns to scale during 1946-65. However, for the the period of 1953-64 evidence goes in favour of constant returns to scale. Goldar (1980) on the basis of both the Cobb-Douglas and the CES production functions finds categorical evidence in favoour of constant returns to scale in aggregate CMI (1951-65) and also in large scale (1959-79) and small scale (1960-78) sectors. Almost similar conclusions in respect of total manufacturing sector for all-India level and Rajasthan are reached by Rajalakshmi (1983). In another study Rajalakshmi (1981), has found evidences in favour of constant returns to scale in non-metallic mineral products and non-ferrous basic metals of Rajasthan. Analysing jute industry at all-India level for the period of 1950-78, Verma (1985) has also reached the similar conclusions. In a study of five industries (namely food products, cotton textiles, basic metals and alloys, transport equipment, and electricity industry) of Punjab for the period of 1967-82, Singh and Singhal (1986) through application of Cobb-Douglas production function have found the first industry operating under decreasing and rest of the industries under constant returns to scale. However, on the basis of CES production function, basic metals and alloys is found to be experiencing increasing returns to scale, whereas food products and transport equipment have operated under decreasing returns to scale. The remaining two industries have experienced constant returns to scale. Categorical evidence in favour of increasing returns to scale has been brought out in the studies of Yeh (1966), Diwan (1968) and Sankar (1970) for the period 1953-58. Yeh in his study notices increasing returns to scale in seventeen industries, whereas constant and decreasing returns have been under operation in two and ten industries respectively. Diwan and Gujarati (1968) observe significant economies of scale on the basis of CES production function for twenty-nine industries for the period 1946-58.

Including time trend in the production function to capture technological change often gives unrealistic estimates. Quite frequently, time trend turns out to be insignificant, leading to the conclusion that neutral technologial progress is not a major source of output growth so far as Indian industries are concerned. However, the degree of technical progress varies from industry to industry.Using the data of manufacturing sector for 1946-67, Venkataswami (1975) notices that new industries have demonstrated much more technological progress as compared to old ones. Sankar (1970) observes positive neutral shifts in six industries and negative in two for the period of 1953-58. Narasimham and Fabrycy (1974) observed not any significant shift in the production function for 1946-58. Banerji (1975) finds evidence of a shift in production function in sugar, paper and bicycles, whereas cotton and jute have not experienced significant technical progress. Mehta (1980) finds only eleven out of twenty seven industries experiencing technical progress. Goldar (1986), however, finds significant shifts in production function in aggregate CMI, large scale sector and to some extent in small sector also. Conversely, according to a study by Subramaniyan (1979), sugar industry has not experienced any significant technical progress during the period of 1953-69.

The present study also supports the findings of earlier studies. Neutral technological progress does not seem to have played any important role in output growth. Thus, positive significant estimates of time trend are seen only in three out of twenty industry groups (on the basis of both Cobb-Douglas and CES production functions) and category-II (on the basis of CES production function). Further, most of the earlier studies concerning organised industrial sector on all-India level have found increases in labour force to be a major source of growth.[29] The present study seems to be a distinction and identifies capital as the most crucial factor to output growth. In the above mentioned production function studies, coefficient of capital is generally found to be insignificant owing to mainly measurement problems, multicollinearity, overcapitalisation and underutilisation of the installed capacity. The findings of the present study are not comparable with those of the earlier ones mainly because of differences in the choice of the period and the coverage of areal units. Necessary adjustments have been made in the time series data of capital to minimise measurement errors in the present study. Improvement in measurement of capital has brough about a significant improvement in coefficient of capital, as experienced by Dholakia (Jan.-Mar. 1977) in his study of Indian iron and steel industry. Further studies covering the recent time period, have usually found significant estimates of capital coefficient. For example, Goldar (1980) in his study has found insignificant estimate of capital coefficient for 1951-

65 (aggregate CMI), whereas the corresponding estimates workout significant for 1959-79 (ASI census sector). Similarly, a recent study on Indian jute industry by Verma (1985) covering the time period of 1950-68 has found significant capital coefficient accompanied by insignificant labour coefficient. Apart from the reason outlined above, since the beginning of the Fifth Plan (i.e. 1974-75) a considerable amount of investment has been made in industrial sector of U.P. Correlating this to our present study, it is noticed that increased capital has made a significant contribution to output growth of the organised industrial sector in U.P. during the reference period. Insignificant labour coefficient in many cases paints a disquieting picture so far as the role of labour in the output growth is concerned. This conforms to the finding that the organised industrial sector of the State in recent years has experienced deceleration in employment growth. Further, the low labour coefficients also indicate that there is less scope of employment in the organised industrial sector and the increased capital is chiefly responsible for the output growth.[30]

2. PERFORMANCE OF ORGANISED INDUSTRIAL SECTOR IN UTTAR PRADESH: 1974-75 TO 1985-86

The contributions of primary, secondary and tertiary sectors to total State income (at constant prices of 80-81) during 85-86 being 47 percent, 19 percent and 34 percent respectively, clearly demonstrate the predominance of primary sector in the State economy. Moreover, there have been some significant changes in inter-sectoral contributions over the period of 1980-86; a loss in the contribution of primary sector by 5 percentage points (from 52 percent to 47 percent) has been compensated by 3 percentage point gains of secondary sector (from 16 percent to 19 percent) and 2 percentage point gains of tertiary sector (from 32 to 34 percent).[31]

2.1 Overall performance of Organised Industrial Sector at the State Level

Increased efforts for development, particularly since the Fifth Plan, have resulted in significant structural changes in the State economy. Rapid industrialisation has been used as an instrument for acceleraling the pace and process of development in shortest possible time. In view of this, it is aimed here to analyse the changes that have taken place in organised manufacturing sector of U.P. over the period. The time series data on gross value-added, total employment and gross fixed capital for this sector, and the trend and average annual growth rates for the entire period and two sub-periods are provided in Table-5.14

Significant trend growth rates can be seen in all the three variables. The highest trend growth rate of 6.69 percent is observed in gross fixed capital followed by 6.56 percent in gross value added and 2.36 in employment. Further, a sharp increase in trend growth rates of value-added and gross fixed capital is accompanied by a significant trend rate of decline of employment in the sub-period II (1980-86) as compared to sub-period I (1974-80). This has happened probably because of additions/expansions of the units requiring more capital and less labour. Further, significant increases in the labour productivity in the second sub-period (see table-5.1) seems to have led to an increase in output with the use of lesser amount of labour.

Table-5.14 : Time Series Data on Different Variables for Organised Manufacturing Sector in U.P. 1974-75 to 1985-86

Year	*Gross Value Added at 1974-75 Prices (in lakh Rs.)*	*TotalEmployment*	*Gross Fixed Capital Stock at 1974-75 Prices (in lakh Rs.)*
1	2	3	4
1974-75	39911.93	453870.0	192251.34
1975-76	38503.50	471250.0	202008.43
1976-77	43698.71	515169.0	214968.43
1977-78	50028.76	562464.0	227838.38
1978-79	53156.00	562550.0	241580.33
1979-80	51194.98	571278.0	250384.78
1980-81	45395.01	640980.0	260251.85
1981-82	47837.05	660250.0	293655.70
1982-83	68946.83	675547.0	323437.33
1983-84	71205.52	590691.0	343325.03
1984-85	70140.82	571065.0	363088.44
1985-86	84030.87	568688.0	384133.67
Trend Growth Rate:			
1974-75 to 1979-80	**6.937** (4.598)**	**5.186* (6.147)**	**5.626* (29.430)**
1980-81 to 1985-86	**12.941* (4.987)**	**-3.282** (2.895)**	**7.844* (11.343)**
1974-75 to 1985-86	**6.560* (6.752)**	**2.363** (3.014)**	**6.699* (29.200)**

Source : ASI Reports : Various Issues.

Note : Figures in Parentheses are t values of the estimates.

* Significant at 1 percent level of significance.

** Significant at 5 percent level of significance.

As transpires from the foregoing analysis, a conflict between the output growth and employment persistently existed in the organised industrial sector of the State during sub-period-II. Considering the National level objective of efficiency and equity, it would, however, be incongruous to make concentrated efforts for achieving the one at the cost of the other. In other words, one has to strike a balance between the two. And for this purpose, if would be worthwhile to mainly depend upon the organised manufacturing sector for maximising the output growth and concentrate on unorganised one (based on labour-intensive technology) for enhancing the employment growth. The latter is better rewarding from the point of view of employment generation, as would be evident from the Table-5.15

Table-5.15 : Persons Usually Employed in the Manufacturing Sector of U.P.

(Persons in lakhs)

Sector/Year	1977-78	1987-88	Compound Growth Rate (1987-88 over 1977-78)
1. Total Manufacturing (+)	32.00	44.00	3.25
1.1 Organised	4.79	5.34	1.09
1.2 Unorganised (++)	27.21	38.66	3.56

Source : NSS data, 32nd round for 1977-78 and 43rd round for 87-88

Draft Eighth Five Year Plan, 1990-95, and Annual Plan 1991-92, Vol I, Uttar Pradesh, pp.106 (+) and 108 (++).

As shown above, the compound growth rate of employment in unorganised manufacturing sector of U.P. during the period 1977-87 was much higher (3.56 percent) as compared to the organised one (1.09 percent).

2.2 Category/Industry Group-wise Performance at the State Level.

The category/industry group-wise trend growth rates of gross value added, total employment and gross fixed capital are presented in Table-5.16. The positive and significant trend growth rates of value added are witnessed in all the categories. The highest trend growth rate of 13.77 percent in category-II is followed by the respective trend growth rates 7.74 and 6.92 percent in categories-IV and III. The lowest trend growth rate of 5.11 percent seen in highly capital intensive category-I is simply because of already high value added figures in the base year.

Table-5.16 : Category/Industry Group-wise Trend Growth Rates in Gross Value Added, Total Employment and Gross Fixed Capital in U.P.: 1974-75- to 1985-86.

Category/Industry Group	Gross Value Added	Total Employment	Gross Fixed Capital Stock
1	2	3	4
1. Manufacture of chemicals and chemical products (except products of petroleum and coal)	4.487** (2.391)	3.084* (8.839)	5.973* (10.043)
2. Basic metals and alloys industries	6.602* (4.034)	2.619* (5.923)	3.349* (16.145)
3. Manufacture of wool, silk and synthetic fibre textiles	5.262*** (1.945)	1.887 (0.924)	6.564* (7.189)
Category I	**5.113* (3.760)**	**2.691* (5.489)**	**5.036* (15.196)**
4. Manufacture of electrical machinery, apparatus, appliances and supplies and parts	14.461* (7.783)	5.469* (12.251)	4.415* (40.887)
5. Manufacture of rubber, plastic petroleum and coal products	17.632** (3.070)	8.319* (4.662)	16.672* (5.011)
6. Manufacture of edible oil and vanaspati ghee	3.077 (1.347)	-2.338** (2.498)	5.253* (14.301)

Table - 5.16 (Contd...)

1	2	3	4
7. Other manufacturing industries	8.709*** (2.150)	3.544* (3.285)	12.089* (6.415)
Category II	**13.769*** **(7.852)**	**4.829*** **(10.969)**	**5.718*** **(29.869)**
8. Manufacture of paper and paper products, and printing, pulishing and allied industries	4.836* (3.649)	3.039* (8.146)	11.934* (13.524)
9. Manufacture of alcohol, beverages, tobacco and tobacco products.	7.234* (4.769)	2.406** (2.730)	6.559* (15.794)
10. Manufacture of machinery, machine tools and parts (except electrical)	9.217* (4.918)	3.613* (7.025)	6.002* (14.848)
11. Manufacture of cotton textiles	4.893** (3.076)	2.863* (5.327)	5.678* (36.430)
12. Manufacture of food products (except sugar, khandsari and gur)	10.372* (13.133)	4.548* (9.590)	6.240* (26.772)
13. Manufacture of textile products (including wearing apparel other than footwear)	10.675** (2.410)	7.036* (3.502)	18.846* (8.329)
Category III	**6.923*** **(7.597)**	**3.292*** **(10.187)**	**7.025*** **(32.505)**
14. Manufacture of metal products and parts (except machinery and transport equipment)	3.505** (2.696)	–1.403** (2.248)	3.550* (13.207)
15. Manufacture of non-metallic mineral products	6.196* (4.964)	3.482* (4.333)	7.952* (11.308)
16. Manufacture of jute, hemp and mesta textiles	6.304*** (1.845)	-1.020 (0.335)	5.917* (5.505)
17. Manufacture of sugar, khandsari and gur	7.233* (3.915)	0.494 (0.260)	9.585* (22.426)
18. Manufacture of transport equipment & parts	13.247* (4.790)	11.419* (5.116)	7.951* (7.083)
19. Manufacture of wood and wood products, furniture and fixtures	3.765* (3.540)	0.221 (0.121)	3.984* (10.350)
20. Manufacture of leather and leather & fur products	12.133* (4.843)	7.000* (4.575)	12.157* (24.026)
Category IV	7.742* (9.618)	2.103 (1.598)	8.369* (58.227)
Total Manufacturing	**6.560*** **(6.752)**	**2.363**** **(3.014)**	**6.699*** **(29.200)**

Source : Based on ASI Reports : Various Issues.

Notes : Figures in parentheses are t value of the estimates.
* Significant at 1 percent level of significance.
** Significant at 5 percent level of significance.
*** Significant at 10 percent level of significance.

So far as the industry groups are concerned, excepting edible oil and vanaspati ghee, the other nineteen industry groups have registered a significant trend growth rate in value added. The highest trend growth rate of 17.63 percent is observed in rubber, plastic, petroleum and coal products followed by the trend growth rate of 14.46 percent in electrical machinery, apparatus, appliances and supplies and parts.

For the entire period of the study, we notice that the trend growth rates of value added in eleven industry groups are higher than that of the whole organised manufacturing sector in the State (6.56). The remaining industry groups qualifying for the lower trend growth rates consist of chemicals and chemical products; wool, silk and synthetic fibre textiles; edible oil and vanaspati ghee; paper and paper products and printing, publishing and allied industries; cotton textiles; metal products (except machinery and transport equipment); non-metallic mineral products; jute, hemp and mesta textiles; and wood and wood products, furniture and fixtures. An important point is that most of these industry groups generally fall in labour intensive categories.

Three out of total four categories registered positive and significant trend growth rates of employment. The highest trend growth rate of employment (4.83) is observed in category-II followed by the trend growth rates of 3.29 percent and 2.69 percent respectively in categories-III and I. The higher labour intensive category-IV registered the lowest (insignificant) trend growth rate in employment.

The highest trend growth rate of employment (11.42 percent) is observed in transport equipment and parts, followed by the trend growth rates of 8.39 percent, 7.04 percent and 7.0 percent in rubber, plastic, petroleum and coal products; textile products; and leather and leather and fur products respectively. Significant growth rates of employment found only in three out of seven industry groups constituting the category-IV might be one of the reasons for low and insignificant growth rate of employment observed in this category. Trend rate of decline in employment is observed in three industry groups out of which significant decline is confining to two industry groups (namely edible oil and vanaspati ghee; and metal products and parts) only. The fourteen out of twenty industry groups have shown growth rates of employment above the State level average during the period of the study.

The positive and significant trend growth rates of gross fixed capital are seen in all of the categories and the industry groups. As a result, highly significant trend growth rate of gross fixed capital (6.7 percent) its found to exist in whole of the organised industrial sector of U.P. The trend growth rate of gross fixed capital in categories-III and IV have exceeded the State level average. The trend growth rates of gross fixed capital is noticed to be the highest (8.37 percent) in category-IV and the lowest (5.04 percent) in category-I. The categories-III and II have occupied the second and the third place with trend growth rates of 7.03 percent and 5.72 percent respectively. These findings are in consonance with the observed growth rates of capital-labour ratios analysed in the previous section.

The highest trend growth rate of gross fixed capital (18.85 percent) is observed in textile products followed by the trend growth rate of 16.67 percent in rubber, plastic, petroleum and coal products. Gross fixed capital has registered the lowest trend growth rate of 3.35 percent in basic metals and alloys. Eight out of twenty industry groups are found to have trend growth rates of gross fixed capital above the State level average.

Category-II has witnessed the high trend growth rates in respect of both the value added and employment. This is supported by the highly significant coefficient of correlation (0.91) between the two in this category. The trend growth rate of gross fixed capital is noticed to be slightly greater than that of employment, whereas the trend growth rate of value added is found to be well above the growth rates of labour and capital. Thus, the category-II seems to have shown greater efficiency in the use of inputs. This is corroborated by the productivity and production function analysis also. In the remaining three categories, the trend growth rate of fixed capital far exceeds that of employment, demonstrating the case of capital deepening. However, with the exception of category-IV, positive and significant trend growth rates of both output and employment can be observed in the remaining categories (I and III). Coefficients of correlation between output and employment in category-I (0.67), category-III (0.95) and category-IV (0.33) also confirms the above findings.

In respect of ten out of twenty industrial groups, the trend growth rates of output and employment are found to be above the State level average; wherein the former is accompanied by the latter. These industry groups are basic metal and alloys industries; electrical machinery, apparatus, appliances and supplies and parts; rubber, plastic, petroleum and coal products; other manufacturing industries; alcohol, beverages, tobacco and tobacco products; machinery, machine tools and parts (except electrical); food products; textile products; transport equipment and parts; leather and leather and fur products. The coefficient of correlation between the growth rates of gross value added and employment across industries is 0.82, which, is statistically significant at one percent level. However, out of these ten industries only in electrical machinery, apparatus, appliances and supplies and parts, the trend growth rate of employment has exceeded that of gross fixed capital. On the whole, the organised industrial sector of the State is characterised by increased capital deeping during whole of the reference period.

3. INTER-RELATIONSHIP BETWEEN TECHNOLOGICAL CHANGE AND DEVELOPMENT OF ORGANISED INDUSTRIAL SECTOR IN U.P.: 1974-75 TO 1985-86

Manufacturing sector in developing countries is, generally, characterised by high growth rate of output accompanied by low growth rate of employment. This kind of unfavourable phenomenon still continues to exist inspite of strenuous efforts including higher investments made in the past to ensure maximisation of employment growth. As a matter of fact, manufacturing in considered as an instrument to absorb not only the growing labour force but also to deploy the surplus labour engaged in low productivity sectors like agriculture. However, the performance of this sector is found to be less rewarding so far as employment generation is concerned. One of the reasons attributed to this failure has been the use of technology unsuited to the factor proportions of developing countries.[32] Giving due weightage to this aspect, it is therefore, decided to analyse through subsequent paragraphs the inter-relationship between the technological change (in terms of partial productivity indices and Solow index of TFP) and performacne of the organised industrial sector in U.P. (in terms of output and employment growth). For this purpose, the subsequent analysis is carried out taking into account the review of previous literature and the results of various models used previously in this chapter.

3.1 Review of Literature

Employment opportunities can be created either through stimulating output in high-productivity and high wage sectors or through use of the greater amount of labour to produce a given amount of output (i.e., the use of more labour intensive techniques).[33] During the Fifties and the Sixties, the over-riding objective of the developing countries had been to achieve higher output growth. It was felt that the 'poor would be better-off...if they received a constant share of rapidly growing pie than if they received a larger share of slower growing one'.[34] This line of thought was mainly influenced by fixed proportions view of technology and the inherent belief that a conflict exists between maximising the growth of employment and that of output and savings (i.e. output employment trade-off).

In consonance with this line of thought, the National Plans as well as the State Plans aimed at accelerated growth through industrialisation, particularly the development of heavy capital goods industries. These industries were associated with greater technological progress and economic growth and it was assumed that accelerated production would build a base for greater employment opportunities. However, the industrial pattern that emerged over the period had a favourable effect on output growth but was not conducive to employment growth.

Disillusionment with this strategy in recent years has led to reversal in thinking, making employment creation a major objective to achieve an equitable growth.[35] Thus, India's Sixth Plan apart from laying emphasis on accelerated growth visualised that 'employment opportunities have not been adequate in recent past either for the educated manpower or for overall population', and therefore, the employment policty during the Sixth plan envisaged to meet two major goals of 'reducing underemployment for majority of the labour force and cutting down long term unemployment'.[36] Similarly, the Sixth Plan of U.P. also proposed to 'give priority to such industries as have greater potential for employment'.[37]

The above mentioned strategy was based on the assumption that adequate substitution possibilities exist and that factor proportions are responsive to changes in factor prices. The literature on the topic indicates that the range varies from 'elasticity pessimists' to 'elasticity optimists'.[38] Elasticity pessimists believe that no substitution between factors is possible and that the only alternative available to developing countries is the fixed proportions high capital intensive western technology.[39]

Elasticity optimists, on the other hand, believe that high substitution possibilities exist and the faster growing factor (i.e. labour) can be substituted easily for the constraining factor (i.e. capital); this makes it possible to increase output alongwith employment. Econometric evidences of elasticity of substitution on the basis of CES function, barring a few cases, are positive, leading to the conclusion that substitution possibilities do exist. The estimates usually cluster between the values of 0.5 to 1.2 but estimates on either side of these values also are not uncommon.[40] Similar results for Indian industries have been provided in section 1.4 (iv) above. However, keeping in view the theoretical and empirical problems, it is necessary to view these results with caution. It has been found that 'even slight variations in the period or concept tend to produce drastically different estimates of elasticity'.[41] Morawetz (1976) could not consistently rank high elasticity and low elasticity two-digit industries on the basis of CES function for 12 sets of U.S. data and 4 sets of data for developing countries. Inspite of these criticisms, econometric investgations based on CES production function are carried out to deduce meaningful policy implications.

Further, disaggregative analysis on elasticity of substitution has also been carried out for large number of industries. On the basis of individual case studies, fairly widespread substitution possibilities have been found out, with the alternative labour intensive technology often proving to be superior, low in cost, in comparison to modern capital intensive techniques.[42] Many of these studies concentrate on consumer goods industries only-which are simpler and more homogeneous in character. A study covering fairly wide range of products reached the similar conclusions.[43]

Besides the econometric investigations, a number of suggestions have also been made to increase substitution possibilities in the developing countries. Some of these are:

(i) Intensive use of capital (extra shifts) will help in lowering capital labour ratios. The subsequent need for maintenance adds to employment opportunities as repair is labour-intensive activity.[44] Fuller utilisation of existing capital stock will also have favourable impact on employment.[45]

(ii) It is felt that even if core production processes can not be made labour intensive, ancillary activities, such as materials receiving and handling, packaging and storage offer a greater scope for varying factor proportions.

(iii) Use of second-hand developed country machinery has also been recommended for reducing capital-labour ratios. In spite of the reservations on the front of efficiency and cost effectiveness a number of studies have found efficient use of second hand machinery in the industries of developing countries.[46]

(iv) For making greater in-roads to sloving the output-employment conflict, it is argued that besides appropriate choice of technique for producing a given product, appropriate product choice is also important. For this, it is proposed that a country should be export oriented as developing countries will have a comparative advantage in labour intensive goods and processes in the World markets.[47]

(v) Small scale firms are advocated because of their low capital intensity. An important reason for the low capital-labour ratios of small firms is that they face factor prices closer to the social opportunity costs (as against large firms).[48]

(vi) Lastly, it is also argued that developing countries can do their own research and development, adapting transferred technology suiting to local conditions and the most important developing entirely new products and processes (or labour using technological changes).

The two main contentions on which capital intensive techniques are advocated (i.e. high capital output ratios of labour intensive techniques and a greater reinvestible surplus of capital intensive techniques) are questionable. Growing evidence points towards, the greater possibility of substituting labour for capital without sacrificing output, provided the cooperating factors are present.[49]

Apart from this, Ranis (1962) in a study of four industries of Pakistan finds that medium-sized (less capital intensive) firms have higher savings and higher reinvestment rate per unit of output than do large firms. Appavadhanulu (1974) finds small firms having higher saving rates than large firms. Sandesara (1966) in a study of ten Indian industries finds more labour intensive industries having higher output and higher surplus per unit of capital. Further, wages have also been found to be low in these industries.

Despite a widespread need and possibility to switching over to more appropriate technologies, the reasons for still finding large scale use of inappropriate technologies are as follows:[50]

(i) Government policies in developing countries have distorted the input prices in such a way that they do not reflect the real social opportunity costs. Large firms are provided credit at low interest rates. Further, low custom duties and excise taxes on capital goods imports, partial tax exemption for income generated from capital investment, tax holidays and similar other policies make capital cheaper and thus preferable to be substituted for labour. To top it, labour is made dear by creating artificially high wages through minimum wage laws, large fringe benefits, restrictions on firing and government encouraged trade union pressures.

(ii) There seems to be some sort of prestige issue involved among the entrepreneures of developing counries in the use of developed country mechanised technology.

(iii) Even if one finds instances of Multinational Corporations (MNCs) adapting to local conditions, lack of competition may make it less worthwhile to adapt and as a result, MNCs may continue to use highly sophisticated parent industry western technology.

(iv) Even in the cases where we find willingness to adopt more labour intensive technologies, lack of information may act as barrier and may prevent firms from producing on the most efficent frontier. This is an aspect of X-inefficiency.

(v) Other government policies also result in inappropriate factor proportions. Some of these mainly include: failure to generate competitive environment due to protective regime, negative attitude towards second-hand machinery imports, lack of proper policies to discourage or restrict the consumption of luxury items, undue emphasis on import-substitution and less encouragement to the development of export markets for manufactured goods.

(vi) Finally, the full potential of local research and development in fostering the technological changes suitable to developing countries has not bee realised.[51] Although there are evidences of adaptations of imported capital-intensive technology to local conditions the pace at which these are occurring is slow. Apart from this, to broaden the range of alternatives available to them, developing countries need to develop new products and processes suitable to their environment (factor endowments).

Technology policies aiming at removing these problems and increasing the use of labour can be broadly divided in to three main schools of thought.[52] The first school known as 'price incentive school' stresses on getting prices right to suit the social opportunity costs. This, it is felt will not only result in the choice of most appropriate technique from amongst the given range, but also create an incentive for development of more appropriate technologies. Direct correction of price distortion may not always be feasible. Under such circumstances, indirect measures like wage subsidy or taxation on the use of capital will go a long way in correcting the problem. Second school or the 'technologist school'. believes that increased investment in technological development (i.e. R & D) will bring about the required transformation. Lastly, the third one is the 'radical reform school' which believes in the radical transformation of the society. No amount of institutional or incentive change in absence of such a transformation will result in desired use of technology.

An integrated approach, involving elements of all the three schools are stressed to tackle the situation.[53] Further, depending on the circumstances, every country may have its own unique solution to the problem.

3.2 Inter-relationship between Technological Change and Performance: A Case of Organised Industrial Sector in U.P.

As transpires from the review from the of literature, the capital intensive technology is usually production oriented and not employment oriented. As rapid technological progress is associated with capital intensive techniques, it is proposed to examine whether technological advancement has led to convert industry into capital intensive. And if so, whether there has been a favourable impact on productivity and output and simultaneously an adverse bearing on employment.

Tables 5.17 and 5.18 give trend growth rates of gross value added, total employment, gross fixed assets, and technological and cost ratios as well as the estimates of elasticity of substitution (σ) based on the CES production functions, respectively, for whole of organised industrial sector and various categories/industry groups. As indicated in the previous section, twenty industry groups have been divided into four categories, according to their levels of capital intensity. Category-I comprises most capital intensive industry groups, category-II medium high capital intensive industry groups, category-III medium low capital intensive industry groups and category-IV low capital intensive (or labour intensive) industry groups.

In case of organised industrial sector of the State, significant trend growth rates have been observed in respect of both output and employment for total manufacturing sector during the whole reference period (1974-86), but a high growth rate of output (6.56 percent) is accompanied by lower growth of employment (2.36 percent). This is due to the fact that during the sub-period-II (1980-86) of the study the State organised industrial sector witnessed significant trend rate of decrease in employment. Total factor productivity (Solow index) witnessed a significant growth of 2.4 percent. A significant, though not very high correlation of 0.60 between TFP and gross value added points towards a positive impact of TFP on output growth, but it seems that significant capital deepening rather than neutral technical change has played a more important role in output growth.[54] The significant decline in employment in sub-period-II, however, is accompanied by highly significant improvements in output and TFP. Technological progress seems to be largely of labour saving nature which does not suit labour surplus economy like U.P.

As already indicated, a conflict between output and employment can be traced back to low substitutability of the production structure. Esimates of elasticity of substitution (σ) for organised manufacturing sector of U.P. have been worked out through application of three models derived from the CES production function. On the basis of all the three models, estimates of (σ) found to be quite close to unity in total manufacturing sector of the State. This indicates greater employment potential in organised manufacturing, but due to high labour cost, capital seems to have been increasingly substituted for labour. Adjustment in input cost, so that these reflect the real social opportunity cost, is deemed to be necessary for accelerating the growth of both output and employment.

As already observed through inter-category analysis, there has been the highest trend growth rate of both output and employment in category-II (i.e. the medium high capital

Table-5.17 : Inter-Relationship between Technological Change and Performance of Organised Industrial Sector in U.P.

Year	Trend Growth Rate of: Solow index of TFP	Gross Value Aded	Total Employment	Gross Fixed Capital	Labour Productivity	Capital Productivity	Capital Intensity	Wage Rate	Rate of Return on Capital	Estimates of Elasticity of Substitution: CES Model-I	CES Model-II	CES Model-III
1	2	3	4	5	6	7	8	9	10	11	12	13
1974-80	1.28 (1.14)	6.94** (4.60)	5.19* (6.15)	5.63* (29.43)	1.67 (1.59)	1.24 (0.95)	0.42 (0.60)	2.44 (1.32)	0.28 (0.07)	–	–	–
1980-86	11.72* (5.14)	12.94* (4.99)	–3.28** (2.90)	7.84* (11.34)	16.77** (7.61)	4.73*** (2.15)	11.50* (12.95)	8.41* (7.36)	15.72** (3.72)	–	–	–
1974-86	2.42*** (2.07)	6.56* (6.75)	2.36** (3.01)	6.70* (29.2)	4.10** (2.77)	-0.13 (0.16)	4.24* (4.63)	4.28* (6.22)	-0.42 (-0.19)	1.07* (0.22)	1.51** (0.48)	1.22* (0.21)

Source: (Cols. 2,6,7,8): Table-5.3; (Col.11): Table-5.11; (Col.12): Table-5.12; (Col.13): Table-5.13; (Cols. 3,4,5): Table-5.16; and (Cols.9& 10): Appendix Table-5.1.

Notes: Figures in parentheses are t values (Cols. 2-10) and standard errors (Col. 11-14) of the estimates.

*, **, ***. Significant at 1,5 and 10 percent levels.

Table-5.18 : Category/Industry Group-wise Inter-Relationship between Technological Change and Performance in U.P.: 1974-75 to 1985-86

Category/Industry Group	Solow Index of TFP	Trend Growth Rate of: Gross Value Added	Total Employment	Gross Fixed Capital	Labour Productivity	Capital Productivity	Capital Intensity	Wage Rate	Rate of Return on Capital	Estimates of Elasticity of Substitution: CES-Model - I	CES-Model - II	CES-Model - III
1	2	3	4	5	6	7	8	9	10	11	12	13
1. Manufacture of chemicals and chemical products (except products of petroleum and coal)	-0.41 (0.25)	4.49** (2.39)	3.08* (8.84)	5.97* (10.04)	1.36 (0.75)	-1.40 (0.91)	2.80* (3.89)	4.70* (9.92)	-3.14 (1.18)	0.41 (0.34)	1.51 (1.13)	0.60 (0.66)
2. Basic metals and alloys industries	3.62** (2.47)	6.60* (4.03)	2.62* (5.92)	3.35* (16.15)	3.88** (2.57)	3.15*** (2.19)	0.71*** (1.94)	4.64* (7.85)	2.44 (0.74)	0.74** (0.30)	0.09 (0.81)	0.40 (0.67)
3. Manufacture of wool, silk and synthetic fibre textiles	-1.62 (0.73)	5.26*** (1.95)	1.89 (0.92)	6.56* (7.19)	3.31 (1.66)	-1.22 (0.63)	4.59** (2.74)	2.58** (2.92)	-1.44 (0.42)	0.90*** (0.49)	0.58 (0.69)	1.38** (0.60)
Category I	**1.29** **(0.99)**	**5.11*** **(3.76)**	**2.69*** **(5.49)**	**5.04*** **(15.20)**	**2.36** **(1.67)**	**0.07** **(0.06)**	**2.28*** **(3.64)**	**4.38*** **(11.89)**	**-1.39** **(0.58)**	**0.50** **(0.30)**	**-0.07** **(1.23)**	**0.98** **(0.61)**
4. Manufacture of electrical machinery apparatus, appliances and supplies and parts	9.26* (5.11)	14.46* (7.78)	5.47* (12.25)	4.42* (40.89)	8.53* (4.48)	9.62* (5.31)	-1.00*** (2.19)	3.31* (8.01)	15.29* (3.66)	2.27*++ (0.52)	0.73 (1.40)	1.66 (1.01)
5. Manufacture of rubber, plastic petroleum and coal products	-2.31 (0.49)	17.63** (3.07)	8.32* (4.66)	16.67* (5.01)	8.60*** (2.02)	0.82 (0.19)	7.71* (3.92)	7.32** (2.69)	1.37 (0.24)	1.20* (0.22)	1.22* (0.31)	1.31** (0.48)
6. Manufacture of edible oil and vanaspati ghee	-0.54 (0.22)	3.08 (1.35)	-2.34** (2.50)	5.25* (14.30)	5.54*** (1.94)	-2.07 (0.87)	7.77* (8.32)	5.11* (4.12)	-1.96 (0.53)	0.85*** (0.42)	0.46 (0.71)	-0.29 (0.50)
7. Other manufacturing industries	-9.96*** (1.91)	8.71*** (2.15)	3.54* (3.28)	12.09* (6.42)	4.99 (1.23)	-3.02 (0.78)	8.25* (4.61)	3.34* (4.64)	-0.62 (0.09)	1.35 (0.93)	1.05 (1.73)	1.35 (1.05)
Category II	**7.98*** **(5.12)**	**13.77*** **(7.85)**	**4.83*** **(10.97)**	**5.72*** **(29.87)**	**8.53*** **(5.48)**	**7.62*** **(4.89)**	**0.85*** **(2.13)**	**4.16*** **(10.80)**	**11.53*** **(3.58)**	**1.81*+++** **(0.39)**	**-0.55** **(1.24)**	**0.47** **(0.77)**
8. Manufacture of paper and paper products, and printing, publishing and allied industries	-1.60 (1.34)	4.84* (3.65)	3.04* (8.15)	11.93* (13.52)	1.74 (1.46)	-6.34* (6.7)	8.63* (12.20)	3.13* (5.84)	-8.81** (2.78)	0.36 (0.34)	-0.33 (0.70)	-0.10 (0.51)
9. Manufacture of alcohol, beverages, tobacco and tobacco products	1.67 (0.99)	7.23* (4.77)	2.41** (2.73)	6.56* (15.79)	4.72** (2.91)	0.63 (0.38)	4.06* (4.56)	4.99* (7.91)	0.33 (0.12)	0.95* (0.27)	0.96 (0.75)	1.02* (0.31)
10. Manufacture of machinery, machine tools and parts (except electrical)	4.53** (2.87)	9.22* (4.92)	3.61* (7.03)	6.00* (14.85)	5.41* (3.22)	3.03*** (2.04)	2.31* (5.43)	4.92* (8.29)	3.61 (1.44)	1.18* (0.25)	1.76** (0.70)	1.45** (0.58)
11. Manufacture of cotton textiles	1.05 (0.78)	4.89** (3.08)	2.86* (5.33)	5.68* (36.43)	1.97 (1.50)	-0.74 (0.48)	2.74* (4.86)	3.79* (4.83)	-7.82 (1.03)	0.57** (0.26)	0.68 (0.49)	0.40 (0.36)
12. Manufacture of food products (except sugar khandsari and gur)	4.72* (6.56)	10.37* (13.13)	4.55* (9.59)	6.24* (26.77)	5.57* (5.91)	3.89* (5.96)	1.62** (2.76)	0.55 (1.28)	6.23* (6.74)	2.67** (0.98)	1.49** (0.49)	2.00** (0.65)
13. Manufacture of textile products	-4.32 (1.25)	10.68** (2.40)	7.04* (3.50)	18.85* (8.33)	3.40 (1.01)	-6.88** (2.35)	11.03* (5.58)	3.86* (4.19)	-8.20*** (1.85)	1.48** (0.54)	2.52** (0.84)	1.54*** (0.72)
Category III	**1.86**** **(2.35)**	**6.92*** **(7.60)**	**3.29*** **(10.19)**	**7.03*** **(32.51)**	**3.52*** **(4.87)**	**-0.10** **(0.10)**	**3.62*** **(8.41)**	**3.56*** **(6.89)**	**-0.07** **(0.04)**	**0.87*** **(0.19)**	**0.30** **(0.43)**	0.25 (0.34)

Table-5.18 (Contd...)

	1	2	3	4	5	6	7	8	9	10	11	12	13
14.	Manufacture of metal products and parts (except machinery and transport equipment)	2.21*** (2.14)	3.51** (2.70)	-1.40** (2.25)	3.55* (13.21)	4.98* (5.22)	-0.04 (0.04)	5.02* (11.47)	2.49* (5.15)	2.04 (1.13)	1.67*+++ (0.31)	0.87 (0.55)	1.75*+++ (0.37)
15.	Manufacture of non-metallic mineral products	1.77 (1.54)	6.20* (4.96)	3.48* (4.33)	7.95* (11.31)	2.63*** (2.14)	-1.63 (1.68)	4.32* (3.81)	2.14** (3.08)	-1.48 (0.26)	1.09* (0.32)	0.97*** (0.47)	1.05** (0.34)
16.	Manufacture of jute, hemp and mesta textiles	1.82 (0.83)	6.30*** (1.85)	-1.02 (0.34)	5.92* (5.51)	7.40* (5.45)	0.37 (0.11)	7.01** (2.39)	5.10* (4.0)	12.69 (1.37)	0.92* (0.28)	0.11 (0.33)	0.98* (0.30)
17.	Manufacture of sugar, khandsari and gur	2.28 (0.91)	7.23* (3.92)	0.49 (0.26)	9.59* (22.43)	6.71** (2.67)	-2.15 (1.15)	9.05* (5.25)	5.21** (2.75)	6.69 (0.80)	1.10* (0.21)	0.96* (0.29)	1.17* (0.28)
18.	Manufacture of transport equipment & parts	2.39 (1.60)	13.25* (4.79)	11.42* (5.12)	7.95* (7.08)	1.64 (1.04)	4.91** (2.46)	-3.11 (1.63)	2.75 (1.78)	-2.54 (0.40)	0.86* (0.12)	0.94* (0.13)	0.94* (0.12)
19.	Manufacture of wood and wood products, furniture and fixtures	4.31** (2.99)	3.77** (3.54)	0.22 (0.12)	3.98* (10.35)	3.54*** (2.01)	-0.21 (0.18)	3.76*** (2.09)	1.79*** (1.84)	6.14 (0.98)	1.08** (0.45)	0.79 (0.51)	0.61 (0.45)
20.	Manufacture of leather and leather & fur products	2.28 (0.82)	12.13* (4.84)	7.00* (4.58)	12.16* (24.03)	4.80** (2.38)	-0.02 (0.01)	4.82* (4.07)	3.24* (4.63)	6.46 (0.63)	0.77 (0.56)	-0.75 (0.87)	-0.34 (1.28)
	Category IV	**3.48**** **(2.67)**	**7.74*** **(9.62)**	**2.10** **(1.60)**	**8.37*** **(58.23)**	**5.52*** **(3.69)**	**-0.58** **(0.75)**	**6.14*** **(4.53)**	**5.05*** **(3.97)**	**1.35** **(0.41)**	**1.01*** **(0.15)**	**0.87*** **(0.25)**	**1.00*** **(0.16)**
	Total manufacturing	**2.42***** **(2.07)**	**6.56*** **(6.75)**	**2.36*** **(3.01)**	**6.70*** **(29.2)**	**4.10**** **(2.77)**	**-0.13** **(0.16)**	**4.24*** **(4.63)**	**4.28*** **(6.22)**	**-0.42** **(0.19)**	**1.07*** **(0.22)**	**1.51**** **(0.49)**	**1.22*** **(0.21)**

Source : (Col. 2, 6, 7, 8) : Table-5.3: (Col.11); Table-5.11; (Col.12): Table-5.12; (Col.13): Table-5.13; (Cols. 3,4,5): Table-5.16; and (Cols. 9&10): Appendix Table-5.1.

Notes : Figures in parentheses are t values (col. 2-10) and standard errors (col. 11-13) of the estimates.

*,**,*** Significant at 1,5 and 10 percent levels.

+,++,+++ Significantly different from unity at 1,5 and 10 percent levels.

intensive category), but the trend growth rate of 13.8 percent in value added far exceeds the trend growth rate of 4.8 percent in employment. A highly significant coefficient of correlation (0.91) betwen output and employment shows absence of any conflict between the two in this category. The high trend growth rate of output can be attributed to the highly significant trend growth rate of 7.98 percent in Solow index of TFP. This is corroborated by the significant coefficient of correlation (0.98) between gross value added and Solow index. Highly significant partial productivity ratios also indicate the increased efficiency in input use. In addition, the significant trend growth rate of 4.16 percent in wage rate, well below the trend growth rate of labour productivity (8.53 percent) indicates a fall in labour cost per unit of output. Also highly significant trend growth rate in regard to rate of return on capital accompanied by significant trend growth rate of capital productivity shows increasing return to capital.

A significant relationship between the growth of labour productivity and output growth, known as 'Verdoorn's law' is indicative of technical progress and returns to scale. A highly significant and positive correlation (0.98) between value added and labour productivity may be ascribed to significant technical progress and economies of scale operating in industry groups of category-II. Generally, there is likelihood that a high growth of labour productivity would have an adverse bearing on employment growth. However, a significant and positive coefficient of correlation (0.86) between the two points towards the fact that a greater output growth has been conducive to increased employment growth in this case.

Regarding the other categories, it is observed that contrary to the theoretical expectations, highly labour-intensive category (i.e. category-IV) has experienced significant trend growth rate of 7.74 percent in value added accompanied by insignificant trend growth rate of employment. TFP seems to have played a significant role in the growth of value added but the partial productivity ratios point towards efficiency only in the use of labour. A significant trend growth rate of wages seems to have induced substitution of capital for labour as is witnessed by significant trend growth rate of 6.14 percent in capital-labour ratio. A significant and positive coefficient of correlation (0.96) between labour productivity and capital intensity points towards the significant role of capital deepening in the growth of labour productivity.

In the remaining two categories (I and III), there have been significant growth rates in both the output and employment with the former far exceeding the latter. However, in category-I (highly capital intensive), the trend growth rate of output is the lowest (contrary to popular belief) and that of employment is just above that of category-IV. In respect of category-III, one finds a positive and significant correlation (0.95) between gross value added and employment. However, TFP growth because of being low (1.8 percent) has resulted in comparatively lower trend growth rate of output. While the significant trend growth of labour productivity does point towards the efficiency in labour use, its trend growth rate is lower as compared to those of categories-II and IV. A significant trend growth of capital-labour ratio and insignificant trend growth of capital productivity indicates greater use of capital. Trend growth rate of wages exceeding that of average product of labour favours this trend. However, a significant coefficient of correlation between labour productivity and employment (0.85) shows that increases in output growth over and above labour productivity has taken care of otherwise negative impact on employment.

In respect of category-I, there does not appear any conflict between the output and the employment growth. But TFP and the partial productivities have shown an insignificant growth over the period. It seems that there has been greater use of capital as well as labour per unit of output. Significant trend growth rate of wages (4.38 percent) accompanied by insignificant growth rate of labour productivity points towards an increase in labour cost per unit of output. Further, insignificant trend growth rate of capital productivity accompanied by insignificant trend growth rate in respect of rate of return per unit of capital shows that there is less scope for further investment in various industry groups of this category.

Out of the twenty industry groups, the fourteen have shown significant growth rates of both output and employment. This is also supported by a significant and positive coefficient of correlation (0.83) between the growth rates of the two across industry groups. Only four out of these fourteen industry groups, have, however, witnessed significant trend growth rate in Solow index of TFP. These industry groups are basic metals and alloys industries; electrical machinery, machine tools and parts, machinery, machine tools and parts (except electrical); and food products.

The highest trend growth rate of output (17.63) is accompanied by significantly high employment growth rate of 8.32 percent in rubber, plastic, petroleum and coal products. Looking at the trend growth rates of capital (16.67 percent) and capital-labour ratio (7.71 percent) accompanied by negative though insignificant growth of Solow index, it appears that high output growth in this group is mainly the result of increased inputs, particularly capital.

The highest trend growth rate of employment (11.42 percent) is observed in transport equipment and parts, besides a significiant trend growth of 13.25 percent in value added. However, insignificant trend growth in TFP is probably an indicator of inefficiency in resource use. While capital productivity has registered a significant trend growth rate of 4.9 percent, the growth rate of labour productivity has proved to be insignificant. This is indicative of a greater use of factor inputs especially labour.

Electrical machinery, apparatus, appliances and supplies and parts is found to be the most efficient industry as far as the input use is concerned. The trend growth rate of Solow index (9.26 percent) is the highest amongst all the industry groups. This is accompanied by highly significant trend growth rate of 14.46 percent in gross value added (second in ranking) and significant though lower trend growth rate of employment (5.47 percent). This is also accompanied by the highest trend growth rates of labour productivity (8.53) and capital productivity (9.62 percent). Thus, there seems to have been an efficient utilisation of resources, more so of capital. This is reflected in a significant trend rate of decline in capital intensity. The trend growth rate of wages (3.31 percent) being almost half the growth rate of labour productivity indicates a fall in labour cost per unit of output. Further, significant trend growth rate of capital productivity accompanied by the high trend growth in regard to rate of return on capital (15.29 percent) shows increasing returns to capital. Thus, in this industry group there does not seem to be any conflict between output and employment or between employment and savings. More or less similar pattern is observed in three more industry groups, namely basic metals and alloys indsutries; machinery, machine tools and parts (except electrical); and food products.

In another eight industry groups (i.e. chemicals and chemical products; other manufacturing industries; paper and paper products, printing, publishing and allied industries; alcohol, beverages, tobacco and tobacco products; cotton textiles; textile products; non-metallic mineral products; leather and leather and fur products) out of the total fourteen, there appears to have been significant trend growth rates in both output and employment accompanied by insignificant trend growth rate of Solow index. Increased application of inputs, particularly capital seems to have been instrumental in the growth of these industry groups.

In the remaining six out of the total twenty industry groups, significant trend trowth rate of value added is accompanied by insignificant trend growth of employment in four industry groups (i.e. wool, silk and synthetic fibre textiles; jute, hemp and mesta textiles; sugar, khandsari and gur; and wood and wood products, furnitures and fixtures) and significant trend rate of decline in two industry groups (i.e., edible oil and vanaspati ghee; and metal products and parts).

Estimates of σ are not found to be significantly different from unity on the basis of all the three model in category-IV. Conversely in category-I, the hypothesis of σ =0 could not be rejected. As pointed out earlier, elasticity of substitution has been proved to show a continuous decline with an increasing replacement of traditional technology by modern one. Employment growth in category-IV has been found to be insignificant probably due to the fact that a greater substitution possibility accompanied by high wage rate has favoured greater substitution of capital for labour. Considering the substitution possibilities, corrective price adjustments can be of great help to brighten the scope of employment in category-IV as factor proportions are fairly responsive to factor price ratios. Whereas in category-I, one can hardly find an alternative to the type of technology already being used as substitution possibilities are almost non-existent.

Regarding the category-II, σ is found to exceed unity on the basis of Model-I only. The remaining models provide insignificant estimates of σ for this category. But there does not arise any conflict between output and employment or between employment and savings in this category, indicating a fairly flexible production structure. Similarly, for category-III also significant estimates of σ (quite close to unity) are observed only on the basis of Model-I only.

Estimates of σ not significantly different form unity are observed in the seven industry groups on the basis of all the three models. These industry groups are rubber, plastic, petroleum and coal products; machinery, machine tools and parts (except electrical); food products; textile products; non-metallic mineral products; sugar, khandsari and gur; and transport equipment and parts. Excepting sugar, khandsari and gur, significant trend growth rates in output are accompanied by significant trend growth rates of employment.

Significant estimates of σ on the basis of Model-I and III are observed in four industry groups, out of which in three industry groups (wool, silk and synthetic fibre textiles; alcohol, beverages, tobacco and tobacco products; and jute, hemp and mesta textiles) the estimates are found to be quite close to unity, whereas in metal products and parts, the estimates have exceeded unity. Excepting alcohol, beverages, tobacco and tobacco products, a conflict between output and employment is observed in all these industry groups.

Estimates of σ are found to be significant through application of Model-I only, in respect of five industry groups as follows. Estimates exceeding unity are observed in

(i) electrical machinery, apparatus, appliances and supplies and parts; and quite close to unity in (ii) basic metal and alloys industries; (iii) edible oil and vanaspati ghee; (iv) cotton textiles; and (v) wood and wood products, furniture and fixture. Excepting (iii) and (v) the rest have experienced significant trend growth rates of output accompanied by significant trend growth rates of employment.

In the remaining four out of twenty industry groups (chemicals and chemical products; other manufacturing industries; paper and paper products, printing, publishing and allied industries; and leather and leather and fur products), significant estimates of σ could not be witnessed on the basis of any of the three models. Poor performance and inefficiency (in terms of insignificant TFP as well as partial productivities) of these industry groups can be ascribed to lesser flexibility of the production structure.

Putting together the results of this chapter, the following broad conclusions emerge. So far as organised industrial sector of U.P. is concerned, significant trend growth rates of labour productivity and capital intensity are accompanied by insignificant growth of capital productivity during whole of the reference period. Significant TFP growth is observed only on the basis of Solow index. However, the period-wise analysis indicates a significant improvement in the average annual growth rates of partial and TFP indices in the sub-period II (1980-86) as compared to sub-period-I (1974-79). Decomposition results also show a significant improvement in the contribution of TFP to output growth in the sub-period-II.

The organised industrial sector of the State is not found to be experiencing significant technical progress and economies of scale on the basis of production function analysis also. The importance of capital to output growth is quite perceptible. All the three models derived from CES function provide estimates of σ which are not significantly different from unity. The (K/L) seems to be fairly responsive to changes in the factor prices in the organised manufacturing sector of the State.

Large inter-category/inter-industry differences prevail as far as the productivity and production function estimates are concerned. Category-II (medium-high capital intensive) has witnessed increases in both partial productivity ratios accompanied by significant trend rate of decline in capital intensity. Further, all the three indices of TFP have experienced significant trend growth rates. It seems that industry groups falling under this category are experiencing significant technical progress and economies of scale. These findings are corroborated through production function analysis also. Further, a significant saving in labour cost per unit of output is accompanied by high rate of return on capital. Increasing returns to capital have resulted in progressively high reinvestment potential of the industry groups constituting this category.

The high trend growth rates of labour productivity and capital intersity are accompanied by insignificant trend growth rates of capital productivity in categories-III and-IV. Increases in labour productivity seem to have resulted from increased capital deepening. However, significant trend growth rates of all the three indices of TFP indicate that these categories have experienced some sort of 'residual growth not accountable by the accompanying growth of inputs'.[55]

Production function estimates show output to be more responsivie to changes in labour input in category-III and to changes in capital input in category-IV. Production function has not shown a significant shift during the reference period as far as these two categories are concerned. However, significant economies of scale are witnessed in category-III, while the category-IV experiences constant returns to scale.

Category-I (or the highly capital intensive category) has experienced significant capital deepening accompanied by insignificant trend growth of partial productivities as well as the TFP. The production techniques used in this category seem to have not been conducive to increases in efficiency. The production function estimates also indicate absence of technical progress and economies of scale as far as this category is concerned.

As far as the technological change and economies of scale are concerned, comparatively less capital intensive categories (particularly category-II) seem to have been in a better position compared to highly capital intensive category.

Estimates of elasticity of substitution are not found to be significantly different from unity in category-IV, whereas the hypothesis of $\sigma = 0$ could not be rejected on the basis of all the three models in category-I. A more flexible production structure is noticeable in more labour intensive industry groups as compared to those based on relatively high capital intensive technology.

Significant trend growth rates in all the three TFP indices are observed in two industry groups, namely electrical machinery, apparatus, appliances and supplies and parts; and food products. These are also accompanied by significant trend growth rates of partial productivity ratios, showing a sign of improvement in overall efficiency. Significant trend growth rates in Kendrick and Solow indices of TFP are observed in basic metals and alloys industries; machinery, machine tools and parts (except electrical); metal products and parts; and wood and wood products, furnitures and fixtures. Out of these four industry groups, the first two have witnessed significant trend growth rates of both labour and capital productivities, whereas the significant trend growth rate of labour productivity alone indicates the labour-saving nature of technical progress in the latter two industry groups. Jute, hemp and mesta textiles; and sugar, khandsari and gur witnessed significant trend growth rate of only Kendrick index of TFP and registered a significant growth of partial productivity of labour only. In case of the remaining twelve industry groups, either TFP growth has not been significant or there has been a decline in it.

According to production function analysis, output is found to be more responsive to capital increases in larger number of industry groups as compared to employment increases. This goes against the earlier production function studies, which have found output to be more responsive to employment increases. On the basis of both the Cobb-Douglas and the CES production functions, time trend is found to be significant only in three out of twenty industry groups. Neutral technological progress does not seem to have made a significant contribution to the growth of organised industrial sector in U.P. during the reference period. Further, significant TFP growth in electrical machinery, apparatus, appliances and supplies and parts; basic metals and alloys; machinery, machine tools and parts (except electrical); metal products and parts; sugar, khandsari and gur is not substantiated by the production function estimates, whereas in respect of food products; jute, hemp and mesta textiles; and wood and wood products, furniture and fixtures, a significant shift in production function corroborates the earlier findings based on TFP indices.

Signifcant economies of scale are seen in basic metals and alloys; rubber, plastic petroleum and coal products; and food products; whereas significant diseconomies can be observed in edible oil and vanaspati ghee; alcohol, beverages, tobacco and tobacco products; and wood and wood products, furnitures and fixtures. The remaining industry groups are found to have been operating under constant returns to scale.

On the basis of all the three models derived from CES production function, estimates of σ are not found to be significantly different from unity in seven industry groups, whereas the similar estimates are found for three more industry groups on the basis of Model-I and III. Only on the basis of Model-I estimates of σ are found to be quite close to unity in four industry groups. In metal products and parts, estimates of σ exceed unity on the basis of Model-I and III. Similarly, greater than unity estimates of σ are found in electrical machinery, apparatus, appliances and supplies and parts on the basis of Model-I. In four industry groups (namely chemicals and chemicals products; other manufacturing industries; paper and paper products, printing, publishing and allied industries; leather and leather and fur products) the hypothesis of σ =0 could not be rejected on the basis of all the three models. Excepting leather and leather and fur products (which is the least capital-intensive) these industry groups are comparatively more capital intensive.

Category/industry group-wise analysis clearly brings out the better performance of category-II in terms of both output and employment growth. This is also substantiated by significant coefficient of correlation between the two. Besides, the significant coefficient of correlation of labour productivity with those of output and employment indicates that technical progress has been effective in augmenting the level of growth with equity in the industry groups comprising this category. Excepting the category-IV, the remaining two categories have also recorded significant development over the period in terms of output and employment growth. However, contrary to the popular belief, the highly labour intensive category witnesses significant growth in value added, while the employment growth has proved to be insignificant.

The ten industry groups have shown above the State level average growth rates in both the output and the employment. The coefficient of correlation between the two across the industry groups is highly significant. Besides, out of these, the five industry groups have also recorded significant trend growth rate in gross fixed capital which is greater than employment growth, indicating significant capital deepening over the period.

Finally, so far as assessing the role of technological change in development (in terms of output and employment growth) of organised industrial sector at the State level is concerned, technological change has significantly contributed to the output growth but not the employment growth. Significant increase in labour productivity accompanied by insignificant growth in capital productivity shows the labour saving bias of technological progress. As a result, we notice a sluggish employment growth in the organised manufacturing sector of the State.

Technological progress seems to have played a positive role in the overall development of industry groups constituting the category-II (mainly electrical machinery, apparatus, appliances and supplies and parts). Apart from significant trend growh rate of value added and employment, significant trend growth rates in both the partial productivities as well as the TFP are also observed. Further, labour productivity is positively associated with both output and employment, resulting in significant development of the industry groups constituting the medium-high capital intensive category-II. Contrary to the popular belief, there has been an insignificant employment growth in the category-IV (labour-intensive category). Technical progress in this category seems to have been more conducive to labour saving, resulting in significant growth in value added only. The behaviour of partial productivities and capital intensity also substantiates this finding. Significant growth rates of both value added and employment are seen in the remaining two categories (I and II). In category-III, technical progress has significantly contributed to output growth, whereas in category-I, inputs seem to have been the major source of output growth as witnessed by insignificant growth rates of both the partial productivities and TFP.

Significant trend growth rates in both value added and employment are witnessed by fourteen industry groups. The performance of the ten industry groups in this regard have been found above the State level average growth. This is accompanied by significant trend growth of Solow index in four industry groups, namely, basic metals and alloys industries; machinery, machine tools and parts (except electrical); electrical machinery, appliances and supplies and parts and; food products.

Excepting the category-I and the four industry groups estimates of σ indicate responsiveness of factor proportions to factor price ratio. In other words, greater possibilities of substitution exist in the organised industrial sector of U.P. Hence, suitable adjustments in factor prices can play a significant role in achieving the twin objectives of growth with equity and thereby overall development of the State.

References

1. Annual compound growth rate of industrial sector in U.P. was 9.4 percent during the Fifth Plan (1974-79) as against 3.4 percent during the Fourth Plan (1969-74). Further the corresponding growth rate during the Sixth Plan (1980-85) was 11.8 percent. Thus, there was a remarkable progress during the period 1969-85. See Government of Uttar Pradesh, *State Income Bulletin*; and A.K. Singh (1988).

2. Trend growth rates have been calculated from the following equation: log Y= a+bt Where Y is concerned variable ant 't' refers to time.

3. A. Banerji (1975), p.72.

4. To ascertain what other factors apart from capital intensity may have caused the increases in labour productivity, we have estimated the regression equation relating wage rate and capital intensity to labour productivity. The estimated equation is:
   $V/L = -721.63 - 0.44w + 0.27^{**}K/L$
   t values (-0.47) (2.91)
   $R^2=0.88$

   Only K/L has shown a significant influence, however, increased capital deepening did not lead to sharp fall in capital productivty.

5. B.R. Hasim and M.M. Dadi (1973); and K. Rajlakshmi (July 1983).

6. The Kendrick, Solow and Translog Indices of TFP have been estimated by applying equation 3, (9a), (33a) given in section 2.2 of Chapter-III.

7. R.R. Singh (1966); and Shivamaggi, Rajgopalan and Venkatachalam (1968).

8. L. Singh (1987); S.S. Dhillon (1983); and D. Gupta (1985).

9. Regression equation relating V/L to wage rate and capital intensity yield following results for category-II.

$V/L = -39648.9 + 4.163^{*} w + 0.284 K/L$
t values (3.278) (0.934)

* Significant at 1 percent level.

10. A. Banerji (1975), p.72

11. Regression equation relating V/L to wage rate and capital intensity for category-III and IV are as follows:

    Category-III

    $V/L = 1124.58 + 1.18^{***} w + 0.05 K/L$
    t values (2.04) (0.61)

    $R^2=0.671$

    Category-IV

    $V/L = 288.84 + 0.301 w + 0.18^{**} K/L$
    t values (0.618) (2.57)
    $R^2 = 0.921$

    ** Significant at 5 percent level.

    *** Significant at 10 percent level.

12. For details see B.H. Dholakia (Jan. 1977); I.J Ahluwalia (1985); and B.N. Goldar (1986).

13. Striking similarity can be seen in the contribution of TFP based on Solow method and the decomposition method.

14. This period is characterised by sharp fall in the employment in the registered manufacturing sector of U.P.

15. The Stochastic formulation of equation (41) from Chapter III.

16. The interpretation of the degree of homogeneity of Cobb Douglas production function in terms of the returns to scale is far from being accurate. Correct interpretation holds only at micro level. See Ferguson (1965). Further, Cobb Douglas function imposes the same degree of returns to scale over the whole range of sizes and observations-an assumption not borne out of facts. See J. Johnston, *Statistical Cost Analysis*, New York, 1960; and M. Nerlove, *Estimation and Identification of Cobb-Douglas Production Functions*, Chicago, 1964.

17. See equation (43a) from section 4.2 (i) in Chapter-III.

18. Also the elimination of trend component from conventional variables by including a separate time trend variable as a proxy for technical progress might have affected our results as this leaves estimated relationship dominated by short term cyclical influence. A production function analysis on the other typically concerns itself with long run equilibrium relations. This might explain the behaviour of the independent variables. See Banerji (1975). p.63.

19. The estimated equation used is as: $\log V/L = \log A + \beta \log K/L + \mu$.

20. See equation (45) in chapter-III.

21. See K.F. Wallis (1973), pp.45-46.

22. S.S. Mehta (1980), p.112.

23. R. Diwan and D.Gujarati (1968), p.52.

24. A. Banerji (1975), p.110.

25. See equations (49), (50) and (51) in chapter-III.

26. P.A. Yotopoulos and J.B. Nugent (1976), p.54.

27. A. Banerji (1975), p.112.

28. Evidence is provided by comparing estimates of elasticity of substitution for a sample of 'modern' Peruvian and U.S. firms in manufacturing obtained by Clague with those obtained by Witte for a sample of 'traditional' Peruivian manufacturing firms. The latter estimates of σ have generally been closer to one, while the former estimates are significantly less than unity averaging around 0.2. For details, see Yotopoulos and Nugent (1976), p.151.

29. Mainly see Banerji (1975), Mehta (1980); and Subramaniyan (1979).

30. Similar results are brought out in a recent study on the manufacturing sector of Pakistan. See A.H. Khan and R. Siddiqui (1990).

31. Data on sectoral contributions has been taken from Government of Uttar Pradesh, *Draft Eight Five Year Plan 1990-95 and Annual Plan 1991-92,* Vol.1, Table-3, and p.11.

32. The technology of Western nations transferred and used without adapting to local needs is mainly unsuitable for following reasons (i) it is developed for labour scarce developed countries and is, therefore, more capital intensive (ii) it is associated with high rate of labour productivity which is essential for it to be viable in developed countries because high wages are involved. Transfer without adaptation leads to high rates of labour productivity, leading to dualism in the economy with wide gap between the labour productivity in the modern sector and incomes of rest of the economy (iii) it requires highly skilleld personnel that are in short supply in developing countries, (iv) it is developed to suit large scale operation of developed countries, and (v) it is most suited to mass production of products that cater to the demand of high income consumers. For details, see Frances Stewart (1974), pp.19-22.

33. M.Gillis, D.H. Perkins, M.Roemer and D.R. Snodgrass (1983), pp.197-198.

34. D.Morawetz (1974), p.499.

35. Income redistribution is assumed to naturally follow from this. Lower income levels are found among these who fail to find employment in modern sector due to the fact that gains from growth of aggregated output have been mainly accrued by those who are fortunate enough to be employed. Poverty many be a proxy for atleast a part of employment problem since excess supply of people seeking modern sector jobs is reflected in low incomes arising from complete lack of work or work of very low productivity. See F. Stewart and P.Streeten (1976), p.381.

36. Government of India, *Sixth Five Year Plan (1980-85)*, Planning Commission, p.203.

37. Government of Uttar Pradesh, *Sixth Five Year Plan (1980-85)*, Planning Department.

38. Terms taken from M.Gillis, D.H. Perkins, M. Roemer, and D.R. Snodgrass (1983), p.200.

39. The reasons for favouring this view are follows:

(i) For certain industries, capital intensive, large scale setting many be absolutely necessary to capture economies of scale. It is argued that in such cases capital intensive technology may be more efficient than less capital intensive one, as they apart from using less labour may also be using less capital per unit of output. Apart from this, it is also argued that capital intensivie technologies are necessary to enusre high quality of products as lack of skilled manpower may be compensated for by substituting capital in place of labour. For these and other issues related to technology and employment, see A.S. Bhalla (ed.) (1975), particularly the case studies by G.K. Boon and F. Stewart.

(ii) High capital intensive processes are also associated with high rate of technological progress.

(iii) It is argued that even though labour intensive alternatives may exist the choice may be restricted due to non-viability or due to lack of information.

(iv) Further, it is also argued that capital intensive technology results in higher returns to capital owners who have high propensity to save and invest. See W. Galenson and H. Leibenstien (1955).

40. See L.J. White (1978), p.33.

41. M. Nerlove (1967).

42. See A.S. Bhalla (1975); L.J. White (1978); W. Bear (1976); F.T. Moore (1983).

43. D.J.C. Forsyth, N.S.Mc Bain and R.F. Solomon (1980).

44. G. Ranis (1957).

45. The reasons for this unused capacity have to be fully explored as insufficiency of demand may be only a part of the problem. Inappropriate price incentives and lack of complementary resources, including entrepreneurship and management, are also likely to be involved. See Gillis, Perkins, Roemer and Snodgrass (1983), p.207.

46. See L. White (1978), pp.41-42.

47. Also the conclusion of Heckscher-Ohlin-Samuelson factor proportions theory of trade flows. For some other studies reaching similar conclusions, see D. Morawetz (1974), p.507.

48. Counterargument for this runs as follows: small firms use more labour as well as capital per unit of output. Output capital and capital-labour ratio would be a deciding factor but evidence regarding this is conflicting. Further, it is also argued that only direct employment implications are taken into account while comparing Big vs. Small firms. Opportunities for indirect employment are large in big firms. See L. White (1978), p.40; and D. Morawetz, (1974), p.526.

49. Apart from the studies already mentioned see also H. Pack (1974).

50. See L. White (1978), pp. 47-50; and F.T. Moore (1984), pp.27-29, for detailed discussion of these points.

51. Developing countries performs only 2 percent of all R&D performed in the non-Communist world, with the firms in these countries spending approximately 0.1 percent to 0.2 percent of their sales in R&D. In contrast manufacturing firms in the U.S. spent on an average 2 percent of sales from their own finances on R&D. Information provided in L.White, *ibid.*, p.51.

52. See F. Stward (1974), p.32; and D. Morawetz (1974), pp.528-530.

53. F. Steward (1974).

54. See Table 5.4. Further significant correlation (r=0.93) between V/L and K/L point towards the importance of capital deepening in the growth of value added per person.

55. A. Banerji (1975).

20. See L.J. White (1976), p.35.

21. M. Merhav (1969).

24. G. Ranis (1957).

33. F. Stewart (1974).

35. A. Bhalla (1975).

CHAPTER 6

Technological Progress and Performance of Organised Industrial Sector: Regional Level Analysis

Uttar Pradesh is divided into five economic regions, namely, Western, Central, Eastern Uttaranchal and Bundelkhand. Out of these, the latter three are recognised as backward regions.

Since the start of planning in India, balanced regional development through accelerated development of backward areas, has been the major plank of development policy of the country. The Government of Uttar Pradesh has also emphasised this line of thought, particularly since the Third Plan. Apart from allocation of higher outlays for development of backward areas, a number of policy instruments, particularly those of protective and promotional measures to attract industrial activities to these areas were introduced. A number of programmes were also launched to ensure diversification of industries in backward areas.

Regarding the different regions, we notice that the agricultural base is comparatively strong in the Western and the Central regions. The Eastern region, in spite of being heavily dependent on agriculture, contributes less in terms of agricultural production as compared to the developed regions, mainly due to low agricultural productivity. The remaining two regions of Bundelkhand and Uttaranchal are also predominantly agrarian, but topography of these regions does not favour much to agricultural development. Therefore, for achieving the objective of balanced regional development in the State, development of industrial sector in these regions seems to be most crucial.

Taking into account the resource base of the backward regions, a well knit programme for establishing resource based industries appears to be worthwhile proposition for initiating a process of sustained industrial development.[1] For example, the agrarian character of the Eastern region can be improved upon through development of agro-based industries. Similarly, looking to the existing resource endowments, the development of mineral based industries in the Bundelkhand region and forest based industries in the Uttaranchal would prove to be a sound economic proposition.

A heavy dependence on resource based industries, however, might jeopardise the objective of balanced regional development because of the likelihood of larger concentration of industrial activity in the resource rich districts. In such circumstances, development of footloose industries (i.e. the industries not bound to a particular location by specific locational requirements) may lead to spread effect and enhance effectiveness in arresting the divergent tendency of intra-regional and inter-regional disparities. Judicious blend of these two types of industries through careful planning is likely to accelerate the process and tempo of balanced regional development in the State.

The State level analysis carried out in the previous chapter has, no doubt, revealed that technological change had made a significant contribution to the performance of organised industrial sector in Uttar Pradesh over the period. On the other hand, as indicated earlier, inter-regional disparities do exist in the State, not only in respect of industral development, but also in respect of the availability of natural resources, including human capital and social capabilities. Looking to these aspects, it would be worthwhile to carry out a disaggregative analysis to study and examine the inter-regional differentials in technological change and its inter-relationship with inter-regional performance of industrial sector.

Therefore, the present chapter aims at analysing the inter-relationship between inter-regional differentials in technological progress and performance of organised industrial sector in the State during the period: 1974-75 to 1985-86. One of the major limitation of our analysis in the present context is non-availability and insufficiency of consistent industry group-wise time series data for different regions of the State. And obviously because of this, our analysis is confining to total manufacturing sector at the regional level. In spite of this limitation, strenuous efforts have been made to use and incorporate in the present analysis, industry group-wise as well as district-wise data for the first and the last years of the reference period of the study.

For convenience sake, the whole chapter is divided into three sections; first, measuring technological progress region-wise; second, assessing the inter-regional performance of organised industrial sector; and third, highlighting the inter-relationship between technological progress and performance of the organised industrial sector of different regions.

1. REGION-WISE TECHNOLOGICAL ADVANCEMENT IN THE ORGANISED INDUSTRIAL SECTOR: 1974-75 TO 1985-86

1.1 Trends in Partial and Total Factor Productivities

To begin with, we tried to examine the trends in partial productivities and capital intensity. The trend growth rates of these ratios for whole of the organised industrial sector region-wise (year-wise indices are placed at Appendix: Table-6.1) are shown in Table-6.1.

Partial productivities simply gives us an idea of efficiency in the use of a factor input. Increase in partial productivity index implies that more output is obtained with less use of a factor input. During the reference period of the study, the labour productivity, as measured by gross value added per person, experienced a significant trend rate of growth in the Western, the Eastern and the Bundelkhand regions, besides the whole of the State.[2] The highest trend growth rate of 9.9 percent was observed in the Eastern region followed by the trend growth rate of 8.78 percent in the Bundelkhand region. The Western region also registered a significant trend growth rate of 4.14 percent. Contrary to this, the Central region and the Uttaranchal experienced insignificant trend growth rate in labour productivity. The trend growth rate in labour-productivity was the lowest in the Central region. The trend growth rate above the State average (5.07 percent) is seen in the Eastern and the Bundelkhand regions only.

Table-6.1 : Region-wise Trend Growth Rates in Partial Productivity Indices and Capital Intensity for Organised Industrial Sector: 1974-75 to 1985-86

	Partial Productivities		*Capital Intensity*
Region	*Labour Productivity*	*Capital Productivity*	
1	2	3	4
Western	4.14**	0.60	3.52*
	(2.33)	(0.56)	(3.73)
Central	2.11	-2.09	4.29*
	(2.00)	(2.23)	(6.18)
Eastern	9.90*	0.85	8.98*
	(3.22)	(0.53)	(4.70)
Uttaranchal	3.72	-0.57	4.32**
	(1.56)	(0.29)	(2.86)
Bundelkhand	8.78*	0.90	7.81*
	(5.52)	(0.47)	(4.12)
U.P.	**5.07****	**-0.01**	**5.08***
	(2.99)	**(0.01)**	**(4.76)**

Source : Appendix Table 6.1.

Note : Figures in parentheses are t values of the estimates.

* Significant at 1 percent level of significance

** Significant at 5 percent level of significance.

Positive trend growth rates in capital productivity can be seen in the Western, the Eastern and the Bundelkhand regions, while negative trend growth rates can be observed in the remaining two regions (Central and Uttaranchal) and also in whole of the State. These trend growth rates of capital productivity, as noticed, were not significant at both the State and regional levels. This means the growth of capital productivity has remained almost constant during the period of the study.

On the other hand, the trend growth rates of capital intensity are found to be significant in all the regions of the State. This was the highest (8.98 percent) in the Eastern region followed by the Bundelkhand (7.81 percent) and the Uttaranchal (4.32 percent). However, comparatively better developed Western and Central regions experienced the respective trend growth rates of 3.52 per cent and 4.29 percent only. It seems that the National policy of backward area development has gone in favour of setting up a reasonably good number of organised industrial units based on capital intensive technology in all the three backward regions of the State.

Regarding the relationship between these ratios, it is noticeable that a significant growth in capital intensity is accompanied by significant growth of labour productivity in the organised industrial sector of the Western, the Eastern and the Bundelkhand regions. This is accompanied by positive though insignificant growth of capital productivity. Much of the gains in output per person seem to be an outcome of capital deepening. The coefficient of correlation between the two, being as high as 0.92, 0.95 and 0.73 in the Western, the Eastern and the Bundelkhand regions, respectively, substantiates this conclusion.[3] Although capital productivity has not shown a significant improvement over the period in these regions, the technical progress seems to have made definite contributions to labour productivity. Excepting the Bundelkhand region, significant coefficient of correlation between the two indices of capital and labour productivities in the Western (r=0.81) and the Eastern (r=0.63) regions indicates that both the indices have, by and large, moved in a similar direction.

In the organised industrial sector of the Central region and the Uttaranchal, significant capital deepening is accompanied by insignificant partial productivity ratios. Hence, one can argue that increased capital intensity in industries of these regions has not been conductive to productivity improvements. In other words, the factor proportion has not been used in a manner that would lead to increased efficiency in terms of significant growth of labour and capital productivities. So far as the State level organised industrial sector is concerned, significant growth rates in labour productivity and capital intensity and high coefficient of correlation between the two (r=0.95) point out that major increases in labour productivity are a result of capital deepening.[4]

In case of cost ratios (Appendix Table-6.2), significant increases in wage rate are observed in all the regions and whole of the State. The highest trend growth rate in wages in seen in the Eastern region. In this context, it is interesting to note that growth rates of wages are found to be less than that of labour productivity in the Western, the Eastern, and the Bundelkhand regions and also in whole of the State. The growth rate of wages is significantly lower (3.9 percent) than that of labour productivity (8.78 percent) in the Bundelkhand, implying a fall in the cost of labour per unit of output in the organised manufacturing sector of this region. Thus, increased capital intensity resulted in increased remuneration for labour, but the labour productivity registered an increase to the extent that it reduced unit labour cost significantly.[5] In the organised manufacturing sector of the Central region and the Uttaranchal an increase in the unit labour cost is noticeable over the period. The significant trend growth rate of 24.87 percent in respect of rate of return on capital as observed in Bundelkhand shows a greater reinvestment potential for the manufacturing sector in this region.

The divergent movements of partial productivity ratios do not permit us to draw any precise and meaningful conclusion as far as improvements in overall efficiency are concerned. Therefore, total factor productivity (TFP) index has been estimated. The trend rates of growth in Kendrick, Solow and translog indices[6] are presented in Table-6.2 (year-wise indices are placed at Appendix: Table-6.1). The organised industrial sector of the Bundelkhand region witnessed significant trend growth rates separately for all the three indices, being 8.23 (Kendrick), 6.92 (Solow) and 4.17 (translog) percent, respectively. This substantiates our conclusion drawn for this region previously. The coefficient of correlation between Solow index and labour productivity is 0.99 (significant at one percent level) and between Solow index and capital productivity is 0.56 (significant at 10 percent level). Thus, the region seems to be experiencing a significant technological progress.

In the Eastern region, significant trend growth rate of 5.20 percent in Kendrick index and 8.06 percent in Solow index indicates that significant neutral technological progress has occurred in the organised manufacturing sector of this region. As observed in the previous Table, the Eastern region witnessed a significant increase in labour productivity, whereas the growth rate of capital productivity was not significantly different from zero. The coefficient of correlation between Solow index and labour productivity was significantly high (r=0.99) as against 0.67 between Solow index and capital productivity.

Table-6.2 : Region-wise Trend Growth Rates in Total Factor Productivity Indices for Organised Industrial Sector: 1974-75 to 1985-86

Region	*Kendrick Index*	*Solow Index*	*Translog Index*
1	2	3	4
Western	1.83 (1.43)	2.36 (1.73)	1.22 (0.95)
Central	0.20 (0.22)	1.18 (1.16)	0.17 (0.17)
Eastern	5.20** (2.33)	8.06** (3.06)	1.99 (0.94)
Uttaranchal	2.09 (0.98)	4.57** (2.60)	-4.94 (1.78)
Bundelkhand	8.23* (5.32)	6.92* (4.48)	4.17** (2.99)
U.P.	**2.15** **(1.84)**	**3.10**** **(2.34)**	**1.77** **(1.46)**

Source : Appendix Table 6.1.

Note : Figures in parentheses are t values of the estimates.

* Significant at 1 percent level of significance.

** Significant at 5 percent level of significance.

Significant trend growth rate of 4.57 percent (significant at 5 percent level) in Solow index was observed in the manufacturing sector of the Uttaranchal. Kendrick and translog indices, however, witnessed insignificant trend growth rates. This substantiates to our previous finding that both the partial productivity ratios did not register significant growth in this region.

The manufacturing sector of all the three backward regions (Bundelkhand, Eastern and Uttaranchal) accounted for about 35 percent of the total value added of the State level manufacturing sector in 1985-86 as compared to only 22 percent in 1974-75. The expansion of industrial activities in terms of number and type of units over the period seems to be responsible for greater participation of these regions.

In the Western and the Central regions, all the three indices of TFP show insignificant growth rates. Thus, it seems that a higher use of inputs in comparatively developed regions has been a major source of growth of the organised manufacturing sector.

The State manufacturing sector witnessed significant growth rate of 3.1 percent (significant at 5 percent level) in Solow index only. Above State level average growth in Solow index is observed in the regions of Eastern, Uttaranchal and Bundelkhand pointing towards the efficient use of inputs in these regions.

1.2 Decomposition of Growth

Using the linear homogeneous production function, absolute and relative contributions of various factors to output growth were estimated.[7] Average relative shares of labour and capital and average and relative contributions of labour, capital and TFP to

Table-6.3 : Region-wise of Sources of Growth of Output for Organised Industrial Sector: 1974-75 to 1985-86

Region	Average Share of Labour in Value Added	Average Share of Capital in Value Added	Absolute Contribution of (percentage points)			Trend Growth Rate of Gross Value Added	Relative Contribution of			Total (percent)
			Labour	Capital	TFP		Labour	Capital	TFP	
1	2	3	4	5	6	7	8	9	10	11
Western	0.46	0.54	1.467	3.683	2.312	7.462*	19.66	49.36	30.98	100.00
Central	0.71	0.29	1.527	1.894	0.888	4.309*	35.44	43.95	20.61	100.00
Eastern	0.54	0.46	-0.031	4.099	5.771	9.839*	-0.32	41.66	58.65	100.00
Uttaranchal	0.59	0.41	2.276	3.421	2.026	7.723*	29.47	44.30	26.23	100.00
Bundelkhand	0.73	0.27	4.360	3.848	7.067	15.275*	28.54	25.19	46.27	100.00
U.P.	**0.53**	**0.47**	**1.250**	**3.554**	**2.747**	**7.551***	**16.55**	**47.07**	**36.38**	**100.00**

Source : Based on the Table 6.11 incorporated subsequently in this Chapter.

* Significant at 1 percent level of significance.

the growth of value added are presented in Table-6.3. For the State as a whole, it is noticed that capital has been the major source of growth. It is supported by the fact that the contribution of capital to growth of value added in organised industrial sector of U.P. was as high as 47 percent. The corresponding contributions of TFP and labour were only 36 percent and 17 percent respectively.

The contribution of TFP in the Eastern region was higher (about 59 percent) than those of the factor inputs, mainly because of poor contribution of labour. In the organised industrial sector of the remaining four regions total factor input was the main source of output growth as compared to TFP. However, capital's contribution was greater than that of labour, with an exception of Bundelkhand where contribution of labour to output growth was greater. Like the Eastern region, the contribution of TFP to output growth was also the highest (about 46 percent) in the Bundelkhand region, followed by labour (about 29 percent) and capital (25 percent).

The contribution of TFP to output growth was the lowest (21 percent) in the Central region where capital emerged as a major source of output growth. However, it is gratifying to note that technological progress has played a significant role in development of the Eastern and the Bundelkhand regions.

1.3 Region-wise Production Function Estimates of the Organised Industrial Sector

No doubt, the unrestricted Cobb-Douglas production function permits us to get the estimates of neutral technological change and returns to scale, although the *apriori* assumption of elasticity of substitution being equal to one is the major shortcoming of this function. It has, therefore, been decided to determine region-wise elasticity of substitution by estimating the side relations derived from the CES production function.

(i) *Cobb-Douglas Production Function*: Region-wise estimates for organised industrial sector based on the unrestricted Cobb-Douglas production function without time trend are provided in Table-6.4.[8] Positive coefficients of capital and labour are observed in the Central, the Uttaranchal and the Bundelkhand regions. Whereas, coefficient of labour is found to be negative and insignificant in the Eastern region and negative and significant (at 10 percent level) in the Western region. Capital coefficient is found to be significant in the Western, the Central, the Eastern regions and the Uttaranchal, indicating capital to be the major source of output growth in organised industrial sector. However, in case of the Bundelkhand, a significant labour coefficient accompanied by insignificant capital coefficient indicates that output is more responsive to changes in labour as compared to capital.

It seems that significant coefficients of capital in four out of five regions have acted as a push factor in the development of organised industrial sector of the State. The returns to scale (given by sum of labour and capital coefficients) was found to be significantly greater than one (at 5 percent level) in the Bundelkhand region, demonstrating increasing returns to scale in the organised industrial sector of this region. The returns to scale for the remaining four regions and the whole State are found to be not significantly different from one, indicating that constant returns to scale are operating in the organised manufacturing sector. On the whole, high value of $\bar{R}^2$ points that the fit is good. Durbin Waston (D.W.) test indicates error terms to be serially independent.

Incorporation of time trend in the above regression give us Model II,[9] the estimates of which are provided in Table-6.5.

Table-6.4 : Region-wise Estimates of the Cobb-Douglas Production Function for Organised Industrial Sector: 1974-75 to 1985-86-Model I

No. of Observations: 12 — Dependent Variable : Log V

Region	*Constant term*	*Log L*	*Log K*	*Returns to scale (3+4)*	R^2	$\bar{R}^2$	*SE*	*F Value*	*D.W.*
1	2	3	4	5	6	7	8	9	10
Western	1.593	-0.608*** (-1.950)	1.381* (6.833)	0.773 (-1.066)	0.871	0.858	0.104	30.322*	2.193
Central	1.351	0.119 (0.243)	0.608** (2.869)	0.727 (-0.760)	0.674	0.641	0.104	9.290*	1.653
Eastern	7.569	-0.893 (-1.591)	1.086* (6.886)	0.193 (-1.283)	0.863	0.850	0.158	28.474*	1.172
Uttaranchal	-0.830	0.010 (0.022)	0.859** (2.778)	0.869 (-0.394)	0.578	0.535	0.222	6.152**	1.653
Bundelkhand	-13.559	2.086** (3.043)	0.151 (0.550)	2.237++ (2.839)	0.919	0.911	0.156	51.293*	2.552
U.P.	**2.791**	**-0.488 (-1.663)**	**1.162* (8.783)**	**0.674 (-1.380)**	**0.909**	**0.900**	**0.088**	**44.899***	**1.753**

Source : Based on ASI Reports : Various Issues.

Note : Figures in parentheses are t values of the estimates.

V : value added; L : labour; K : capital.

*, **, *** Significant at 1,5 and 10 percent level of significance.

++ Significantly different form unity at 5 percent level of significance.

Table-6.5 : Region-wise Estimates of the Cobb-Douglas Production Function for Organised Industrial Sector: 1974-75 to 1985-86-Model II

No. of Observations : 12 | Dependent Variable : Log V

Region	*Constant term*	*Log L*	*Log K*	*t*	*Returns to scale (3+4)*	R^2	$\bar{R}^2$	*SE*	*F Value*	*D.W.*
1	2	3	4	5	6	7	8	9	110	11
Western	0.587	-0.609 (-1.852)	1.471 (1.196)	-0.006 (-0.074)	0.862 (-0.121)	0.871	0.842	0.104	17.981*	2.211
Central	14.267	-0.0616 (-0.118)	-0.429 (-0.407)	0.071 (1.004)	-0.491 (-1.246)	0.707	0.641	0.099	6.390**	2.035
Eastern	10.130	-1.010 (-1.136)	0.974 (1.493)	0.010 (0.177)	-0.036 (-0.738)	0.864	0.834	0.157	16.938*	1.239
Uttaranchal	6.666	-0.027 (-0.061)	0.072 (0.084)	0.070 (0.977)	0.045 (-1.139)	0.618	0.533	0.211	4.314**	1.595
Bundelkhand	-11.074	1.788 (1.335)	0.170 (0.572)	0.016 (0.264)	1.958 (0.873)	0.920	0.902	0.156	30.654*	2.541
U.P.	**-4.661**	**-0.326** **(-0.774)**	**1.603***** **(1.979)**	**-0.036** **(-0.553)**	**1.277** **(0.263)**	**0.912**	**0.892**	**0.086**	**27.624***	**1.607**

Source : Based on ASI Reports : Various Issues.

Note : Figures in parentheses are t value of the estimates.

V : value added; L: labour; C: capital; and t: time.

*, **, *** Singnificant at 1, 5 and 10 percent level of significance.

Excepting the Bundelkhand, negative coefficients of labour are now found in the organised industrial sector of the remaining regions and for the whole State. The only significant estimate observed through application of this model is the coefficient of log (K) for the State manufacturing, demonstrating the importance of capital once again. The presence of multicollinearity between the independent variables seems to have resulted in inflated standard errors. Positive time trend is observed in the Central, the Eastern, the Uttaranchal and the Bundelkhand regions while the time trend is negative in the Western region and for whole of the State but it is not found to be significant in any case. It seems that production function has not experienced any significant shift over the period. The estimate of returns to scale is not found to be significantly different from one, indicating the existence of constant returns to scale in the manufacturing sector of the State as well as the five economic regions.

To remove the effect of multicollinearity between the independent variables of capital and labour, the ratio form of unconstrained Cobb-Douglas with time trend[10] has also been estimated (Appendix Table-6.3). But nothing meaningful could be noticed through application of this alternative method of estimation. The results of two regressions (Table-6.5 and Appendix Table-6.3) are more or less similar. Multicollinearity among independent variables, particularly log (K/L) and t seems to have jeopardised the quality of results

Barring the Bundelkhand (where significant economies were observed in Table-6.4), constant returns to scale seem to have operated in the organised industrial sector of the remaining four regions and the whole State. Therefore, the ratio form of constrained Cobb-Douglas production function with time trend[11] has been estimated. The results are provided in the Table-6.6. Positive coefficients of capital are seen in all the regions and the State, but they are found to be significant in case of the organised industrial sector of the Western, the Eastern regions and the Uttaranchal and the State only. Capital seems to have played an important role in development of organised industrial sector of these regions. In case of Bundelkhand, it is already seen that the role of labour is more important than that of capital. Time trend is found to be negative (though insignificant) in most of the cases excepting Bundelkhand where significant neutral technological progress of about 6 percent seems to have played a crucial role. This is fairly comparable with the conclusion drawn earlier regarding this region.

The important among the general conclusions emerging from application of different models of Cobb-Douglas production function is that the capital has played the crucial role in output growth of the organised industrial sector. Neutral technological progress seems to have played insignificant role in the development of organised industries of U.P. during the period of the study. The only exception is Bundelkhand which has experienced both significant technological progress as well as economies of scale.

(ii) *Constant Elasticity of Substitution (CES) Production Function* : The elasticity of substitution (σ), showing the scope of factor substitution in the production process is a crucial parameter, so far as deriving policy implications, particularly in respect of developing countries are concerned. These countries are characterised by abundant labour force, which need to be absorbed efficiently to fulfil the twin objectives of growth and equity. High substitutability of the production structure is associated with high output and employment. Since Cobb-Douglas production function is based on the restrictive assumption of unitary elasticity of substitution, the estimates of side relations have been derived from CES

Table-6.6 : Region-wise Estimates of the Cobb-Douglas Production Function for Organised Industrial Sector: 1974-75 to 1985-86- Model III

No. of Observations : 12

Dependent Variable : Log (V/L)

Region	*Constant*	*Log K/L*	*t*	R^2	$\bar{R}^2$	*SE*	*F Value*	*D.W.*
1	2	3	4	5	6	7	8	9
Western	-7.959	1.605* (5.178)	-0.015 (-1.063)	0.824	0.807	0.104	21.018*	2.229
Central	1.647	0.708 (1.641)	-0.009 (-0.433)	0.438	0.381	0.106	3.504	1.559
Eastern	-6.201	1.404* (5.730)	-0.026 (-1.033)	0.885	0.874	0.162	34.746*	0.987
Uttaranchal	-0.606	0.867*** (2.069)	-0.0001 (-0.005)	0.437	0.380	0.224	3.489	1.747
Bundelkhand	5.551	0.306 (1.246)	0.061** (2.628)	0.786	0.764	0.162	16.547*	2.613
U.P.	**-5.948**	**1.410* (6.109)**	**-0.020 (-1.487)**	**0.888**	**0.877**	**0.087**	**35.865***	**1.687**

Source : Based on ASI Reports : Various Issues.

Note : Figures in parentheses are t values of the estimates.

V : value added ; L : labour; K : capital and t : time.

* , **, *** Significant at 1, 5 and 10 percent level of significance.

production function under the assumption of perfect competition to measure the most important element of technological change, i.e., the elasticity of substitution.

Table-6.7 presents the estimates of the regression used originally by Arrow, Chenery, Minhas and Solow (and thus know as SMAC model), where the log of wage rate is regressed against the log of value-added per person[12] for the organised industrial sector of five economic regions and the State of Uttar Pradesh. The coefficient of wage rate (giving estimate of σ) is found to be significant in all the regions and the State, rejecting the hypothesis of σ = 0. However, the estimate of σ is not significantly different from unity in the Western region and the Uttaranchal and for the whole State. The estimate of σ is significantly different from unity, being less than one (at 5 percent level) in the Central region, and greater than one in both the Eastern (at 5 percent level) and the Bundelkhand (at 10 percent level) regions. Low R^2 indicates poor fit of data in case of the Central region and the Uttaranchal. On the basis of D.W. Test, there seems to be significant auto-correlation of the error terms in the Western region as well as the whole State.

Table-6.7 : Region-wise Estimates of the CES Production Function for Organised Industrial Sector: 1974-75 to 1985-86-Model I

No. of Observations : 12 Dependent Variable : Log (V/L)

Region	*Constant*	*Log W*	R^2	$\bar{R}^2$	*SE*	*F Value*	*D.W.*
1	2	3	4	5	6	7	8
Western	-3.053	1.458* (0.314)	0.662	0.662	0.144	19.575*	0.835
Central	5.298	0.433*** (0.239)	0.230	0.230	0.124	2.988	1.986
Eastern	-4.514	1.595* (0.213)	0.836	0.836	0.193	51.061*	1.079
Uttaranchal	3.374	0.671** (0.272)	0.355	0.355	0.239	5.495**	2.203
Bundelkhand	-6.826	1.814* (0.432)	0.615	0.615	0.217	15.997*	1.834
U.P.	**-1.837**	**1.290* (0.250)**	**0.707**	**0.707**	**0.140**	**24.203***	**0.847**

Source : Based on ASI Reports : Various Issues.

Note : Figures in parentheses are standard errors of the estimates.

V : value added; L: labour; and W: wage rate.

*, **, *** Significant at 1, 5 and 10 percent level of significance.

Incorporation of the time trend in the above equation gives us Model II (Table-6.8).[13] The coefficient of wage rate is, thus, found to be significant only in the Western and the Eastern regions, besides the State as a whole. High coefficient of correlation between log (w) and 't' in Central (r=0.88); Uttaranchal (r=0.75) and Bundelkhand (r=0.91) regions shows the presence of multicollinearity between the two independent variables. Estimates of σ are not significantly different from one in the organised industrial sector of the State and the Western region. For the Eastern region, σ is found to be greater than one.

Table-6.8 : Region-wise Estimates of the CES Production Function for Organised Industrial Sector: 1974-75 to 1985-86-Model II

No. of Observations : 12 Dependent Variable : Log (V/L)

Region	*Constant*	*Log W*	*t*	R^2	$\bar{R}^2$	*SE*	*F Value*	*D.W.*
1	2	3	4	5	6	7	8	9
Western	-5.778	1.795**	-0.016	0.679	0.647	0.140	9.519*	1.116
		(0.562)	(0.022)					
Central	8.711	0.027	0.020	0.286	0.215	0.119	1.806	1.794
		(0.519)	(0.022)					
Eastern	-11.216	2.421*	-0.070**	0.892	0.881	0.157	37.165*	1.670
		(0.407)	(0.031)					
Uttaranchal	3.263	0.685	-0.001	0.355	0.290	0.239	2.474	2.227
		(0.436)	(0.023)					
Bundelkhand	9.569	-0.112	0.088**	0.753	0.729	0.174	13.747*	2.119
		(0.896)	(0.037)					
U.P.	**-4.841**	**1.656****	**-0.019**	**0.723**	**0.695**	**0.137**	**11.760***	**1.096**
		(0.550)	**(0.025)**					

Source : Based on ASI Reports : Various Issues.

Note : Figures in parentheses are standard errors of the estimates.

V : value added; L : labour ; W : wage rate ; and t : time.

*, **, *** Significant at 1, 5 and 10 percent level of significance.

Significant estimates of time trend are observed in case of the Eastern and the Bundelkhand regions. However, in the Eastern region, the time trend is negative and significant (at 5 percent level). This observation goes against the conclusion drawn with the help of TFP indices, where the Eastern region is found to be experiencing the significant technologcial progress. As against this, the positive and significant (at 5 percent level) time trend in case of the Bundelkhand region, conforms to our conclusions based on TFP indices and Cobb-Douglas production function. Insignificant time trend in all other cases indicates that neutral technological change has not been an important source of output growth. The data fit in the Central region and the Uttaranchal is not good as indicated by low $\bar{R}^2$. D.W. test indicates absence of auto-correlation in all the cases.

The estimates of generalised SMAC with labour variable[14] allowing for non-constant returns to scale are presented in Table-6.9. The significant coefficient of wage rate is observed in the Western, the Eastern ad the Uttaranchal regions and also for the whole State. The estimates of σ are, however, not significantly different from one in the Uttaranchal and the State, whereas these estimates are found to be greater than unity in the Western and the Eastern regions (at 10 percent level).

Negative and significant coefficient of labour variable in the Western and the Eastern regions imply diseconomies of scale. This conclusion does not conform to our previous findings based on the Cobb-Douglas production function, where constant returns to scale for the manufacturing sectors of these regions were noticed. Fairly imitating our earlier observation, significant economies of scale are found to prevail in the organised industrial sector of the Bundelkhand region as witnessed by the positive significant (at 5 percent level) coefficient of labour. Insignificant coefficient of labour in the Central and the Eastern regions and the whole State indicates absence of any significant economies of scale. Low $\bar{R}^2$ in the Central region and the Uttaranchal again shows that the fit is not good. Error terms, on the whole, are, however, serially independent.

Table-6.9 : Region-wise Estimates of the CES Production Function for Organised Industrial Sector: 1974-75 to 1985-86-Model III

No. of Observations : 12 Dependent Variable : Log (V/L)

Region	*Constant*	*Log W*	*Log L*	*R^2*	*$\bar{R}^2$*	*SE*	*F Value*	*D.W.*
1	2	3	4	5	6	7	8	9
Western	1.791	1.641*	-0.507***	0.753	0.728	0.123	13.738*	1.586
		(0.297)	(0.263)					
Central	7.412	0.507	-0.234	0.251	0.176	0.122	1.509	2.046
		(0.284)	(0.442)					
Eastern	13.269	1.394*	-1.378**	0.896	0.885	0.154	38.776*	1.806
		(0.197)	(0.575)					
Uttaranchal	5.383	0.674**	-0.205	0.376	0.313	0.235	2.708	2.029
		(0.281)	(0.353)					
Bundelkhand	-5.331	0.358	1.235**	0.801	0.782	0.156	18.153*	2.399
		(0.576)	(0.404)					
U.P.	**5.023**	**1.444***	**-0.617**	**0.779**	**0.757**	**0.122**	**15.850***	**1.486**
		(0.244)	**(0.343)**					

Source : Based on ASI Reports : Various Issues.

Note : Figures in parentheses are standard errors of the estimates.

V : value added ; L : labour; and W: wage rate.

*, **, *** Significant at 1, 5 and 10 percent level of significance.

Based on the results of CES production function, it may be concluded that excepting Bundelkhand, manufacturing sector of no other region has shown significant 'neutral technological progress' and 'economies of scale'. For the organised manufacturing sector at the State level, estimates of σ are found to be significant in all the three models, but in none of the cases estimates are found to be significantly different from unity. Similarly, in the Western and the Eastern regions, hypothesis of $\sigma = 0$ does not hold good in respect of all the three models. For the Western region, σ is not found to be significantly different from unity in the first two models, while in case of the third model, the estimate is indeed greater than unity. On the whole, the estimates go in favour of $\sigma = 1$ in this region. On the other hand, in the Eastern region, σ is found to be greater than unity in all the three models. Thus, a proportionate change in factor price ratio may result in a more than proportionate change in factor ratio in this region.

Estimate of σ in the organised manufacturing sector of the Uttaranchal is found to be significant on the basis of the first and the third models. In either of the case, σ is not significantly different from one. In the remaining two regions (the Central and the Bundelkhand), value of σ is found to be statistically significant only in the first model, being significantly less than one in the former and significantly greater than one in the latter. On the basis of these estimates, the use of Cobb-Douglas production function can be justified only at the State level and also for the Western region and the Uttaranchal.

To test the constancy of factor share under unitary elasticity of substitution, the study relied mainly on the labour's share in the value added. The labour share in value added of the organised industrial sector remained more or less constant in the State as well as the Western region (see Appendix Table-6.2), broadly supporting our finding of the unitary elasticity of substitution. However, in case of Uttaranchal fluctuations in the series with perceptible uptrend resulted in significant increase of the labour share over the period. While this might not support our conclusion of $\sigma = 1$, with regard to this region, the quality of data is such that this cannot be taken as a gross violation of the above conclusion.[15]

2. REGION-WISE PERFORMANCE OF ORGANISED INDUSTRIAL SECTOR: 1974-75 TO 1985-86.

Agriculture is still the mainstay of the population in the State as about 71 percent of the total net output originates from this sector[16] as against only 26 percent from the manufacturing as revealed by Table-6.10. The corresponding contribution of manufacturing in the Western region is found to be above the State level average (33 percent). Although, the contribution of the manufacturing sector of the Central and the Eastern regions is less (26 and 22 percent) than that of the Western region, it is indeed much greater than 12 percent in the Uttaranchal and 15 percent in the Bundelkhand.

Table-6.10 : Percentage Share of Key Sectors in Total Regional Income in 1985-86 (at current prices)*

Region	*Agriculture & Allied Sector*	*Manufacturing (Registerd & unregistered)*	*Others (Forestry & Logging, Fishing, Mining & Quarrying)*
1	2	3	4
Western	65.9	32.7	1.4
Central	73.0	26.0	1.0
Eastern	74.9	21.9	3.2
Uttaranchal	74.1	10.8	15.1
Bundelkhand	79.1	15.3	5.6
U.P.	**70.9**	**26.2**	**2.9**

Source : Govt. of Uttar Pradesh, *Economic Profile And Plan in Outline: 1990-91*, pp.21-23.

Note : * Commodity Producing Sectors only.

2.1 Region-wise Growth of Organised Industrial Sector

Strenuous efforts have been made in the past for achieving the objective of balanced regional development in the State through accelerated industrial development. It is, therefore, deemed worthwhile to assess the performance of organised manufacturing sector region-wise, particularly in terms of output and employment growth.

Region-wise trend growth rates in gross value added, total employment and gross fixed capital of organised manufacturing sector for the reference period are provided in Table-6.11. Significant trend growth rates of value added in the organised manufacturing sector is seen for all the regions and also for whole of the State. The highest trend growth rate of 15.28 percent in value added of this sector is seen in the Bundelkhand followed by the trend growth rate of 9.84 percent in the Eastern region.[17] The Uttaranchal and the Western regions have also registered significantly high trend growth rates of 7.72 percent and 7.46 percent respectively. The lowest but significant trend growth rate of 4.31 percent is seen in the Central region. Interestingly, the trend growth rate of value added in the organised manufacturing sector of the three backward regions (Eastern, Uttaranchal and Bundelkhand) is found to be much greater than what we have experienced at the State level. However, the low base of the value added might be one of the reasons of higher trend growth rates of value added in these regions.

Table-6.11 : Region-wise Trend Growth Rates in Gross Value Added, Total Employment and Gross Fixed Capital for Organised Industrial Sector : 1974-75 to 1985-86.

Region	*Gross Value Added*	*Total Employment*	*Gross Fixed Capital*
1	2	3	4
Western	7.462*	3.189*	6.820*
	(6.516)	(3.362)	(26.433)
Central	4.309*	2.150*	6.531*
	(4.841)	(3.760)	(22.576)
Eastern	9.839*	-0.057	8.912*
	(4.122)	(0.069)	(7.630)
Uttaranchal	7.723*	3.858**	8.343*
	(4.019)	(2.689)	(11.076)
Bundelkhand	15.275*	5.973*	14.252*
	(8.035)	(12.301)	(6.278)
U.P.	**7.551***	**2.358****	**7.561***
	(6.592)	**(3.091)**	**(18.574)**

Source : ASI Reports : Various Issues.

Note : Figures in parentheses are t values of the estimates.

*, ** Significant at 1 and 5 percent level of significance.

Significant trend growth rates of total employment are generally observed in all the cases excepting the Eastern region. Here also, the Bundelkhand region has registered the highest growth rate of 5.97 percent. The next in importance is the Uttaranchal (3.86 percent) followed by the Western (3.19 percent) region. A significant, though lower trend growth rate of 2.15 percent is seen in the Central region. The Eastern region has witnessed a negative but insignificant growth rate in employment. These trend growth rates of employment are found to be higher in the Western, the Uttaranchal and the Bundelkhand regions as compared to U.P. as a whole. The lower trend growth rates in the Central and the Eastern regions have depressed the State level trend growth rate to 2.36 percent. The Uttaranchal and the Bundelkhand regions have witnessed above the State level average growth in both output and employment. While a high coefficient of correlation (r=0.92) between output and employment confirms the aforesaid conclusion for Bundelkhand, it shows contradiction in case of the Uttaranchal, where the coefficient of correlation between the two is found to be 0.45 only.

The gross fixed capital has registered significant trend growth rates (at 1 percent level) in all the regions and at the State level, showing greater use of capital in the organised manufacturing sector. The trend growth rate of gross fixed capital is found to be highest (14.25 percent) in Bundelkhand followed by the Eastern (8.91 percent) and the Uttaranchal

(8.34 percent). Comparatively the lower trend growth rates of 6.82 percent and 6.53 percent are observed in the Western and the Central regions respectively. The trend growth rates of gross fixed capital in the backward regions are much higher as compared to the State level average (7.56 percent). It is interesting to note that the trend growth rates of gross fixed capital in all the regions and the State are found to be greater than those of the labour. Thus, the organised industrial sector is characterised by the growth of capital intensive industries during the period.

Moreover, regarding the inter-regional differentials in the performance of organised industrial sector, it is discernible from Table 6.12 that industrial activities in terms of number of units, employment and value added during the period 1974-86 have largely concentrated in the Western and the Central regions and also to some extent in the Eastern region.

Table-6.12 : Percentage Shares of Units, Employment and Value Added in the Totals of Organised Industrial Sector in U.P.

Region	*Units*		*Employment*		*Gross Value Added*	
	1974-75	*1985-86*	*1974-75*	*1985-86*	*1974-75*	*1985-86*
1	2	3	4	5	6	7
Western	58.92	63.80	48.41	51.80	54.96	50.77
Central	21.96	19.15	24.26	23.40	23.36	14.18
Eastern	15.02	12.16	22.47	18.15	18.25	29.89
Uttaranchal	3.05	4.05	3.36	4.42	2.53	2.94
Bundelkhand	1.05	0.85	1.51	2.23	0.90	2.22
U.P.	**100.0**	**100.0**	**100.0**	**100.0**	**100.0**	**100.0**
Range	**57.87**	**62.95**	**46.90**	**49.57**	**54.06**	**48.55**

Source : ASI Reports : 1974-75 and 1985-86.

The Western region occupies the top position while Budelkhand stands at the bottom at both the selected pointes of time. This indicates the persistence of regional disparities. However, some changes overtime are also perceptible. While the share of the Western region in industrial units and employment has increased, the share in value added has reduced from about 55 percent in 1974-75 to 51 percent in 1985-86. There has been a fall in the share of the Central region in respect of all the three variables over the period. A significant increase in the share of the Eastern region in value added from 18 percent to about 30 percent is observed during this period, but the region has experienced a downfall in the shares in respect of the other two variables. Moreover, during this period both the Uttaranchal and the Bundelkhand regions have shown an increase in the share in respect of all three variables, excepting the share in number of units, which instead of increasing has gone down in the latter. In spite of these changes, there still persists a wide gap between the developed and the backward regions, so far as the development of organised industrial sector is concerned. In its support, it is noticed through the Table-6.12 that the value of the range in respect of units and employment has widened over the period, although the range in respect of gross value added has reduced from 54.06 to 48.55.

It is also endeavoured to analyse the inter-regional changes in the industrial structure of the State during the reference period (See Table-6.13). As shown in the Table the ratio between the number of consumer goods and capital goods industries at the State level increased from 1.03 in 1974-75 to 1.18 during the year 1984-85, showing an increase of 15.8 percent. An increase in this ratio is also noticed in case of the Western, the Central and the Bundelkhand regions during this period. Inspite of predominance of capital goods units in the Bundelkhand, a remarkable increase is noticed in the ratio of consumer to capital goods units from 0.25 in 1974-75 to 0.82 in 1984-85. A reverse trend can be observed in the Eastern region and the Uttaranchal where this ratio has shown a significant decline.

Table-6.13 : Region-wise Ratios between Consumer Goods and Capital Goods Industries

Region	*No. of Units*		*Percentage increase/ decrease*	*ValueAdded*		*Percentage increase/ decrease*
	1974-75	*1984-85*		*1974-75*	*1984-85*	
1	2	3	4	5	6	7
Western	0.898	1.190	32.51	1.117	1.059	-5.19
Central	1.102	1.139	3.36	1.724	0.841	-51.22
Eastern	1.792	1.270	-29.13	1.954	0.679	-65.25
Uttaranchal	1.560	1.286	-17.56	0.642	1.165	81.46
Bundelkhand	0.250	0.818	227.20	0.054	0.113	109.26
U.P.	**1.025**	**1.187**	**15.80**	**1.361**	**0.938**	**-31.08**

Source : ASI Reports : 1974-75 and 1984-85.

Contrary to the above, the consumer goods industries have lagged far behind the capital goods industries, so far as the contribution to value added at the State level is concerned. In its support, it is seen that the ratio of value added between consumer and capital goods industries has significantly reduced from 1.36 in 1974-75 to 0.94 during 1984-85, registering a decrease of 31.08 percent.[18] This ratio has also reduced in the Western, the Central and the Eastern region during the reference period. However, an opposing trend of increase in this ratio is noticed in respect of both the Uttaranchal and the Bundelkhnad regions. As already noticed, both the regions have also experienced above State level average growth rates of output and employment. It seems that increased number of consumer goods industries has played major role in augmenting the levels of output as well as employment in organised industrial sector of these regions.

2.2 Location Pattern : Specialisation and Industrial Base of Districts

Based on the previous discussions, one can safely conclude that developed regions are still best claimant for a major share in total industrial activity of the State. Apart from the inter-regional disparities, the intra-regional disparities have also shown a tendency of divergence, as is seen in Table-6.14.

About 78 percent of the total industrial units are found to be concentrated in the seven (namely Ghaziabad, Agra, Meerut, Muzzafarnagar, Moradabad, Saharanpur and Bijnor) out of total nineteen districts of the Western region in 1985-86. Moreover, the districts of Kanpur and Lucknow account for 79 percent of the total industrial units available in all the nine districts of the Central region. Similarly, only the three districts of Varanasi, Allahabad and Gorakhpur (out of the total fifteen districts) account for 64 percent of the total industrial units of the Eastern region. The position of the Uttaranchal and the Bundelkhand regions is found to be of disquieting nature. Only Dehradun and Nainital of the Uttaranchal (out of the total eight districts) and Jhansi of the Bundelkhand region (out of the total five districts) are having respectively 88 percent and 75 percent of the total industrial units available in these regions. The foregoing analysis indicates that clusters of industries have developed in the State during the period of the study.

Table-6.14 : Intra-Regional Representation/Concentration of Industrial Units in 1985-86

Region/District	*No. of Factories*	*Percentage to Total*
1	2	3
Western (19 Districts)	3,925	100.00
1. Ghaziabad	904	23.03
2. Agra	551	14.04
3. Meerut	406	10.34
4. Muzaffarnagar	332	8.46
5. Moradabad	311	7.92
6. Saharanpur	295	7.52
7. Bijnor	243	6.19
	3,042	77.50
Central (9 Districts)	1,178	100.00
1. Kanpur	654	55.52
2. Lucknow	279	23.68
	933	79.20
Eastern (15 Districts)	748	100.00
1. Varanasi	211	28.21
2. Allahabad	170	22.73
3. Gorakhpur	97	12.97
	478	63.90
Uttaranchal (8 Districts)	249	100.00
1. Dehradun	118	47.39
2. Nainital	101	40.56
	219	87.95
Bundelkhand (5 Districts)	52	100.00
1. Jhansi	39	75.00

Source : ASI Report : 1985-86.

Note : Figures in brackets give total number of districts in the respective regions.

Theoretically speaking the clustering of industries takes place only because industries have a tendency to get located in areas having certain locational advantages, such as, the easy availability of raw materials, skilled labour, closeness to markets and other physical advantages. Despite a fairly well diversified industrial structure comprising footloose industries in a large number, the State has not been successful in achieving adequate spatial diversification of industries. Also resource based industries have not been developed in accordance with the availability of potential in resource rich districts. As a result, the State of Uttar Pradesh has as many as forty-two industrially backward districts (see Appendix

Table-6.5). Inspite of strenuous efforts to achieve the balanced regional development, it appears that the protective as well as promotional measure have not been significantly effective in accelerating the industrial development of backward areas. However, some improvements are noticeable during the period of 1974—86 as is observed in Table.6.15

Although the share of non-backward districts in total industrial units, employment and output of the state is found to be above 70 percent during 1985-86, there seems to have been a gradual improvement in the industrial situation of the backward districts also. The shares of backward districts in the total units, employment and value added of the State organised industrial sector have gone up during the period under reference, as would be evident from the Table-6.15

Table-6.15 : Percentage Distribution of Industrial Activity Between Backward/Non-backward Districts

Districts	*No. of Units*		*Employment*		*Gross value Added*	
	1974-75	*1985-86*	*1974-75*	*1985-86*	*1974-75*	*1985-86*
1	2	3	4	5	6	7
Backward	22.99	25.54	24.14	28.14	14.34	23.36
Non-Backward	77.01	74.46	75.86	71.86	85.66	76.64
Total	**100.00**	**100.00**	**100.00**	**100.00**	**100.00**	**100.00**

Source : ASI Reports : 1974-75 and 1985-86.

For the speedier development of particular district, diversified industrial structure is considered desirable due to the fact that industries have direct as well as indirect linkages with each other, and therefore, existence of greater number of directly or indirectly inter-connected industries may provide a better potential for overall industrial development of a district, than a narrow base comprising fewer industries.[19]

Industrial diversification/specialisation of a district can be measured through the coefficient of specialisation. This coefficient indicates the degree to which the industry mix of particular district is different from the State of which it forms a part. The coefficient of specialisation for a district (Sj) can be expressed as

$$Sj = \sum_{i=1}^{n} \left| \frac{eij}{Ej} - \frac{Ei}{E} \right|$$

(the two vertical lines indicates absolute values, that is, ignoring positive or negative sings) where eij is employment in ith industry in jth district Ej is employment in all industries in jth district, Ei is employment in ith industry in the State and E is employment in all industries in the State. When the value of Sj is found to be zero, it means the industrial structure of the district is as diversified as that of the State. The greater the value of the coefficient, greater the extent to which the district structure varies from the State average. In case, the value approximates one, industrial activity (usually measured in terms of employment) of a district is concentrated in a few or only one industry. A comparison of Sj at two points of time, therefore, would indicate whether the industrial structure of a district has become more concentrated or diversified over the period of time.

Table-6.16 : Extent of Industrial Diversification/Specialisation of Districts in 1974-75 and 1985-86

Districts	*1974-75*	*1985-86*	*Districts*	*1974-75*	*1985-86*
1	*2*	*3*	*4*	*5*	*6*
1. Agra	0.36718	0.26972	1. Allahabad	0.40033	0.33091
2. Aligarh	0.03253	0.09520	2. Azamgarh	0.54392	0.53118
3. Bareilly	0.62792	0.26474	3. Bahraich	0.62076	0.66422
4. Bijnor	0.36699	0.35882	4. Ballia	0.64656	0.69145
5. Badaun	0.40694	0.47393	5. Basti	0.40694	0.45646
6. Bulandshahr	0.50847	0.17136	6. Deoria	0.40694	0.47393
7. Etah	0.60683	0.67111	7. Faizabad	0.54392	0.56059
8. Etawah	0.62076	0.64545	8. Ghazipur	0.64656	0.67282
9. Farrukhabad	0.38030	0.43784	9. Gonda	0.38115	0.44677
10. Mainpuri	0.56931	0.56475	10. Gorakhpur	0.24063	0.19736
11. Mathura	0.22572	0.26300	11. Jaunpur	0.62242	0.61619
12. Meerut	0.01613	0.09299	12. Mirzapur	0.50748	0.57865
13. Ghaziabad	–	0.00540	13. Pratapgarh	0.64656	0.69145
14. Moradabad	0.24679	0.28217	14. Sultanpur	0.64656	0.69145
15. Muzzafarnagar	0.28862	0.33543	15. Varanasi	0.44658	0.31584
16. Pilibhit	0.63075	0.44670	1. Almora	0.64656	0.65536
17. Rampur	0.40694	0.35867	2. Pithoragarh	–	0.69145
18. Saharanpur	0.21201	0.14720	3. Dehradun	0.56049	0.53036
19. Shahjahanpur	0.35700	0.42304	4. P. Garhwal	0.64656	0.66420
1. Barabanki	0.64656	0.62632	5. Chamoli	–	–
2. Fatehpur	0.63075	0.66422	6. Nainital	0.37215	0.27848
3. Hardoi	0.64656	0.69145	7. T. Garhwal	–	0.69145
4. Kanpur	0.15457	0.27609	8. Uttarkashi	–	–
5. Kheri	0.40694	0.44670	1. Banda	0.63075	0.66422
6. Lucknow	0.36400	0.43787	2. Hamirpur	–	0.69145
7. Rae Bareli	0.64656	0.51025	3. Jalaun	0.64656	–
8. Sitapur	0.39705	0.40922	4. Jhansi	0.55146	0.63090
9. Unnao	0.54800	0.47279	5. Lalitpur	–	0.69145

Source : ASI Reports: 1974-75 and 1985-86.

Note : The districts are placed region-wise. The nineteen districts of the Western region are followed by the nine districts of the Central region, the fifteen districts of the Eastern region, the eight districts of the Hill region and the five districts of the Bundelkhand region.

The computed coefficients of specialisation for 1974-75 and 1985-86 are presented in Table-6.16. The Table reveals that the State is still largely characterised by districts with highly concentrated rather than diversified structure, particularly in the backward regions. Thirteen districts, namely, Agra, Aligarh, Bijnor, Badaun, Farrukhabad, Mathura, Meerut,

Ghaziabad, Moradabad, Muzaffarnagar, Rampur, Saharanpur, Shahjahanpur of the Western region; four districts namely Kanpur, Lakhimpur Kheri, Lucknow and Sitapur in the Central region; six districts–Allahabad, Basti, Deoria, Gonda, Gorakhpur and Varanasi of the Eastern region and only Nainital district of the Uttaranchal have the value of coefficient less than 0.5 at both the points of time, indicating that these districts have comparatively more diversified structure of industrial employment. However, all the districts of the Bundelkhand region seem to have developed concentrated industrial structure as in none of the cases, the value of coefficient is found to be less than 0.50. Furthermore, as noticed there has been some improvement in diversification of industries during 1985-86 over the base 1974-75 as witnessed by the reduction in values of coefficients. Eight districts of the Western region, three districts of the Central region, five districts of the Eastern region and two districts of the Uttaranchal had lower values of Sj at the latter point of time. More diversification seems to have taken place in more developed regions (especially the Western region) as compared to less developed regions. As a matter of fact, the districts of Bundelkhand have shown increase in the concentration of industrial activity over the period. Considerable diversification seems to have taken place in Bareilly, Bulandshahar, etc., whereas the relatively more advanced districts, namely Kanpur and Lucknow have developed concentrated structure of factory employment over the period.

It is also argued that it is not always beneficial to develop a highly diversified industrial structure at the micro level.[20] Depending upon the resource base there might be certain industries in a particular district that have some locational advantage. These may form the industrial base of that district. For accelerating the development of a district, it might be more desirable to concentrate on these industries first, then to aim at achieving the diversified industrial structure.

Industries forming the industrial base of a particular district can be identified through location quotients. Location quotient measures the extent to which a particular economic activity (in most cases measured in terms of employment) in an industry is over or under represented in a district in comparison to the State. Location quotient for an industry in a district is calculated as:

$$Iij = \frac{eij}{Ej} \bigg/ \frac{Ei}{E}$$

with various terms having the same meaning as in case of coefficient of specialisation. Industries with Iij > 1 are supposed to constitute the industrial base of that district. In other words one can say that the industries with Iij > 1 have a higher proportion in the district's industrial employment than at the State level.

District-wise location quotients for different industry groups have been estimated and the results are provided in Appendix Table-6.6. Industry groups having Iij > 1 (i.e., constituting the industrial base of a district) are listed separately for various districts. Larger number of industries constitute the industrial base in the districts that are more developed and have fairly diversified structure. However, in such districts also, all industry groups do not have locational advantage as Iij is not greater than 1 for all the industry groups. For the accelerated development of a district and the State, it might be advantageous to concentrate on industries forming the industrial base in the initial stages. In the resource poor districts, where locational advantage may not act as a catalyst, emphasis should be placed on the development of footloose industries to prevent these districts from lagging behind.

The conclusions emerging from the analysis of this section point towards the fact that inter-regional disparities of widening nature exist in the State. Major part of the industrial activity seems to be concentrated in relatively developed regions. It is heartening to note that during the period of the study, backward regions particularly the Uttaranchal and the Bundelkhand have shown remarkable growth in output and employment. As a result of these trends, significant improvements in industrial scenario of backward regions are quite perceptible, but the pace and process of industrialisation still lags behind the more developed regions.

3. REGION-WISE INTER-RELATIONSHIP BETWEEN TECHNOLOGICAL CHANGE AND PERFORMANCE OF ORGANISED INDUSTRIAL SECTOR

Technological change is made possible by more efficient utilisation of resources. More output is obtainable, therefore, with lesser amount of inputs. As a matter of fact, technological change has to play an effective role in achieving the National level goals and hence it should have a positive impact on both the output growth and employment growth. Generally, the studies have come out with the conclusion that technological change goes in favour of output growth and has an adverse bearing in employment growth. Here we plan to examine and analyse this hypothesis in greater detail, taking regional dimension into consideration.

In this context, the trend growth rates of Solow index (taken as an indicator of technical progress in this section), capital, labour, partial productivity and cost ratios are provided in Table-6.17. Flexibility of production structure has positive impact on output and employment growth. Estimates of elasticity of substitution throwing light on this aspect are also given in this table. A significant trend growth rate of 7.55 percent in value added of organised industrial sector at the State level is accompanied by slower but significant trend growth rate of 2.36 percent in employment. A weak relation between the two is also indicated by the low coefficient of correlation (r=0.35). TFP has recorded a trend growth rate of 3.1 percent (significant at 5 percent level).

The impact of technological progress on output growth is positive but there has been a considerable amount of labour-saving. A significantly higher trend growth of capital indicates greater application of capital overtime. The behaviour of partial productivity ratios also confirm this conclusion. Although the growth of labour productivity is significant, capital productivity has witnessed an insignificant trend growth rate. A significantly high coefficient of correlation (r=0.95) between labour productivity and value added indicated presence of technical progress in the organised manufacturing sector of the State.[21] The growth rate of value added over and above the growth of labour productivity has prevented employment from falling,[22] although the employment growth lags behind the output growth. The behaviour of cost ratios (a highly significant trend growth rate of 4.25 percent in wage rate) also seems to have favoured capital deepening.

The highest trend growth rate of both value added and employment is witnessed in the organised industrial sector of the Bundelkhand region. However, the trend growth rate of 5.97 percent in employment is far less than the trend growth rate of 15.28 percent in value added. The coefficient of correlation between the two is as high as 0.92. A significantly high trend growth rate in Solow index at 6.92 percent and labour productivity at 8.78 percent

Table-6.17 : Region-wise Inter-Relationship Between Technological Change and Performance of Organised Industrial Sector

Region	Trend Growth Rates in									Estimates of Elasticity of Substitution Based on CES Production Function		
	Solow Index	Gross Value	Total Employment	Gross Fixed	Labour Productivity	Capital Productivity	Capital Intensity	Wage Rate	Rate of Return on Capital	Model I	Model II	Model III
1	2	3	4	5	6	7	8	9	10	11	12	13
Western	2.36 (1.728)	7.46* (6.516)	3.19* (3.362)	6.82* (26.433)	4.14** (2.326)	0.60 (0.560)	3.52* (3.728)	3.19* (4.56)	1.16 (0.541)	1.46* (0.314)	1.80** (0.562)	1.64*+++ (0.297)
Central	1.18 (1.161)	4.31* (4.841)	2.15* (3.760)	6.53* (22.576)	2.11 (2.003)	-2.09 (2.225)	4.29* (6.175)	3.90* (5.99)	-5.78 (1.517)	0.43***++ (0.239)	0.03 (0.519)	0.51 (0.284)
Eastern	8.06** (3.06)	9.84* (4.122)	-0.057 (0.069)	8.91* (7.630)	9.90* (3.219)	0.85 (0.530)	8.98* (4.697)	7.03* (6.35)	2.38 (0.477)	1.60*++ (0.213)	2.42*+ (0.407)	1.39*+++ (0.197)
Uttaranchal	4.57** (2.596)	7.72* (4.019)	3.858** (2.689)	8.34* (11.076)	3.72 (1.559)	-0.57 (0.291)	4.32** (2.859)	5.69* (3.64)	-2.18 (0.473)	0.67** (0.272)	0.69 (0.436)	0.67** (0.281)
Bundelkhand	6.92* (4.483)	15.28* (8.035)	5.973* (12.301)	14.25* (6.278)	8.78* (5.521)	0.90 (0.469)	7.82* (4.115)	3.90* (7.09)	24.87* (3.354)	1.81*+++ (0.432)	-0.11 (0.896)	0.36 (0.576)
U.P.	**3.100**** **(2.343)**	**7.55*** **(6.592)**	**2.358**** **(3.091)**	**7.561*** **(18.574)**	**5.07**** **(2.992)**	**-0.009** **(0.010)**	**5.08*** **(4.761)**	**4.25*** **(6.04)**	**0.57** **(0.240)**	**1.29*** **(0.250)**	**1.66**** **(0.550)**	**1.44*** **(0.244)**

Source : Cols 6,7,8 (Table 6.1); Col 2 (Table 6.2); Cols, 3,4,5 (Table 6.11); cols 9,10 (Appendix Table 6.2); and cols 11,12,13 (Tables 6.7, 6.8, 6.9).

Notes : Figures in parentheses are t values for cols 2 to 10 and standard errors for cols 11 to 13.

*, **, *** Significant at 1,5 and 10 percent level of significance.

+, ++, +++ Significantly different from unity at 1,5 and 10 percent levels.

(next only to the Eastern region) indicates significant technical progress to have taken place in this region. This accompanied by significant increases in output and employment growth show a favourable impact of technological progress on the industrial development of this region. Significant coefficient of correlation of 0.96 between Solow index and gross value added and 0.81 between Solow index and employment also support these results. A very high correlation (r=0.98) between value added and labour productivity indicates presence of significant technical progress and economies of scale in the region. The significantly high trend growth rate of labour productivity is expected to have brought about a negative impact on employment growth but correlation between the two in this region is found to be as high as 0.84, exhibiting greater promises for employment. A significantly high growth rate of value-added over and above labour productivity has prevented a fall in employment negating the adverse impact of technological change on employment growth.[23]

Insignificant growth rate of capital productivity accompanied by significant growth rates of gross fixed capital (14.25 percent) and capital intensity (7.82 percent) indicates importance of capital in output growth. One has to bear in mind that Bundelkhand is one of the backward regions of the State. The significant efforts for industrialisation of this region have resulted in larger capital investment over the period. The growth of wage rate is much below the growth of labour productivity effecting lower cost per unit of labour. The significant trend growth rate regarding the rate of return (24.9 percent) indicates that the region has higher potential for reinvestment.

A high trend growth rate of value added (9.84 percent) is accompanied by the highest trend rate of increase in Solow index (8.06 percent) and labour productivity (9.90 percent) in the organised industrial sector of the Eastern region. TFP seems to have played a significant role in output growth of this region, as witnessed by the high coefficient of correlation (r=0.99) between the two. This correlation between value-added and labour productivity is as high as 0.99 implying prevalence of technical progress in the organised industrial sector of this region. However, increased labour productivity has made it possible to achieve greater output with less amount of labour. This is also revealed by a negative coefficient of correlation (r = -0.56) between labour productivity and employment. The highly significant trend growth of gross fixed capital (8.91 percent) and capital intensity (8.98 percent) accompanied by insignificant trend growth of capital productivity points towards the labour saving (capital using) bias of technological progress in this region.

A highly significant trend growth rate of 7.72 percent in value added is accompanied by a significant (though of smaller magnitude) growth of employment (3.86 percent) in the organised manufacturing sector of the Uttaranchal. The relationship between the two, as shown by the low coefficient of correlation (0.45) is positive but not very strong. TFP growth of 4.57 percent (significant at 5 percent) indicates that technological change has taken place at least to some extent. The significant coefficient of correlation (0.90) between the Solow index and value added shows signs of the positive relationship between the two. Inspite of the significant growth of Solow index in this region, we observe insignificant trend growth rates in both the partial productivity ratios. Thus, increased use of inputs seems to have been an important factor of growth of industries in this region. Increased labour cost per unit of output is indicated by the significant trend growth rate in wage rate accompanied by insignificant growth of labour productivity. The insignificant trend growth rate pertaining to rate of return on capital shows low potential for reinvestment in the organised industrial sector of the Uttaranchal.

The organised industrial sector of both the Western and the Central regions have witnessed significant trend growth rates of output as well as employment. However, in case of the Central region, the growth in respect of these variables is below the State level average, whereas the trend growth rate of employment is above and that of output below the State level average in the Western region. But insignificant TFP (Solow index) indicates that increased inputs are the major source of contribution to growth.

As for as the estimates of elasticity of substitution are concerned, there are greater possibilities of substitution in the State manufacturing as witnessed by the value of σ, which is quite close to unity through application of all the three models derived from CES production function. There is a possibility of substituting easily the factor, whose cost increases as a result of the price increase, without sacrificing output.

In the Western region too, σ = 1 is upheld on the basis of the first two models while the third model shows σ to be greater than one. Similarly, for the Uttaranchal too, σ is found to be close to unity on the basis of the two out of the three models. In all these cases, a proportionate change in input prices will cause an equi-proportionate change in input ratio. A highly flexible production structure is reflected in the Eastern region, where the organised industrial sector was found to have the value of greater than one on the basis of all the three models.

As far as the Bundelkhand region is concerned, while significant growth of both output and employment is observed, value of σ is significant and greater than unity only in the first model and that too at the probability level of 10 percent. But less than unity estimates of σ are found for the Central region again on the basis of the first model only. The remaining two models provide insignificant estimates of σ for both these regions. While these results indicate an inflexible production structure, any conclusions arrived at in respect of these need to be interpreted with caution, particularly for the Bundelkhand region.

As far as the Western, the Eastern and the Uttaranchal regions are concerned, any conflict between output and employment growth can easily be resolved by correcting distortions in factor prices. As indicated in the previous chapter, the modern sector firms in underdeveloped countries experience problems regarding factor prices, not reflecting their real social opportunity cost. The existing policies contribute to making the labour dearer and the capital cheaper and hence modern sector firms find it more cost effective to apply greater quantity of capital to the production process. Any remedial change in the policy will go a long was in resolving the problem of unemployment and will facilitate more labour adsorption without sacrificing output.

Main conclusions emerging from the foregoing are as follows: There has been a significant growth of labour productivity accompanied by significant capital deepening, but insignificant growth of capital productivity in the organised industrial sector of the Western, the Eastern, and the Bundelkhand regions. There has been a significant economy in the use of labour as against the diseconomies in the use of capital in these regions. As far as the industrial sector of the Central and the Uttaranchal regions is concerned, insignificant partial productivities indicate that there has been inefficient use of resources, both capital and labour.

The manufacturing sector of the Eastern and the Bundelkhand regions has experienced significant technological change as shown by the significant trend growth rate of TFP indices. In case of the Uttaranchal, significant growth of only Solow index (accompanied by insignificant labour and capital productivities), and in case of the Western and the Central regions, insignificant growth of all the three TFP indices indicate that increased inputs rather than technological progress has been the major source of output growth of the organised industrial sector in these regions.

The manufacturing sector of only Bundelkhand has shown significant technical change, besides effecting economies of scale. The manufacturing sector of the remaining regions has operated under the constant returns to scale and no significant shift in the production function is noticeable over the period. Output seems to be more responsive to changes in capital in almost all the regions, excepting Bundelkhand where output is found to be more responsive to increase in the labour force.

Significant technical progress and economies of scale have also been experienced in the organised industrial sector of the Bundelkhand region as revealed by the CES production function. The hypothesis $\sigma = 0$ does not hold good for the manufacturing sector of the State and those of the Western, the Eastern and the Uttaranchal regions. To add further, the value of σ is found to be greater than unity only in the Eastern region, whereas its value does not show significant difference from unity in case of remaining regions and the State. In the organised manufacturing sector of the Central and the Bundelkhand regions, significant estimates of σ are found using the model-I only. While it is very difficult to draw any precise conclusions in regard to these two regions, there seems to be a good scope for factor substitution in cases of remaining three regions and the State.

Inter-regional disparities of alarming nature are still witnessed in the State of Uttar Pradesh. Industrial activity is mainly concentrated in the more developed regions (i.e., the Western and the Central). Besides a more diversified industrial structure necessary for the speedier process of development is noticed mainly in the districts of the developed regions and the less developed regions generally lack this opportunity. However, as a result of structural change, it is seen that industrial activity among the less developed regions has been gradually spreading. In this context, it is already seen that both the output growth and employment growth have been above the State average in the Uttaranchal and the Bundelkhand regions. In the Eastern region, however, a significant output growth was accompanied by insignificant employment growth. The more developed regions have recorded output growth below the State level average while only the Western region has witnessed above the State level average growth of employment. On the whole, the less developed regions have demonstrated a better performance of the organised industrial sector during the period of the study. However, one has to take into account the low industrial base of these regions while analysing and interpreting these results.

Technological progress seems to have brought about significant improvements in the performance of organised industrial sector especially in terms of output growth. This is supported by the fact that at the State level while technical progress has resulted in greater output growth, there has been considerable labour saving. In the Bundelkhand region significant technical progress is accompanied by significant improvement in performance of organised industrial sector, both in terms of output and employment growth, A highly significant correlation between labour productivity and value added indicates presence of significant technical progress and economies of scale in this region. In the Eastern region, while technological progress has effected a higher output growth in the organised industrial sector, there has been an adverse impact on employment growth simultaneously.

A significant increase of the TFP has resulted in greater output growth in the organised industrial sector of the Uttaranchal but employment growth has been lagging behind it. Positive and significant growth in Solow index is accompanied by insignificant partial productivities in this region. Inputs seem to have played a more important role as compared to technical progress in the development of the industrial sector of the Uttaranchal. In case of the Western and the Central regions, insignificant growth of TFP has resulted in slower development of the organised industrial sector. On the whole, the technological progress has been of the labour saving nature, enhancing the output growth more in comparison to employment growth in the organised industrial sector of various regions in the State.

References

1. J.C. Budhraja, V.S. Singh, R.Dutta (1984), p.40.
2. The figures for the organised manufacturing at State level in this chapter differ from those in the previous chapter. The figures in this chapter are arrived at by simply aggregating data of total manufacturing sector of all the five economic regions. For greater details see note 4 of Chapter III.
3. Highly significant correlation of 0.83, 0.92 and 0.77 between the wage rate and labour productivity in the Western, the Eastern and the Bundelkhand regions indicates that some increases in labour productivity can also be ascribed to increases in wage rate.
4. Coefficient of correlation between labour productivity and wage rate in the organised manufacturing sector of the state is 0.87.
5. A. Banerji (1975), p.72
6. See equations 3, (9a), (33a) in chapter III.
7. See section 1.3 of chapter V and references cited therein.
8. See equation 41 in chapter III.
9. See equation (43a) in chapter III.
10. See equation 45 in chapter III.
11. See equation 44 in chapter III.
12. See equation 49 in chapter III.
13. See equation 50 in chapter III.
14. See equation 51 in chapter III.
15. A.Banerji (1975), p.118.
16. As a matter of fact the income originating from key sectors of the economy, i.e. primary, secondary and tertiary, are available at the State level, whereas estimates of income originating from tertiary sector are lacking at the regional and district levels. With the result, whatsoever estimates of income flow from regional/district levels are confining to agriculture and allied and manufacturing sectors only. This is the reason that the actual contribution of primary sector to total income at the State level in considerably low (47 percent in 1985-86 at constant 1980-81 prices) as compared to that of regional/district level. Since the present chapter deals with region level analysis, we have to rely on district level income estimates.

17. Similar results are observed in a report published by Government of Uttar Pradesh. The highest annual growth of 12.6 percent is found in registered manufacturing sector of Bundelkhand followed by the Eastern region (10.6 percent) during 1974-79. See Government of U.P., *State of the Economy,* 1987, Annexure-X, p.52.

18. Similar trend can be observed at all India level and for other States as well. See R.T. Tewari (1988), pp.86-87.

19. T.S. Papola (1979), p.185.

20. *Ibid.*, p.195.

21. A specific relationship between the movements of labour productivity and output is known as 'Verdoons coefficient' from which important implications regarding returns to scale and technological progress can be derived. See S.S. Mehta (1980), p.94.

22. In the neo-classical model technical change results in aggregate unemployment only because the growth of output falls short of the rate of increase in labour productivity. For further details see A. Hussain, in D.L. Bosworth (ed.) (1983), p.15.

23. Neo-classical view is that technological unemployment can not occur because of the mechanism of compensation. A fall in the costs due to labour saving or capital saving technological change would lead to fall in prices due to competitive forces. If demand is elastic then expansion of demand will result in re-employment of displaced workers to produce extra output. If the demand for output of the innovative industry is inelastic, then price fall has an income effect which causes demand for other factors to rise. Displaced workers find new jobs producing the expansion of output necessary to meet this demand. For more details and critique of this approach see Douglas Jones, in D.L. Bosworth (ed.), *Ibid.*, p.27.

CHAPTER 7

Main Conclusions

While the importance of investment in the process of economic development cannot be undermined, the technological change is deemed to be the most crucial. It involves use of inputs/resources in a manner that leads to increased efficiency. Realising the overwhelming importance of the subject, economic development *via* indutrialisation has, therefore, been emphasised in India since inception of the Second Five Year Plan , resulting in heavy investment over a wide spectrum of industries accompanied by all round efforts including technological advancement. This has widened the scope of this study for analysing the role of technological change in development of the industrial sector of the U.P.'s economy over the period. This is also hypothesised that inter-regional disparities in levels of industrial development have, *inter alia,* been due to inter-regional disparities in levels of technological progress. Thus, the study has become more relevant in the context of Uttar Pradesh, besides noticing absence of researches on this very theme prior to conduct of this study. The present study of 'Technological Change and Industrial Development : Indian Experiences' has therefore, been an attempt to bridge this gap.

The study has basically aimed at analysing the inter-relationship between differentials in technological progress and those of differentials in output and employment growth of the organised industrial sector in Uttar Pradesh both at the State and the regional levels during the reference period of 1974—1986. Besides, the analysis has been carried out for twenty industry groups and the four categories delineated out of them on the basis of their capital-labour ratios of the final year, i.e., 1985-86.

To measure technological change during the reference period, partial productivity indices of labour and capital have been estimated to analyse efficiency in the use of factor inputs overtime. Moreover, to throw light on overall efficiency in factor use, Kendrick, Solow and Translog indices of total factor productivity have also been estimated. Besides, the Cobb-Douglas and CES production functions have also been estimated, using the rich cross-section and time series data base of the study. Not only this, the efforts have also been made to assess and analyse performance of the organised industrial sector at the State as well as the regional levels in terms of the trend growth rates of both output and employment.

Finally, it would also be relevant to add that analysis in the book, which focuses mainly on the growth performance of the organised industrial sector, is absolutely based on the National Accounts/ASI data rather than the industrial production data/indices obviously because the latter are found to be suffering from problems of limited coverage and lack of representativeness of the listed items. Moreover, owing to paucity/insufficiency of data, our analysis at the regional level is restricted to whole of the organised industrial sector alone, and industry group wise analysis is not attempted. Besides, the study also suffers from one major limitation of not utilising the latest ASI data of the year 1990-91 owing to its non availability till completion of this work. Inspite, the emerging conclusions are expected to remain as revealing and rewarding as would have been after using such data. These conclusions are recapitulated here broadly in two sections. The first section describes the major conclusions arrived at through the State level analysis, whereas the second section is devoted to highlighting those policy capsules emerging out of the regional level analysis.

1. STATE -LEVEL ANALYSIS

1.1 Partial Productivity and Total Factor Productivity

In respect of the total organised industrial sector ofU.P., the significant trend growth rates of labour productivity and capital intensity are found to have been accompanied by insignificant trend growth rate of capital productivity during whole of the reference period. Of the three indices of TFP (Kendrick, Solow and translog), only Solow index is found to have registered a significant trend growth rate and its value is found to be quite low. However, the sub-period wise analysis reveals that there have been significant improvements in the trend growth rates of partial productivities and all the three TFP indices during the sub-period-II (1980—86) over the base of sub-period-I (1974—80).

Besides, there have been marked and meaningful inter-category/inter-industry group-wise differences in levels of both the partial productivities and TFP during the reference period. The highly capital intensive category-I has experienced significant capital deepening accompanied by insignificant trend growth rates of partial and TFP indices. Conversely, the medium capital intensive category-II has witnessed significant trend growth rates of partial productivities accompanied by significant but lower trend growth rate of capital intensity. Moreover, the significant trend growth rates in respect of all the three indices of TFP have demonstrated a better performance in terms of greater efficiency of the industry groups falling under this category.

The remaining two categories-III and-IV (i.e., medium-low capital-intensive and low capital-intensive) have witnessed significant trend growth rates of labour productivity and capital intensity, whereas the trend growth rate of capital productivity is found to be insignificant. Further, the trend growth rates of all the three TFP indices are found to be significant, demonstrating significant technological advancement in these categories. However, this has finally resulted in an efficient use of labour input only.

As demonstrated by the trend growth rates of TFP, almost all the industry groups excepting chemicals and chemical products; paper and paper products, printing, publishing and allied industries; and textile products; have experienced positive technological progress in the State during the reference period. But, trend growth rates of TFP are found to be significant in eight industry groups only. There are two industry groups [namely, (i) manufacture of electrical machinery, apparatus, appliances and supplies and parts; and (ii) manufacture of food products], which have experienced significant trend growth rates of all the three TFP indices (Kendrick, Solow and translog). Interestingly , these industry groups have also shown significantly positive trend growth rates of partial productivities (labour and capital), in opposition of a significant decline in the trend growth rate of capital intensity in case of the former and significantly positive but with its lower order trend growth rate in case of the latter. There are two more industry groups (i.e., basic metals and alloys industries; and machinery, machine tools and parts (except electrical)) in which significant trend growth rates of TFP are accompanied by significant trend growth rates of partial productivities, with relatively lower order but significant trend growth rates of capital intensity. Thus, these four industry groups have demonstrated significant technological progress resulting in overall increase in efficiency.

Another four industry groups (namely, metal products and parts; jute, hemp and mesta textiles; sugar, khandsari and gur; and wood and wood products, furnitures and fixtures),which have experienced significant TFP growth, have demonstrated greater efficiency in the use of labour input only. This is supported by the highly significant trend growth rates of labour productivity and capital intensity accompanied by insignificant trend growth rate of capital productivity. By and large, the technological advancement appears to be closely associated with labour productivity as witnessed by the similar movements of the two at differing situations over the period.

1.2. Sources of Output Growth

The contribution of factor inputs (labour and capital) to the growth of gross value added is found to be much higher (nearly two-third) than that of total factor productivity (TFP) in the State-level organised industrial sector during whole of the reference period (i.e.,1974—86). Besides, the corresponding contribution of factor inputs exhibits a considerable downfall in sub-period-II (1980—86) over sub-period-I (1974—80) mainly because of a significant reduction in labour's contribution. Contrary to this, the contribution of TFP to the growth of gross value added has appreciably increased from 22 percent in the former to about 88 percent during the latter period. Thus, the latter period appears to have demonstrated much higher efficiency in the use of factor inputs.

Factor inputs are identified as major source of output growth in category-I (79 percent) followed by category-III (70 percent). On the other hand, increased efficiency in the use of factor inputs has made a significant contribution to output growth in category-II (61 percent) followed by category-IV (51 percent). In all the four categories, contribution of capital has outstripped that of labour and in cases of category-I and-III, the former has surpassed the contribution of TFP as well. Thus, one may safely conclude that growth of capital has been the major source of output growth in categories-I and III.

Importance of capital is also brought out by industry group-wise analysis. Almost all the industry groups excepting the five (i.e., basic metals and alloys industries; cotton textiles; non-metallic minerals products; transport equipment and parts; and leather and leather and fur products) have demonstrated higher contribution of capital than that of labour. Moreover, the contribution of labour input is found to be negative in edible oil and vanaspati ghee; metal products and parts; and jute, hemp and mesta textiles, indicating a lesser scope for employment generation in these three industry groups. Besides, the contribution of TFP to the growth of gross value added has exceeded the contributions of labour as well as capital in seven industry groups (i.e., basic metals and alloys industries; electrical machinery, apparatus, appliances and supplies and parts; food products; metal products and parts; jute, hemp and mesta textiles; sugar, khandsari and gur ; and wood and wood products), showing increased efficiency in input use.

One of the most striking conclusion emerging from the aforesaid is that increased investment or capital deepening has been a major source of output growth in the State level organised industrial sector during whole of the reference period.

1.3 Production Function Estimates

The analysis based on Cobb-Douglas production function estimates indicates that output has been more responsive to increased capital in the State level organised industrial sector during the period of the study (1974—86). Moreover, both the Cobb-Douglas and the CES production functions do not indicate the presence of any significant neutral technological progress. Besides, the whole organised industrial sector of the State has experienced constant returns to scale during the reference period.

The estimates of elasticity of substitution are found to be significant , as demonstrated by the application of all the three models derived from the CES production function. These estimates are not found to be significantly different from unity, indicating that factor proportions are fairly responsive to changes in factor prices in the organised manufacturing sector of the State. Thus, there seems to be a wider scope for factor substitution in the State level organised industrial sector.

Inter-category analysis of production function estimates indicates that output is more responsive to increased capital in almost all the four categories excepting the III. The coefficient of labour is found to be significant in category-III, showing a greater scope for additional employment in the industry groups constituting this category.

Neutral technological progress has not played any significant role in the output growth of all the categories excepting the -II, which qualifies for significant time trend on the basis of CES production function (Model-II). Economies of scale are found to be significant in categories-II and III on the basis of Cobb-Douglas as well as CES production functions. The rest two categories are found to have experienced constant returns to scale.

Estimates of elasticity of substitution are not found to be significantly different from unity in category-IV on the basis of all the three models derived from the CES production function. Conversely, the estimates of elasticity of substitution are found to be insignificant ($\sigma = 0$) through application of all the three Models in category-I, indicating existence of fixed factor proportions and demonstrating least scope for factor substitution. In the remaining two categories -II and-III, the estimates of elasticity of substitution are found to be significant on the basis of model-I only. Thus, it seems that as we move from less capital intensive to more capital intensive industry groups, the possibilities of factor substitution (labour for capital or vice-versa) gradually reduce and the production structure becomes less flexible.

Industry group-wise estimates of Cobb-Douglas production function indicate output to be more responsive to increased capital as compared to labour in greater number of cases. In this context, out of the twenty industry groups, significant labour coefficients are observed in four industry groups (i.e., rubber, plastic, petroleum and coal products; cotton textiles; jute, hemp and mesta textiles; and transport equipment and parts). Thus, these four industry groups have greater possibilities of employment generation and hence deserve promotion in future.

Out of the total twenty, the three industry groups (i.e., alcohol, beverages, tobacco and tobacco products; jute, hemp and mesta textiles; and wood and wood products, furniture and fixtures) have experienced significant neutral technological progress during the period of the study on the basis of Cobb-Douglas production function; and another three (food products; jute, hemp and mesta textiles; and leather and leather and fur products) on the basis of CES production function. Moreover, production function estimates do not go in favour of our earlier finding of significant technological progress based on TFP index in electrical machinery, apparatus, appliances and supplies and parts ; basic metals and alloys industries; machinery, machine tools and parts (except electrical); and sugar, khandsari and gur. But the industry groups consisting of foods products; jute, hemp and mesta textiles; and wood and wood products, furniture and fixtures are found to have experienced significant technological progress based on both TFP and production function estimates.

Out of the twenty industry groups, significant economies of scale (i.e., increasing returns to scale) are experienced by four industry groups (basic metals and alloys industries; rubber, plastic, petroleum and coal products; food products; and transport equipments and parts) during the reference period. Whereas those having experienced significant diseconomies of scale (i.e., decreasing returns to scale) consist of two industry groups (edible oil and vanaspati ghee; and wood and wood products, furniture and fixtures) only. Finally, the remaining industry groups, which have operated under constant returns to scale, are as many as fourteen. It appears that loss of industry groups experiencing diseconomies of scale has been compensated by the gains of those experiencing economies of scale; this has brought them at par with those experiencing constant returns to scale. Deducing from this is a generalised conclusion that U.P.'s organised manufacturing sector has experienced constant returns to scale during the period of the study. One of the plausible reasons attributable to this vexed situation of constancy is the low capital productivity probably resulting from under-utilisation of installed capacity in majority of the industry groups.

Out of the total twenty industry groups, in cases of fourteen the estimates of elasticity of substitution are found to be closer to unity (or not significantly different from unity). Whereas those demonstrating estimates of σ greater than unity are only two in number. Adding these two sets together, all the sixteen industry groups seem to have a considerable scope of factor substitution.

Contrary to the above, insignificant estimates of σ are noticed in the remaining four industry groups (i.e., chemicals and chemical products; other manufacturing industries; paper and paper products and leather and leather and fur products), showing least scope for factor substitution.

1.4 Performance of Organised Industrial Sector

Regarding the performance of organised manufacturing sector, it is seen that trend growth rates of both the gross value added and employment have shown a significant increase at the State level during the period of 1974—86; but the growth of the former has been much higher (6.56 percent) than the corresponding growth of the latter (2.36 percent). Moreover, the period-wise analysis indicates that the growth of gross value added has considerably increased from 6.94 percent in sub-period-I to 12.94 percent during sub-period-II, whereas the corresponding growth rate of employment has shown a drastic reduction from 5.19 percent to -3.28 percent during this period. This periodic shortfall in employment growth has happened probably because of a significant increase in trend growth rates of both the gross fixed capital (7.84 percent) and capital intensity (11.50 percent) during the sub-period-II . Besides, an unprecedented increase in growth rate of labour productivity from 1.67 percent in sub-period-I to 16.77 percent during sub-period-II is also expected to have led to increased output with lesser amount of labour.

Thus, the performance of organised manufacturing sector in the State by and large goes in favour of the hypothesis that there exists a conflict between the output growth and employment growth during sub-period-II. But the question is whether the programme for expansion of employment should be entertained at the cost of output growth . This seems to be neither feasible nor worthwhile proposition. In order, therefore, to sincerely partake with the national level objective of efficiency and equity, it would be desirable to largely depend upon organised manufacturing sector for maximisation of output growth and simultaneously concentrate on accelerating development of unorganised manufacturing sector for generating maximum possible employment.

However, looking to inter-category scenario it is noticed that during whole of the reference period all the categories excepting-IV have registered significant trend growth rates of both output and employment, with the highest in category-II followed by category-III.In juxtaposition, the trend growth rate of output in category-IV has been highly significant, whereas in case of employment the corresponding growth is found to be positive but not significant during the period of the study. Thus, while considering total period of the study, there does not seem to be any conflict between output growth and employment This is also supported by the findings based on inter-industry group analysis. The significant trend growth rates of both output and employment have been noticed in cases of fourteen industry groups out of the total twenty. However, visualising the experiences of sub-period-II (1980—86), the organised manufacturing sector of the State has definitely experienced a distinct conflict between the two, suggesting for enforcement of two-pronged approaches (promotion of organised sector for output growth and unorganised sector for employment growth) simultaneously.

1.5 Inter-relationship between Technological Progress and Performance

As objectively assessed, there has been a significant technological advancement as witnessed by a significant trend growth rate of Solow index of TFP in the organised industrial sector of the State during the reference period. On the other hand, there has been a significant progress in performance of organised manufacturing sector as witnessed by the significant trend growth rates of both output and employment. Correlating the Solow index of TFP with gross value added, the coefficient of correlation, which emerges as 0.60, indicates that both are positively associated and have moved in a similar direction. Contrary to this, the relation of Solow index of TFP with employment growth is not found to be significant (-0.14).

This is also supported by the movement behaviour of partial productivity ratios, which indicates existence of labour saving bias of technological change, resulting in lower order trend growth rate of employment. Probably costlier labour (high wage cost per unit of output (4.28 percent)) has been instrumental in generating pressure for use of increased capital, which has adversely affected the employment growth. Analysis of this issue in the context of sub-period-II of the study also provides adequate support in favour of this conclusion.

Inter-category estimates in the above context are indicative of the fact that category-II has recorded the highest level of technological advancement as witnessed by the highly significant trend growth rates of partial productivities and Solow index of TFP. With the result, highly significant trend growth rate of value added is accompanied by significant trend growth rate of employment. Besides, the trend growth rate of value added is found to be higher than those of labour and capital, pointing towards improvement in overall efficiency. Generally, high labour productivity is expected to affect employment unfavourably but here in this case the former is not only significantly positive but has also made a significant contribution to output and employment. Cost ratios have also been favourable to the growth in category-II. A low wage cost is accompained by significant rate of return on capital, showing existence of strong reinvestment potential in this category.

Contrary to the theoretical expectations, category-IV has registered a significant trend growth rate of value added accompanied by insignificant trend growth rate of employment. Significant trend growth rates of Solow index and labour productivity are accompanied by insignificant trend growth rate of capital productivity. Technical progress seems to have been more conducive to labour saving in this category. High wage cost seems to have promoted substitution of capital for labour, as witnessed by the significant trend growth rate of capital intensity (6.14 percent).

Categories-I and III have witnessed significant trend growth rates of both value added and employment. In case of the latter, significant trend growth rates of Solow index of TFP and labour productivity are noticeable, whereas insignificant trend growth rate of TFP and partial productivity indices are observed in case of the former. Thus, in case of category-III technical progress seems to have played a significant role in output growth, whereas input seems to have been major source of growth in category-I. Besides showing inefficiency in input use, category-I also witnesses insignificant trend growth rate in regard to rate of return on capital.

Excepting the six industry groups (i.e., wool, silk and synthetic fibre textiles; edible oil and vanaspati ghee; metal products and parts; jute, hemp and mesta textiles; sugar, khandsari and gur; and wood and wood products, furnitures and fixtures) all the remaining fourteen have witnessed significant trend growth rates of both output and employment. A significant technological advancement (Solow index of TFP) has been a major source of both output and employment growth in respect of four industry groups (i.e., basic metals and alloys industries; electrical machinery, apparatus, appliances and supplies and parts; machinery, machine tools and parts (except electrical); and food products). Whereas, the gross fixed capital and capital intensity appear to have made significant contribution to performance in the remaining ten industry groups.

Besides, in cases of the above mentioned six exceptional industry groups, the trend growth rates of output are found to be significant, but the corresponding growth rate of employment is noticed to be insignificant. Corollary to this, technological progress (Solow index of TFP) has contributed significantly to output growth in cases of two industry groups and those mainly contributed by greater use of gross fixed capital and capital deepening are four in number.

In sixteen out of twenty industry groups, the estimates of elasticity of substitution are either equal to or greater than unity, which indicates that factor proportions are responsive to factor prices. This leads to a conclusion that greater possibilities of factor substitution exist in these industry groups. In the remaining four industry groups (i.e., chemicals and chemical products; other manufacturing industries; paper and paper products, printing, publishing and allied industries and leather and leather and fur products) the value of elasticity of substitution is equivalent to zero, indicating that there is least scope for factor substitution in these industry groups.

Finally, there seems to be a conflict between output and employment growth in respect of six industry groups (i.e., wool, silk and synthetic fibre textiles; edible oil and vanaspati ghee; metal products and parts; jute, hemp and mesta textiles; sugar, khandsari and gur; and wood and wood products, furnitures and fixtures). Since the estimates of elasticity of substitution indicate greater possibilities of substitution, there is a room for carrying out required adjustments in factor proportions to overcome the conflict.

2. REGIONAL LEVEL ANALYSIS

2.1 Partial Productivity And Total Factor Productivity

The trend growth rate of labour productivity is found to be much higher than the corresponding growth rate of capital productivity in the organised manufacturing sector of all the five economic regions of the State during the period of study. The trend growth rate of labour productivity is found to be above the State level in the Eastern and the Bundelkhand regions and those below it include the Western, the Central and the Uttranchal. Whereas, the trend growth rate of capital productivity is found to be insignificant in all the regions of the State. Significant trend growth rates of labour productivity and capital intensity are accompanied by positive but insignificant trend growth rate of capital productivity in the organised industrial sector of the Western, the Eastern and the Bundelkhand regions, indicating more efficient use of labour input only. In the remaining two regions (i.e., Central and Uttranchal), insignificant trend growth rates of partial productivity ratios are accompanied by the significant trend growth rates of capital intensity. Hence, increased capital intensity in industries of these regions seems to have not been effective in bringing about significant productivity improvements. At the State level, the movement behavior of partial productivity indices and capital intensity has been similar to those of the Western, the Eastern and the Bundelkhand regions.

Significant technological progress in the organised industrial sector of the Eastern, the Uttranchal and the Bundelkhand regions is demonstrated by the significant growth of TFP. However, significant trend growth rates of labour productivity are observed in the Eastern and the Bundelkhand regions only. Moreover, in the organised industrial sector of the Western and the Central regions, insignificant trend growth rates of all the three indices of TFP indicate factor inputs to be the major source of growth. In sum, owing to significant technological advancement, backward regions have shown greater efficiency in the use of factor inputs.

2.2 Sources of Output Growth

The decomposition results show that excepting the Bundelkhand, in all other economic regions and whole of the State, contribution of capital to output growth has been greater than the corresponding contribution of labour during the reference period. But the contribution of TFP is found to be greater than those of capital and labour separately in the organised industrial sector of the Eastern and the Bundelkhand regions.

2.3 Production Function Estimates

Inter-regional analysis of production function reveals that output has been more responsive to increased capital in almost all the regions excepting the Bundelkhand. The significant labour coefficient in respect of the Bundelkhand region shows the availability of greater employment potential.

Insignificant time trend for almost all the regions and whole of the State indicates that neutral technological progress has not made any significant contribution to the State level progress of the organised manufacturing sector. Returns to scale show predominance of constant returns to scale. The only exception is the Bundelkhand region, which has experienced significant technical progress as well as economies of scale (i.e., increasing returns to scale) on the basis of both the Cobb-Douglas and the CES production functions.

Based on the CES production function, inter-regional analysis reveals that the estimates of elasticity of substitution in the organised industrial sector of the Eastern and the Bundelkhand regions are greater than unity and those of the Western and the Uttranchal regions are quite close to unity. Whereas, the value of σ is found to be significantly less than unity in case of the Central region. Thus, one may infer that factor proportion are fairly responsive to changes in factor prices, demonstrating a considerable scope of substituting labour for capital and *vice versa* in the State.

2.4 Inter-regional Performance

The State still suffers from inter-regional disparities in levels of industrial development. Industrial activities in terms of number of units, employment and value added are relatively more concentrated in developed regions. It is also noticed that over the period clusters of industries have developed in a fewer districts of each and every region. For example, nearly 64 percent of the total organised manufacturing units available in the Eastern region are concentrated in Varanasi, Allahabad, and Gorakhpur districts only. Likewise, nearly 79 percent of the total units of the Central regions are concentrated in Kanpur and Lucknow districts and the proportion of those concentrating in Dehradun and Nainital districts of the Uttranchal is as high as about 88 percent. Besides, the process of diversification has been confining to only relatively better developed regions of the State. Not only this, even the larger number of industry groups constituting the industrial base have, through our study, emerged in better developed districts of the State.

However, regarding the structural changes over the period, there appears to have been some improvement in the industrial scenario. The trend growth rates of output and employment are found to be above the State level average in backward regions of Uttranchal and Bundelkhand. The Eastern region has registered a highly significant trend growth rate of value added accompanied by insignificant trend growth rate of employment. The performance in terms of the trend growth rates of output and employment of comparatively more developed Western and Central regions has been below the State average during the period of the study. This shows that there has been some definite improvement in industrial scenario of the backward regions but the pace and the process of industrialisation in the State seems to have been slow and lagging behind the expectations.

2.5 Inter-regional Dimensions of Technological Change and Performance

Significant trend growth rate of Solow index of TFP in the orgnised industrial sector of the Eastern, the Uttranchal and the Bundelkhand regions indicates that the backward regions have started experiencing significant technological progress. However, a slightly different picture emerges from the partial productivity analysis. The trend growth rates of labour productivity are noticed to be significant in the Western, the Eastern and the Bundelkhand regions only, whereas capital productivity is found to be insignificant in all the regions of the State. In juxtaposition, the performance of different regions of the State in terms of the trend growth rates of both output and employment is found to be significant, excepting the Eastern region accounting for insignificant trend growth rate of employment. Technological advancement is identified as major source of output growth in the Eastern and the Bundelkhand regions, whereas the capital intensity is found to have made a major contribution to it in the Western, the Central and the Uttranchal region. In case of the Eastern region, technological progress seems to have been biased to labour saving, resulting in an insignificant growth of employment.

In almost all the economic regions (excepting the Central) as well as the whole State, estimates of elasticity of substitution are either equal to or greater than unity, indicating greater scope for factor substitution. However, a less than unity estimate of elasticity of substitution indicates lesser scope for factor substitution in the Central region. Almost all the regions of the State (excepting the Eastern) have experienced significant trend growth rates of both output and employment. In the Eastern region, there seems to have been a conflict between output and employment growth. But the value of elasticity of substitution, as noticed in case of Eastern region, is significantly greater than unity, demonstrating a fairly responsive production structure. Therefore, necessary modifications in factor substitution are likely to help in resolving the conflict between output and employment growth to a large extent.

Appendices

Appendix Table-3.1 : The Wholsale Price Index of U.P. (by sub-Groups) (1974 - 75 = 100)

Year/ Industry Group	Total Manu. Sector	Manu.of Food Products	Manu.of Sugar,Khan-dsari & Gur	Manu.of Bdible Oil & Vanaspati Ghee	Manu.of Alcohol, Beverages Tobacco & Tobacco Products	Manu.of Cotton Textiles	Manu.of Wool Silk & Synthe-tic Fibre Textiles	Manu.of Jute,Hemp & Mesta Textiles	Manu.of Textile Products,	Manu.of Wood&Wood Products, Furniture & Fixtures	Manu.of Paper & Paper Products, Printing Publishing etc.	Manu.of Leather & Leather & Fur Prod-ucts(except) repair)	Manu.of Rubber, Plastic, Petroleum and Coal Products	Manu.of Chemicals & Chemical Products (except Products of Petrol & Coal)	Manu.of Non-Metallic Mineral Products	Manu.of Metals & Alloys Indust-ries	Manu.of Metal Products (except Mach. & Transport Equipment)	Manu.of Machinery, Machine Tools & Parts (except electri-cal)	Manu.of Electrical Machinery, Apparatus, Appliances etc.	Manu.of Transport Equipment and Parts	Other Manufac-turing Industries
1	2	3	4	5	6	7	8	9	10	11	12	13	14	15	16	17	18	19	20	21	22
1974-75	100	100	100	100	100	100	100	100	100	100	100	100	100	100	100	100	100	100	100	100	100
1975-76	101.5	88.9	106.8	76.8	111.1	91.3	106.4	85.4	92.2	103.4	99.4	117.4	112.1	103.9	115.7	109.7	103.9	113.0	107.2	108.9	98.1
1976-77	103.7	101.8	108.8	81.9	113.4	98.2	107.6	81.7	96.9	101.7	101.5	131.9	112.4	101.4	117.8	113.8	107.3	113.5	102.6	107.2	96.5
1977-78	106.2	114.9	92.8	102.0	115.5	111.0	114.9	92.9	108.1	113.4	99.8	131.9	112.1	102.3	120.1	114.7	114.1	114.6	104.2	109.6	103.8
1978-79	108.9	116.6	81.5	104.3	121.1	114.9	122.6	92.2	110.9	116.9	111.5	139.4	119.9	108.9	131.2	128.8	117.2	115.3	107.8	116.3	107.1
1979-80	132.6	126.7	135.2	120.4	124.9	122.3	131.1	119.6	124.9	128.2	142.1	170.9	137.1	126.9	170.9	162.4	123.6	137.1	118.2	134.8	112.4
1980-81	160.7	146.2	250.3	139.6	136.9	125.9	132.3	109.4	124.1	139.0	170.2	194.9	146.8	151.8	189.9	198.7	131.7	153.6	132.0	136.2	124.8
1981-82	168.3	151.8	212.5	153.9	165.7	147.3	151.3	98.6	135.8	161.7	173.8	199.0	169.6	170.9	227.4	219.5	132.8	164.8	139.9	158.5	115.6
1982-83	170.2	165.9	168.4	156.2	182.9	156.2	162.8	104.4	144.1	187.9	170.3	211.5	194.1	177.3	266.7	216.6	150.4	173.1	149.2	162.6	115.1
1983-84	179.5	174.3	176.6	172.9	202.9	158.1	163.3	118.4	149.7	209.7	176.6	225.4	199.5	184.4	295.7	228.3	157.9	170.3	142.7	168.9	116.4
1984-85	200.9	168.4	200.3	179.9	207.1	171.9	171.8	195.2	182.9	232.3	196.9	254.0	213.3	195.5	336.0	252.9	187.8	177.1	149.3	172.7	126.7
1985-86	220.6	171.4	251.4	180.2	244.4	183.2	180.9	189.0	188.8	245.0	218.9	297.7	226.7	214.6	338.5	308.4	204.9	184.8	165.3	188.0	135.8

Source : 1977-78 to 1985-86-Statistical abstracts: Various Issues.

Note : The wholsale price indices for the years 1974-75, 1975-76 and 1976-77 are extrapolated following the wholesale price indices of India.

Appendix Table-3.2 : Index Number of Machinery and Transport Equipment (1974-75=100)

Year	*Index*
1	2
1952-53	37.6
1953-54	36.8
1954-55	36.4
1955-56	36.4
1956-57	37.2
1957-58	38.3
1958-59	39.1
1959-60	40.2
1960-61	42.1
1961-62	43.2
1962-63	44.9
1963-64	46.8
1964-65	48.3
1965-66	50.8
1966-67	54.7
1967-68	57.0
1968-69	57.3
1969-70	59.0
1970-71	64.0
1971-72	67.3
1972-73	71.7
1973-74	78.5
1974-75	100.0
1975-76	110.4
1976-77	108.7
1977-78	110.4
1978-79	117.2
1979-80	138.0
1980-81	153.1
1981-82	169.5
1982-83	177.7
1983-84	185.1
1984-85	194.1
1985-86	216.0

Source : RBI Bulletins: Various Issues. (Prepared by the Office of Economic Advisor, Government of India).

Appendix Table-3.3 : Consumer Price Index for Industrial Workers in Kanpur (1974-75 = 100)

Year	Index
1	2
1974-75	100.0
1975-76	100.3
1976-77	92.3
1977-78	104.8
1978-79	108.4
1979-80	112.6
1980-81	124.8
1981-82	138.4
1982-83	149.7
1983-84	165.5
1984-85	176.8
1985-86	192.3

Source: Statistical Abstract and Indian Labour Journal : Various Issues. (Prepared by the Labour Bureau, Government of India).

Appendix Table-3.4 : Category-wise Capital-Labour Ratios for Different Industry Groups-1985-86

Category/K/L (in Rs.)	*Industry Groups**
Category I-Highly Capital Intensive (1,21, 377.08 and above)	(1) Manufacture of chemicals and chemical products (239, 277.31); (2) Basic metals and alloys industries (131,991.36); (3) Manufacture of wool, silk and synthetic fibre textiles (123,617.65).
Category II-Medium High Capital Intensive (69,751.73 to 1,21,377.08)	(4) Manufacture of electrical machinery, apparatus appliances and supplies and parts (111,501.63); (5) Manufacture of rubber, plastic, petroleum and coal products (91,341.14); (6) Manufacture of edible oil and vanaspati ghee (82,193.19); (7) Other manufacturing industries (69,717.25).
Category III-Medium Low Capital Intensive (41,953.47 to 69,751.73)	(8) Manufacture of paper and paper products, printing, publishing and allied industries (65, 121.27); (9) Manufacture of alcohol, beverages, tobacco and tobacco products (61,183.57); (10) Manufacture of non-electrical machinery, machine tools and parts (56,508.20); (11) Manufacture of cotton textiles (49,291.38); (12) Manufacture of food products (44,912.19); (13) Manufacture of textile products (including wearing apparel other than footwear) (43,180.86).
Category IV-Low Capital Intensive (41, 953.47 and below)	(14) Manufacture of metal products and parts except machinery and transport equipment (41,087.77); (15) Manufacture of non-metallic mineral products (40,304.21); (16) Manufacture of jute, hemp and mesta textiles (34,817.71); (17) manufacture of sugar, khandsari and gur (30,734.66); (18) Manufacture of transport equipment and parts (30,165.01); (19) Manufacture of wood and wood products, furnitre and fixtures (27,131.38); (20) Manufacture of leather and leather and fur products (except repair) (20,956.95).

Source : ASI Report : 1985-86.

Note : Figure in parentheses give capital-labour ratios for the respective industry groups. Capital-labour ratios represent gross fixed assets at contant prices per employee.

Appendix Table-5.1 : Category/Industry Group-wise Wage Rates, Rates of Return on Capital and Shares of Labour in Value Added-Growth Rates: 1974-75 to 1985-86

Category/Industry Group	*Wage Rate*	*Rate of Return on Capital*	*Share of Labour in Value Added*
1	2	3	4
1. Manufacture of chemicals and chemical products (except products of petroleum and coal)	4.70* (9.92)	-3.14 (1.18)	6.47
2. Basic metals and alloys industries	4.64* (7.85)	2.44 (0.74)	0.98
3. Manufacture of wool, silk and synthetic fibre textiles	2.58** (2.92)	-1.44 (0.42)	1.85
Category I	**4.38* (11.89)**	**-1.39 (0.58)**	**2.88**
4. Manufacture of electrical machinery, apparatus, appliances and supplies and parts	3.31* (8.01)	15.29* (3.66)	-6.07
5. Manufacture of rubber, plastic, petroleum and coal products	7.32** (2.69)	1.37 (0.24)	0.35
6. Manufacture of edible oil and vanaspati ghee	5.11* (4.12)	-1.95 (0.53)	-3.10
7. Other manufacturing industries	3.34* (4.64)	-0.62 (0.09)	15.76
Category II	**4.16* (10.80)**	**11.53* (3.58)**	**-6.29**
8. Manufacture of paper, paper products and printing, publishing and allied Industries	3.13* (5.84)	-8.81** (2.78)	0.65

Appendix Table-5.1 (Contd...)

1	2	3	4
9. Manufacture of alcohol, beverages tobacco and tobacco products	4.99* (7.91)	0.33 (0.12)	0.18
10. Manufacture of machinery, machine tools and parts (except electrical)	4.92* (8.29)	3.61 (1.44)	-0.27
11. Manufacture of cotton textiles	3.79* (4.83)	-7.82 (1.03)	2.51
12. Manufacture of food products (except sugar, khandsari and gur)	0.55 (1.28)	6.22* (6.74)	-4.09
13. Manufacture of textile products	3.86* (4.19)	-8.20*** (1.85)	10.16
Category III	**3.56* (6.89)**	**-0.07 (0.04)**	**-0.35**
14. Manufacture of metal products and parts (except machinery and transport equipment)	2.49* (5.15)	2.04 (1.13)	-1.45
15. Manufacture of non-metallic mineral products	2.14** (3.08)	-1.48 (0.26)	1.26
16. Manufacure of jute, hemp and mesta textiles	5.10* (4.00)	12.69 (1.37)	1.16
17. Manufacture of sugar, khandsari and gur	5.21** (2.75)	6.69 (0.80)	-0.08
18. Manufacture of transport equipment and parts	2.75 (1.78)	-2.54 (0.40)	1.83
19. Manufacture of wood and wood products, furnitures and fixtures	1.79*** (1.84)	6.14 (0.98)	3.76
20. Manufacture of leather and leather and fur products (except repair)	3.23* (4.63)	6.46 (0.63)	0.65
Category IV	**5.05* (3.97)**	**1.35 (0.41)**	**-0.22**

Appendix Table-5.1 (Contd...)

1	2	3	4
Total Manufacturing	**4.28*** **(6.22)**	**-0.42** **(0.19)**	**0.22**

Source : Based on the ASI Reports : Various Issues.

Notes : 1. Cols. 2-3: trend growth rates; Col 4: average annual growth rates.

2. Figures in parentheses are t values of the estimates.

* Significant at 1 percent level of significance.

** Significant at 5 percent level of significance.

*** Significant at 10 percent level of significance.

Appendix Table-5.2 (A) : Industry Group-Wise Indices of Partial Productivities, Capital Intensity and Total Factor Productivity: 1974-75 to 1985-86

Table-5.2 (A).1 : Manufacture of Food Products

Year	*Labour Productivity index (LPI)*	*Capital Productivity Index (KPI)*	*Index of Capital Labour Ratio (IKLR)*	*Kendrick Index (KI)*	*Solow Index (SI)*	*Translog Index (TI)*
1	2	3	4	5	6	7
1974-75	100.00	100.00	100.00	1.000	1.000	1.000
1975-76	109.46	104.59	104.66	1.064	1.066	1.063
1976-77	124.54	117.45	106.04	1.201	1.205	1.191
1977-78	104.91	108.68	96.53	1.072	1.083	1.057
1978-79	135.05	136.88	98.66	1.362	1.379	1.308
1979-80	126.22	132.37	95.36	1.299	1.321	1.250
1980-81	109.98	114.11	96.39	1.125	1.142	1.069
1981-82	141.55	140.28	100.91	1.408	1.436	1.306
1982-83	139.83	132.68	105.39	1.354	1.373	1.250
1983-84	183.48	151.44	121.16	1.625	1.657	1.463
1984-85	167.72	140.93	119.01	1.503	1.537	1.351
1985-86	197.98	165.29	119.78	1.767	1.807	1.568
Trend Growth Rate	**5.571* (5.910)**	**3.890* (5.955)**	**1.618** (2.764)**	**4.506* (6.276)**	**4.721* (6.562)**	**3.279* (4.785)**

Table-5.2(A).2 : Manufacture of Sugar, Khandsari & Gur

Year	*(LPI)*	*(KPI)*	*(IKLR)*	*(KI)*	*(SI)*	*(TI)*
1	2	3	4	5	6	7
1974-75	100.00	100.00	100.00	1.000	1.000	1.000
1975-76	99.26	105.83	93.79	1.003	1.003	0.999
1976-77	120.96	139.51	86.71	1.238	1.225	1.211
1977-78	144.35	169.09	85.37	1.480	1.469	1.434
1978-79	132.05	119.70	110.32	1.298	1.123	1.153
1979-80	94.59	78.23	120.92	0.914	0.770	0.749
1980-81	80.66	80.91	99.69	0.807	0.664	0.647
1981-82	86.95	82.43	105.48	0.862	0.708	0.689
1982-83	151.44	118.39	127.92	1.446	1.208	1.040
1983-84	196.24	104.81	187.25	1.709	1.393	1.196
1984-85	222.03	100.74	220.41	1.843	1.511	1.282
1985-86	228.74	92.20	248.08	1.828	1.487	1.264
Trend Growth Rate	**6.705** (2.670)**	**-2.146 (1.153)**	**9.046* (5.246)**	**4.612 (2.070)**	**2.276 (0.911)**	**0.504 (0.221)**

Table-5.2 (A).3 : Manufacture of Edible Oil and Vanaspati Ghee

Year	*(LPI)*	*(KPI)*	*(IKLR)*	*(KI)*	*(SI)*	*(TI)*
1	2	3	4	5	6	7
1974-75	100.00	100.00	100.00	1.000	1.000	1.000
1975-76	137.95	134.11	102.87	1.359	1.365	1.304
1976-77	130.63	120.39	108.51	1.251	1.239	1.185
1977-78	171.21	176.72	96.88	1.740	1.714	1.604
1978-79	200.13	145.75	137.31	1.677	1.435	1.415
1979-80	257.42	182.13	141.34	2.120	1.813	1.739
1980-81	277.77	178.65	155.49	2.157	1.816	1.745
1981-82	235.34	147.46	159.59	1.798	1.502	1.422
1982-83	174.52	110.95	157.30	1.346	1.130	1.011
1983-84	115.13	71.55	160.89	0.875	0.729	0.577
1984-85	176.83	95.42	185.32	1.226	1.065	0.779
1985-86	338.87	131.85	257.02	1.869	1.783	1.105
Trend Growth Rate	**5.544 (1.941)**	**-2.068 (0.869)**	**7.773* (8.318)**	**0.838 (0.332)**	**-0.536 (0.216)**	**-3.729 (1.432)**

Table-5.2(A).4 : Manufacture of Alcohol, Beverages, Tobacco and Tobacco Products

Year	*(LPI)*	*(KPI)*	*(IKLR)*	*(KI)*	*(SI)*	*(TI)*
1	2	3	4	5	6	7
1974-75	100.00	100.00	100.00	1.000	1.000	1.000
1975-76	115.43	103.42	111.61	1.093	1.098	1.087
1976-77	151.75	130.66	116.14	1.408	1.420	1.359
1977-78	138.07	113.73	121.40	1.251	1.250	1.194
1978-79	160.06	133.98	119.47	1.463	1.461	1.381
1979-80	215.77	184.22	117.13	1.993	1.986	1.811
1980-81	195.51	146.07	133.84	1.680	1.605	1.472
1981-82	138.36	110.77	124.90	1.235	1.204	1.024
1982-83	162.58	143.05	113.65	1.525	1.475	1.244
1983-84	184.17	137.18	134.25	1.580	1.511	1.276
1984-85	149.07	92.34	161.44	1.149	1.041	0.887
1985-86	231.61	121.48	190.65	1.610	1.540	1.204
Trend Growth Rate	**4.715** (2.911)**	**0.633 (0.376)**	**4.056* (4.556)**	**2.409 (1.497)**	**1.671 (0.985)**	**-0.396 (0.236)**

Table-5.2 (A).5 : Manufacture of Cotton Textiles

Year	*(LPI)*	*(KPI)*	*(IKLR)*	*(KI)*	*(SI)*	*(TI)*
1	2	3	4	5	6	7
1974-75	100.00	100.00	100.00	1.000	1.000	1.000
1975-76	86.50	93.92	92.10	0.882	0.884	0.873
1976-77	71.93	71.87	100.09	0.719	0.721	0.704
1977-78	91.46	91.95	99.47	0.916	0.916	0.874
1978-79	115.91	121.55	95.36	1.172	1.173	1.094
1979-80	123.69	118.51	104.37	1.224	1.206	1.131
1980-81	131.83	127.31	103.55	1.307	1.289	1.205
1981-82	98.71	88.15	111.98	0.959	0.934	0.837
1982-83	103.41	96.16	107.55	0.015	0.983	0.879
1983-84	110.55	104.40	105.89	1.090	1.052	0.939
1984-85	98.78	76.15	129.71	0.921	0.914	0.818
1985-86	111.44	81.94	136.00	1.024	1.029	0.914
Trend Growth	**1.974 (1.501)**	**-0.743 (0.475)**	**2.737* (4.859)**	**1.247 (0.912)**	**1.052 (0.782)**	**-0.092 (0.069)**

Table-5.2(A).6 : Manufacture of Wool, Silk and Synthetic Fibre Textiles

Year	*(LPI)*	*(KPI)*	*(IKLR)*	*(KI)*	*(SI)*	*(TI)*
1	2	3	4	5	6	7
1974-75	100.00	100.00	100.00	1.000	1.000	1.000
1975-76	86.06	74.58	115.40	0.796	0.780	0.778
1976-77	82.24	65.21	126.12	0.723	0.711	0.709
1977-78	106.66	92.38	115.46	0.986	0.952	0.928
1978-79	86.74	71.04	122.11	0.777	0.742	0.709
1979-80	101.18	119.42	84.73	1.100	0.968	0.930
1980-81	75.62	58.50	129.27	0.655	0.515	0.500
1981-82	90.96	89.96	101.11	0.904	0.664	0.641
1982-83	77.40	55.14	140.37	0.638	0.465	0.467
1983-84	142.21	86.40	164.61	1.061	0.832	0.717
1984-85	94.05	68.83	136.63	0.788	0.642	0.494
1985-86	179.55	82.03	218.89	1.104	1.050	0.686
Trend Growth Rate	**3.312 (1.655)**	**-1.222 (0.630)**	**4.590** (2.741)**	**0.509 (0.295)**	**-1.616 (0.734)**	**-4.281** (2.523)**

Table-5.2(A).7 : Manufacture of Jute, Hemp and Mesta Textiles

Year	(LPI)	(KPI)	(IKLR)	(KI)	(SI)	(TI)
1	2	3	4	5	6	7
1974-75	100.00	100.00	100.00	1.000	1.000	1.000
1975-76	144.58	149.89	96.46	1.447	1.447	1.372
1976-77	153.93	155.15	99.21	1.540	1.532	1.448
1977-78	138.00	150.51	91.69	1.382	1.412	1.322
1978-79	155.90	185.86	83.88	1.564	1.623	1.515
1979-80	199.70	231.59	86.23	2.002	2.065	1.876
1980-81	246.74	276.55	89.22	2.473	2.524	2.244
1981-82	217.89	229.70	94.86	2.181	2.146	1.903
1982-83	171.38	165.53	103.53	1.713	1.614	1.390
1983-84	244.24	75.58	323.17	2.343	1.260	1.228
1984-85	266.68	212.93	125.24	2.654	1.779	1.777
1985-86	234.48	115.95	202.23	2.300	1.309	1.367
Trend Growth Rate	**7.399*** **(5.448)**	**0.365** **(0.110)**	**7.009**** **(2.385)**	**7.184*** **(5.249)**	**1.822** **(0.834)**	**2.020** **(1.087)**

Table-5.2 (A).8 : Manufacture of Textile Products (including Wearing Apparel other than Footwear)

Year	(LPI)	(KPI)	(IKLR)	(KI)	(SI)	(TI)
1	2	3	4	5	6	7
1974-75	100.00	100.00	100.00	1.000	1.000	1.000
1975-76	91.57	47.16	194.16	0.580	0.338	0.524
1976-77	94.35	46.79	201.65	0.581	0.341	0.528
1977-78	94.84	46.64	203.35	0.580	0.341	0.529
1978-79	153.46	46.96	326.80	0.642	0.440	0.631
1979-80	173.04	48.21	358.96	0.668	0.467	0.668
1980-81	154.59	43.34	356.70	0.600	0.419	0.595
1981-82	270.59	76.47	353.84	1.058	0.736	0.932
1982-83	259.82	71.58	362.97	0.994	0.692	0.875
1983-84	130.71	38.25	341.71	0.526	0.379	0.309
1984-85	118.21	27.61	428.09	0.392	0.292	0.240
1985-86	86.10	20.11	428.13	0.286	0.213	0.164
Trend Growth Rate	**3.400** **(1.012)**	**-6.875**** **(2.352)**	**11.034*** **(5.583)**	**-4.750** **(1.642)**	**-4.320** **(1.250)**	**-9.046**** **(2.488)**

Table-5.2(A).9 : Manufacture of Wood & Wood Products, Furniture & Fixtures

Year	*(LPI)*	*(KPI)*	*(IKLR)*	*(KI)*	*(SI)*	*(TI)*
1	2	3	4	5	6	7
1974-75	100.00	100.00	100.00	1.000	1.000	1.000
1975-76	144.50	108.13	133.64	1.417	1.426	1.317
1976-77	143.94	101.44	141.90	1.405	1.394	1.295
1977-78	167.61	95.48	175.53	1.606	1.586	1.424
1978-79	141.71	107.39	131.96	1.391	1.494	1.318
1979-80	160.20	149.59	107.10	1.596	1.764	1.567
1980-81	123.06	103.99	118.34	1.218	1.286	1.112
1981-82	174.52	125.80	138.73	1.707	1.786	1.451
1982-83	119.47	101.60	117.58	1.183	1.328	0.969
1983-84	180.80	103.44	174.78	1.733	1.893	1.254
1984-85	250.78	108.40	231.34	2.331	2.366	1.510
1985-86	153.47	89.79	170.92	1.474	1.730	0.900
Trend Growth Rate	**3.536 (2.010)**	**-0.211 (0.181)**	**3.754 (2.085)**	**3.206 (1.958)**	**4.309** (2.991)**	**-0.741 (0.469)**

Table-5.2 (A). 10 : Manufacture of Paper & Paper Products and Printing, Publishing and Allied Industries

Year	*(LPI)*	*(KPI)*	*(IKLR)*	*(KI)*	*(SI)*	*(TI)*
1	2	3	4	5	6	7
1974-75	100.00	100.00	100.00	1.000	1.000	1.000
1975-76	106.00	103.33	102.58	1.048	1.049	1.047
1976-77	112.93	104.98	107.57	1.092	1.095	1.094
1977-78	123.90	109.63	113.02	1.171	1.181	1.171
1978-79	106.80	83.95	127.23	0.952	0.941	0.931
1979-80	97.82	68.15	143.54	0.818	0.810	0.811
1980-81	94.56	65.66	144.02	0.790	0.782	0.782
1981-82	95.87	63.39	151.24	0.780	0.784	0.783
1982-83	96.18	60.70	158.44	0.762	0.776	0.777
1983-84	117.36	65.13	180.19	0.863	0.927	0.906
1984-85	123.19	51.76	238.00	0.761	0.872	0.860
1985-86	156.80	61.55	254.76	0.926	1.087	1.043
Trend Growth Rate	**1.744 (1.463)**	**-6.342* (6.700)**	**8.633* (12.197)**	**-2.812** (2.962)**	**-1.596 (1.340)**	**-1.811 (1.625)**

Table-5.2 (A). 11 : Manufacture of Leather & Leather and Fur Products (except repair)

Year	*(LPI)*	*(KPI)*	*(IKLR)*	*(KI)*	*(SI)*	*(TI)*
1	2	3	4	5	6	7
1974-75	100.00	100.00	100.00	1.000	1.000	1.000
1975-76	68.37	43.32	157.83	0.529	0.391	0.419
1976-77	66.78	63.92	104.47	0.653	0.430	0.458
1977-78	56.49	49.38	114.38	0.527	0.357	0.377
1978-79	62.78	54.88	114.38	0.585	0.396	0.417
1979-80	85.64	63.16	135.59	0.726	0.532	0.533
1980-81	67.21	50.23	133.81	0.574	0.419	0.405
1981-82	78.27	55.56	140.87	0.648	0.487	0.464
1982-83	91.37	63.50	143.89	0.747	0.566	0.533
1983-84	101.62	53.85	188.71	0.701	0.577	0.546
1984-85	91.48	51.04	179.25	0.653	0.528	0.498
1985-86	157.84	88.05	179.26	1.126	0.912	0.769
Trend Growth Rate	**4.798** (2.384)**	**-0.021 (0.010)**	**4.820* (4.073)**	**1.949 (0.986)**	**2.280 (0.823)**	**0.589 (0.238)**

Table-5.2 (A). 12 : Manufacture of Rubber, Plastic, Petroleum & Coal Products

Year	*(LPI)*	*(KPI)*	*(IKLR)*	*(KI)*	*(SI)*	*(TI)*
1	2	3	4	5	6	7
1974-75	100.00	100.00	100.00	1.000	1.000	1.000
1975-76	137.17	49.22	278.71	0.637	0.217	0.754
1976-77	140.93	68.08	207.01	0.833	0.248	0.886
1977-78	306.47	131.63	232.83	1.649	0.523	1.507
1978-79	306.58	113.65	269.76	1.462	0.461	1.345
1979-80	331.86	139.50	237.90	1.755	0.539	1.573
1980-81	294.73	114.96	256.38	1.466	0.449	1.305
1981-82	300.85	102.07	294.74	1.332	0.413	1.215
1982-83	295.04	93.06	317.02	1.228	0.386	1.137
1983-84	225.82	65.50	344.75	0.875	0.275	0.782
1984-85	123.23	34.61	356.08	0.464	0.146	0.296
1985-86	713.70	207.57	343.83	2.771	0.848	0.821
Trend Growth Rate	**8.600 (2.020)**	**0.823 (0.192)**	**7.711* (3.919)**	**2.398 (0.565)**	**-2.311 (0.488)**	**-4.576 (1.270)**

Table-5.2 (A).13 : Manufacture of Chemicals & Chemical Products (except Products of Petroleum & Coal)

Year	(LPI)	(KPI)	(IKLR)	(KI)	(SI)	(TI)
1	2	3	4	5	6	7
1974-75	100.00	100.00	100.00	1.000	1.000	1.000
1975-76	106.18	98.32	108.00	1.003	1.004	1.006
1976-77	119.86	121.68	98.50	1.212	1.193	1.193
1977-78	110.93	113.47	97.76	1.128	1.111	1.107
1978-79	108.69	113.32	95.92	1.120	1.103	1.100
1979-80	104.30	108.90	95.77	1.076	1.060	1.055
1980-81	78.36	80.14	97.78	0.800	0.782	0.741
1981-82	68.37	63.71	107.31	0.649	0.641	0.606
1982-83	127.84	109.93	116.30	1.143	1.175	0.958
1983-84	125.62	94.33	133.16	1.012	1.039	0.856
1984-85	148.62	114.07	130.29	1.218	1.243	1.012
1985.86	114.40	88.05	129.92	0.939	0.959	0.749
Trend Growth Rate	**1.361 (0.753)**	**-1.402 (0.907)**	**2.802* (3.893)**	**-0.724 (0.458)**	**-0.405 (0.247)**	**-2.863 (1.928)**

Table-5.2 (A). 14 : Manufacture of Non-Metallic Mineral Products

Year	(LPI)	(KPI)	(IKLR)	(KI)	(SI)	(TI)
1	2	3	4	5	6	7
1974-75	100.00	100.00	100.00	1.000	1.000	1.000
1975-76	107.08	103.95	103.01	1.067	1.067	1.065
1976-77	113.96	94.94	120.03	1.114	1.112	1.103
1977-78	122.88	100.15	122.69	1.197	1.194	1.181
1978-79	138.61	122.47	113.18	1.365	1.366	1.345
1979-80	109.75	100.03	109.72	1.085	1.092	1.038
1980-81	96.53	95.84	100.71	0.965	0.968	0.910
1981-82	95.80	90.42	105.94	0.951	0.958	0.901
1982-83	136.80	102.46	133.52	1.317	1.349	1.193
1983-84	150.86	111.14	135.74	1.449	1.483	1.304
1984-85	149.50	86.50	172.84	1.379	1.321	1.200
1985-86	133.01	74.07	179.56	1.219	1.164	1.053
Trend Growth Rate	**2.623 (2.142)**	**-1.627 (1.684)**	**4.320* (3.809)**	**1.976 (1.749)**	**1.772 (1.535)**	**0.537 (0.484)**

Table-5.2 (A). 15 : Basic Metals & Alloys Industries

Year	*(LPI)*	*(KPI)*	*(IKLR)*	*(KI)*	*(SI)*	*(TI)*
1	2	3	4	5	6	7
1974-75	100.00	100.00	100.00	1.000	1.000	1.000
1975-76	118.42	121.85	97.19	1.197	1.195	1.180
1976-77	161.91	160.64	100.79	1.614	1.616	1.530
1977-78	172.29	170.59	100.99	1.716	1.718	1.624
1978-79	200.44	196.47	102.02	1.989	1.989	1.860
1979-80	146.63	146.97	99.77	1.468	1.481	1.298
1980-81	135.63	134.44	100.89	1.352	1.364	1.192
1981-82	134.58	140.52	95.77	1.368	1.374	1.201
1982-83	161.63	167.22	96.66	1.637	1.647	1.418
1983-84	187.76	185.27	101.34	1.868	1.882	1.601
1984-85	201.67	188.68	106.88	1.965	1.974	1.677
1985-86	183.12	159.32	114.94	1.733	1.724	1.461
Trend Growth Rate	**3.881**** **(2.574)**	**3.147** **(2.185)**	**0.712** **(1.936)**	**3.591**** **(2.439)**	**3.622**** **(2.468)**	**1.967** **(1.331)**

Table-5.2 (A). 16 : Manufacture of Metal Products and Parts (except Machinery and Transport Equipment)

Year	*(LPI)*	*(KPI)*	*(IKLR)*	*(KI)*	*(SI)*	*(TI)*
1	2	3	4	5	6	7
1974-75	100.00	100.00	100.00	1.000	1.000	1.000
1975-76	78.86	78.99	99.83	0.789	0.790	0.763
1976-77	78.10	69.56	112.27	0.733	0.738	0.717
1977-78	88.98	82.98	107.23	0.857	0.855	0.826
1978-79	95.18	87.53	108.74	0.909	0.908	0.875
1979-80	113.60	97.16	116.92	1.041	1.050	0.998
1980-81	105.23	78.71	133.70	0.891	0.896	0.854
1981-82	113.43	79.98	141.82	0.926	0.938	0.892
1982-83	104.61	71.38	146.57	0.837	0.848	0.804
1983-84	116.12	72.17	160.90	0.875	0.900	0.851
1984-85	134.62	85.71	157.06	1.030	1.054	0.988
1985-86	158.20	101.09	156.49	1.214	1.241	1.149
Trend Growth Rate	**4.978*** **(5.224)**	**-0.043** **(0.038)**	**5.023*** **(11.470)**	**1.961** **(1.890)**	**2.214** **(2.143)**	**1.700** **(1.633)**

Table-5.2 (A). 17 : Manufacturing of Machinery, Machine Tools and Parts (except Electrical)

Year	*(LPI)*	*(KPI)*	*(IKLR)*	*(KI)*	*(SI)*	*(TI)*
1	2	3	4	5	6	7
1974-75	100.00	100.00	100.00	1.000	1.000	1.000
1975-76	108.93	100.15	108.77	1.047	1.049	1.047
1976-77	147.82	121.90	121.26	1.346	1.367	1.308
1977-78	132.73	114.49	115.93	1.237	1.261	1.199
1978-79	215.81	173.25	124.56	1.939	2.001	1.730
1979-80	192.85	150.44	128.19	1.707	1.748	1.504
1980-81	137.98	116.66	118.28	1.273	1.330	1.063
1981-82	129.15	96.25	134.19	1.116	1.164	0.931
1982-83	168.66	134.74	125.18	1.511	1.557	1.210
1983-84	206.54	155.25	133.04	1.792	1.860	1.417
1984-85	196.17	142.04	138.11	1.669	1.726	1.315
1985-86	208.94	156.29	133.69	1.809	1.867	1.421
Trend Growth Rate	**5.409*** (3.223)**	**3.033 (2.041)**	**2.305* (5.430)**	**4.200** (2.671)**	**4.527** (2.868)**	**1.523 (0.980)**

Table-5.2 (A). 18 : Manufacture of Electrical Machinery, Apparatus, Appliances and Supplies & Parts

Year	*(LPI)*	*(KPI)*	*(IKLR)*	*(KI)*	*(SI)*	*(TI)*
1	2	3	4	5	6	7
1974-75	100.00	100.00	100.00	1.000	1.000	1.000
1975-76	217.41	230.99	94.12	2.203	2.187	1.802
1976-77	202.91	219.11	92.61	2.063	2.063	1.696
1977-78	212.62	239.36	88.83	2.180	2.213	1.819
1978-79	182.12	208.05	87.53	1.873	1.916	1.553
1979-80	190.73	222.00	85.91	1.969	2.026	1.641
1980-81	182.74	220.47	82.88	1.900	1.978	1.600
1981-82	211.73	246.48	85.90	2.186	2.256	1.806
1982-83	235.57	298.17	79.09	2.473	2.613	2.087
1983-84	355.57	380.03	93.56	3.607	3.652	2.714
1984-85	361.34	402.71	89.73	3.698	3.817	2.837
1985-86	356.21	421.11	84.59	3.688	3.914	2.913
Trend Growth Rate	**8.526* (4.477)**	**9.621* (5.311)**	**–0.999 (2.188)**	**8.749* (4.651)**	**9.256* (5.107)**	**7.338* (5.021)**

Table-5.2 (A).19 Manufacture of Transport Equipment & Parts

Year	(LPI)	(KPI)	(IKLR)	(KI)	(SI)	(TI)
1	2	3	4	5	6	7
1974-75	100.00	100.00	100.00	1.000	1.000	1.000
1975-76	213.26	151.65	140.63	1.958	2.043	1.687
1976-77	162.91	89.74	181.53	1.382	1.446	1.155
1977-78	150.74	90.69	166.21	1.316	1.358	1.085
1978-79	170.72	102.37	166.76	1.489	1.538	1.219
1979-80	181.87	150.12	121.15	1.738	1.736	1.391
1980-81	170.00	168.77	100.73	1.697	1.697	1.343
1981-82	149.13	168.72	88.39	1.530	1.511	1.178
1982-83	199.82	205.45	97.26	2.010	2.022	1.509
1983-84	161.63	175.21	92.25	1.644	1.659	1.204
1984-85	169.47	148.13	114.40	1.643	1.681	1.224
1985-86	170.09	137.73	123.49	1.617	1.668	1.217
Trend Growth Rate	**1.641 (1.044)**	**4.906** (2.463)**	**-3.112 (1.625)**	**2.516 (1.724)**	**2.387 (1.595)**	**0.375 (0.300)**

Table-5.2 (A). 20 : Other Manufacturing Industries

Year	(LPI)	(KPI)	(IKLR)	(KI)	(SI)
1	2	3	4	5	6
1974-75	100.00	100.00	100.00	1.000	1.000
1975-76	453.39	352.86	128.49	4.106	4.430
1976-77	121.16	84.41	143.53	1.045	0.753
1977-78	137.48	140.90	97.57	1.387	0.937
1978-79	139.11	110.38	126.03	1.270	0.828
1979-80	133.43	102.33	130.39	1.201	0.780
1980-81	131.14	91.59	143.18	1.132	0.741
1981-82	168.53	94.56	178.22	1.310	0.905
1982-83	262.18	177.06	148.08	2.229	1.474
1983-84	244.38	161.15	151.64	2.055	1.351
1984-85	151.80	55.98	271.16	0.933	0.188
1985-86	393.67	128.06	307.41	2.237	0.477
Trend Growth Rate	**4.989 (1.234)**	**-3.015 (0.781)**	**8.253* (4.610)**	**0.936 (0.242)**	**-9.957 (1.905)**

Source: Based on the ASI Reports: Various Issues.

Note : Figures in parentheses are t values of the estimates.

* Significant at 1 percent level of significance.

** Significant at 5 percent level of significance.

Appendix Table 5.2 (B) : Category-wise Indices of Partial Productivities, Capital Intensity and Total Factor Productivity: 1974-75 to 1985-86

Table-5.2 (B).1 : Category-I

Year	*Labour Productivity index (LPI)*	*Capital Productivity Index (KPI)*	*Index of Capital Labour ratio* (IKLR)	*Kendrick Index (KI)*	*Solow Index (SI)*	*Translog Index (TI)*
1	2	3	4	5	6	7
1974-75	100.00	100.00	100.00	1.000	1.000	1.000
1975-76	103.41	99.02	104.43	1.006	1.007	1.007
1976-77	124.27	119.00	104.43	1.209	1.210	1.192
1977-78	122.10	120.47	101.36	1.211	1.211	1.195
1978-79	125.39	123.07	101.88	1.239	1.240	1.222
1979-80	111.17	118.95	93.46	1.159	1.165	1.136
1980-81	90.21	87.04	103.65	0.882	0.879	0.842
1981-82	84.73	84.46	100.32	0.846	0.839	0.801
1982-83	128.43	114.07	112.59	1.191	1.232	1.090
1983-84	139.23	112.49	123.77	1.213	1.266	1.119
1984-85	150.76	123.38	122.19	1.325	1.380	1.216
1985-86	138.87	103.15	134.63	1.142	1.187	1.048
Trend Growth Rate	**2.359 (1.668)**	**0.074 (0.064)**	**2.283* (3.639)**	**0.861 (0.707)**	**1.293 (0.996)**	**-0.092 (0.075)**

Table-5.2 (B).2 : Category-II

Year	*(LPI)*	*(KPI)*	*(IKLR)*	*(KI)*	*(SI)*	*(TI)*
1	2	3	4	5	6	7
1974-75	100.00	100.00	100.00	1.000	1.000	1.000
1975-76	209.39	208.05	100.64	2.090	2.092	1.736
1976-77	178.97	185.89	96.27	1.810	1.847	1.511
1977-78	210.00	226.98	92.52	2.149	2.210	1.790
1978-79	191.72	198.26	76.70	1.937	1.951	1.577
1979-80	207.64	217.20	95.60	2.105	2.127	1.713
1980-81	200.16	209.56	95.51	2.030	2.051	1.651
1981-82	222.14	219.51	101.20	2.213	2.209	1.769
1982-83	236.55	250.54	94.42	2.407	2.439	1.953
1983-84	302.11	280.88	107.56	2.953	2.909	2.269
1984-85	309.51	284.41	108.83	3.014	2.957	2.305
1985-86	399.03	374.44	106.57	3.912	3.854	2.925
Trend Growth Rate	**8.528* (5.477)**	**7.615* (4.886)**	**0.848 (2.129)**	**8.242* (5.334)**	**7.983* (5.117)**	**6.477* (5.320)**

Table-5.2(B). 3 : Category-III

Year	*(LPI)*	*(KPI)*	*(IKLR)*	*(KI)*	*(SI)*	*(TI)*
1	2	3	4	5	6	7
1974-75	100.00	100.00	100.00	1.000	1.000	1.000
1975-76	95.96	95.05	100.95	0.956	0.956	0.955
1976-77	98.75	90.93	108.59	0.955	0.957	0.957
1977-78	104.98	97.78	107.36	1.021	1.021	1.020
1978-79	131.91	121.56	108.52	1.277	1.279	1.248
1979-80	136.70	118.22	115.64	1.288	1.281	1.254
1980-81	128.22	111.55	114.95	1.212	1.205	1.177
1981-82	118.72	97.24	122.09	1.093	1.086	1.058
1982-83	126.24	105.22	119.98	1.171	1.162	1.130
1983-84	137.73	109.94	125.28	1.254	1.249	1.210
1984-85	128.34	86.37	148.60	1.079	1.073	1.046
1985-86	149.11	96.62	154.32	1.230	1.231	1.187
Trend Growth Rate	**3.516*** **(4.869)**	**-0.095** **(0.104)**	**3.615*** **(8.410)**	**1.917**** **(2.411)**	**1.861**** **(2.347)**	**1.515** **(2.024)**

Table-5.2 (B). 4 : Category-IV

Year	*(LPI)*	*(KPI)*	*(IKLR)*	*(KI)*	*(SI)*	*(TI)*
1974-75	100.00	100.00	100.00	1.000	1.000	1.000
1975-76	112.49	107.96	104.20	1.113	1.115	1.110
1976-77	108.81	111.24	97.82	1.094	1.088	1.089
1977-78	122.29	128.81	94.94	1.238	1.233	1.228
1978-79	121.70	110.72	109.92	1.188	1.143	1.155
1979-80	112.04	97.13	115.35	1.080	1.034	1.045
1980-81	94.72	96.77	97.89	0.952	0.904	0.903
1981-82	99.26	97.69	101.61	0.989	0.941	0.939
1982-83	146.31	119.85	122.09	1.386	1.354	1.264
1983-84	168.83	106.43	158.64	1.475	1.445	1.352
1984-85	189.02	103.09	183.36	1.568	1.556	1.447
1985-86	197.99	98.27	201.48	1.584	1.582	1.470
Trend Growth Rate	**5.524*** **(3.685)**	**-0.578** **(0.750)**	**6.137*** **(4.530)**	**3.603**** **(3.124)**	**3.480**** **(2.669)**	**2.667**** **(2.312)**

Source : ASI Reports : Various Issues.

Note : Figures in parentheses are t value of the estimates.

* Significant at 1 percent level of significance.

** Significant at 5 percent level of significance.

Appendix Table-5.3 : Percentage Shares of Value Added and Employment in Totals of Organised Industrial Sector in U.P.

Category/Industry Group	*Gross Value Added*		*Employment*	
	1974-75	*1985-86*	*1974-75*	*1985-86*
1	2	3	4	5
1. Manufacture of chemicals & chemical products (except products of petroleum& coal)	14.34	10.58	5.11	5.53
2. Basic metals & alloys industries	4.72	5.19	5.80	5.85
3. Manufactue of wool, silk & synthetic fibre textiles	3.75	2.66	2.31	1.54
Category I	**22.80**	**18.44**	**13.21**	**12.93**
4. Manufacture of electrical machinery, apparatus, appliances, and supplies and parts	6.39	20.38	5.37	8.09
5. Manufacture of rubber, plastic, petroleum and coal products	0.60	7.35	0.71	2.05
6. Manufacture of edible oil & vanaspati ghee	1.45	1.62	1.25	0.70
7. Other manufacturing industries	0.51	1.42	0.79	0.94
Category II	**8.95**	**30.77**	**8.13**	**11.78**
8. Manufacture of paper & paper products & printing, publishing & allied industries	3.48	3.46	3.84	4.08
9. Manufacture of alcohol, beverages, tobacco and tobacco products	1.76	1.95	1.60	1.29
10. Manufacture of machinery, machine tools and parts (except electrical)	2.72	4.03	3.03	3.60
11. Manufacture of cotton textiles	10.38	7.56	11.75	12.90
12. Manufacture of food products (except sugar, khandsari & gur)	2.91	4.50	2.86	3.75

Appendix Table-5.3 (Contd...)

1	2	3	4	5
13. Manufacture of textile products (including wearing apparel other than footwear)	1.41	0.67	1.13	1.05
Category III	**22.67**	**22.17**	**24.20**	**26.67**
14. Manufacture of metal products and parts (except machinery and transport equipment)	3.21	2.29	3.41	2.58
15. Manufacture of non-metallic mineral products	2.37	1.91	6.63	6.75
16. Manufacture of jute, hemp and mesta textiles	0.62	0.77	1.12	0.99
17. Manufacture of sugar, khandsari and gur	9.43	10.84	29.47	24.88
18. Manufacture of transport equipment and parts	2.58	4.73	4.06	7.37
19. Manufacture of wood and wood products, furnitures and fixtures	0.15	0.10	0.52	0.37
20. Manufacture of leather and leather and fur products (except repair)	1.30	1.73	1.58	2.25
Category IV	**19.66**	**22.38**	**46.78**	**45.19**
Total Manufacturing*	**100.0**	**100.0**	**100.0**	**100.0**

Source : ASI Reports : 1974-75 and 1985-86.

Note : * Including repair services and Miscellaneous industries.

Appendix Table-5.4 : The Contribution of Factor Inputs and Increased Efficiency to Economic Growth : 1950-65 (measured in percentage points)

	Countries	*Growth Rate (percent)*	*The Contribution of*		
			Human Resources	*Non-Residential Capital*	*Grwth due to Changes in Efficiency*
	1	2	3	4	5
1.	Argentina	3.20	1.05	2.80	-0.65
2.	Brazil	5.20	2.35	3.05	-0.20
3.	Ceylon	3.60	1.60	2.00	-0.20
4.	Chile	4.00	1.05	2.45	0.50
5.	Colombia	4.70	1.80	2.90	-0.10
6.	Egypt	4.35	1.55	2.80	1.15
7.	Ghana	4.20	1.50	3.00	-0.30
8.	Greece	6.40	1.30	2.85	2.25
9.	India	3.50	2.35	2.35	-1.20
10.	Israel	10.70	3.20	5.60	1.90
11.	Malaya	3.50	2.05	1.80	-0.35
12.	Mexico	6.10	2.45	3.20	0.45
13.	Pakistan	3.70	1.70	1.85	0.15
14.	Peru	5.60	1.20	3.40	1.00
15.	Phillippines	5.00	2.40	2.55	0.05
16.	South Korea	6.20	2.90	2.20	1.10
17.	Spain	7.50	1.20	3.80	2.50
18.	Taiwan	8.50	1.70	3.50	3.30
19.	Thailand	6.30	2.70	7.40	0.20
20.	Turkey	5.20	1.75	2.50	0.95
21.	Venezuela	6.70	3.10	4.65	-1.05
22.	Yugoslavia	7.10	1.70	4.85	0.55
	Average	5.55	1.94	3.06	0.55

Source : A Maddison, 'Economic Progress and Policy in Developing Countries' Table 11.11, p.53 and reprinted in A.P. Thirlwall, 'Growth and Development : With Special Reference to Developing Economies', Third edn., ELBS/Macmillan, 1983, Table-2.1, p.77.

Appendix-5.5 : Category/Industry Group-wise Estimates of the Cobb-Douglas Production Function : 1974-75 to 1985-86 Model-IV

No. of Observation : 12 | Dependent Variable : Log (V/L)

Category/Industry Group	Constant	Log K/L	Log L	t	R^2	$\bar{R}^2$	SE	F Value	D.W.
1	2	3	4	5	6	7	8	9	10
1. Manufacture of chemicals & chemical products (except products of petroleum & coal)	-40.479	2.039** (2.582)	2.603 (1.597)	-0.122 (-1.836)	0.455	0.334	0.155	2.241	2.397
2. Basic metals and alloys industries	-143.67	7.732* (4.471)	6.160* (4.245)	-0.176* (-3.548)	0.841	0.805	0.096	11.428*	2.303
3. Manufacture of wool, silk & synthetic fibre textiles	-25.156	2.030** (3.231)	1.361** (2.675)	-0.084*** (-2.122)	0.640	0.560	0.151	4.801**	2.969
Category I	**-40.167**	**2.519** (2.326)**	**1.847 (1.329)**	**-0.083 (-1.373)**	**0.560**	**0.462**	**0.120**	**3.393**	**1.174**
4. Manufacture of electrical machinery, apparatus, appliances & supplies and parts	-4.667	1.261 (0.201)	-0.061 (-0.009)	0.098 (0.331)	0.704	0.638	0.230	–	–
5. Manufacture of rubber, plastic, petroleum and coal products	-0.152	-0.392 (-0.620)	1.621** (2.320)	-0.018 (-0.280)	0.563	0.465	0.365	3.430	1.863
6. Manufacture of edible oil and vanaspati ghee	56.976	-1.689 (-0.869)	-3.477*** (-1.882)	0.098 (0.906)	0.637	0.557	0.224	4.673**	1.997
7. Other manufacturing industries	8.772	0.451 (0.593)	-0.532 (-0.431)	0.031 (0.343)	0.196	0.017	0.433	0.648	2.478
Category II	**-112.505**	**5.673** (3.044)**	**5.421** (3.161)**	**-0.222** (-2.315)**	**0.878**	**0.851**	**0.114**	**20.843***	**1.429**
8. Manufacture of paper & paper products & printing, publishing & allied industries	-2.189	0.955*** (1.948)	0.168 (0.185)	-0.067 (-1.483)	0.436	0.311	0.111	2.071	1.450
9. Manufacture of alcohol, beverages, tobacco & tobacco products	49.827	-1.867 (-1.726)	-2.414*** (-2.226)	0.178** (2.598)	0.661	0.585	0.143	5.152**	2.738
10. Manufacture of machinery, machine tools & parts (except electrical)	-65.111	4.339* (4.725)	2.930* (3.849)	-0.150* (-3.360)	0.866	0.836	0.099	16.755*	1.876
11. Manufacture of cotton textiles	10.336	-0.465 (-0.165)	0.306 (0.104)	0.023 (0.148)	0.268	0.105	0.141	0.978	1.048

Appendix Table-5.5 (Contd...)

	1	2	3	4	5	6	7	8	9	10
12.	Manufacture of food products (except sugar, khandsari & gur)	-28.353	2.240** (2.377)	1.476 (1.251)	-0.047 (-0.706)	0.910	0.890	0.067	26.305*	2.727
13.	Manufacture of textile products (including wearing apparel other than footwear)	-7.873	1.105*** (2.182)	0.838 (1.714)	-0.139 (-1.781)	0.440	0.315	0.296	2.091	1.079
	Category III	**-13.075**	**0.493 (0.496)**	**1.462 (1.101)**	**-0.030 (-0.399)**	**0.757**	**0.703**	**0.073**	**8.429***	**1.366**
14.	Manufacture of metal products and parts (except machinery & transport equipment)	-1.449	0.345 (0.159)	0.694 (0.470)	0.041 (0.474)	0.760	0.707	0.100	8.439*	0.669
15.	Manufacture of non-metallic mineral products	-12.106	1.176** (2.849)	0.826 (1.423)	-0.052 (-1.430)	0.677	0.605	0.095	5.575**	1.293
16.	Manufactue of jute, hemp & mesta textiles	19.9414	-0.662 (-1.688)	-0.583 (1.600)	0.110* (4.234)	0.809	0.766	0.130	11.271*	1.460
17.	Manufacture of sugar, khandsari & gur	54.606	-1.861 (-0.975)	-2.477 (-1.489)	0.238 (1.367)	0.721	0.659	0.193	6.805**	1.239
18.	Manfacture of transport equipment & parts	-12.180	1.185* (3.420)	0.923** (2.893)	-0.046 (-1.652)	0.608	0.521	0.117	4.138**	1.341
19.	Manufacture of wood & wood products, furniture & fixtures	26.845	-0.760 (-0.900)	-1.501 (-1.842)	0.066*** (1.927)	0.796	0.751	0.105	10.427*	4.479
20.	Manufacture of leather & leather & fur products (except repair)	-19.269	1.794 (0.886)	1.246 (0.787)	-0.122 (-0.605)	0.417	0.288	0.214	1.911	0.852
	Category IV	**5.588**	**0.653 (0.367)**	**-0.295 (-0.165)**	**0.021 (0.147)**	**0.883**	**0.857**	**0.088**	**20.053***	**1.403**
	Total Manufacturing	**-23.640**	**2.076 (1.774)**	**0.821 (0.606)**	**-0.065 (-0.814)**	**0.855**	**0.823**	**0.083**	**15.876***	**1.774**

Source : Based on ASI Reports : Various Issues.

Note : Figures in parentheses are t values of the estimates.

V : value added : L : labour ; K: capital; and t : time.

* Significant at 1 percrnt of significance.

** Significant at 5 percent of significance.

*** Significant at 10 percent of significance.

Appendix Table-5.6 : Category/Industry Group-wise Estimates of Cobb-Douglas Production Function : 1974-75 to 1985-86-Model V

No. of Observation : 12 | Dependent Variable : Log (V/L)

	Category/Industry Group	*Constant*	*Log K/L*	*t*	R^2	$\bar{R}^2$	*SE*	*F Value*	*D.W.*
	1	2	3	4	5	6	7	8	9
1.	Manufacture of chemicals and chemical products	-5.477	1.295*** (1.884)	-0.022 (-0.910)	0.302	0.232	0.176	1.944	3.712
2.	Manufacture of wool, silk and synthetic fibre textiles	3.769	0.512 (1.488)	0.010 (0.407)	0.357	0.293	0.203	2.503	2.824
	Category I	**-5.485**	**1.290*** (2.204)**	**-0.006 (-0.332)**	**0.474**	**0.421**	**0.131**	**4.047**	**1.532**
3.	Other manufacturing industries	3.619	0.533 (0.756)	0.006 (0.094)	0.179	0.097	0.438	0.982	2.298
	Category II	-	-	-	-	-	-	-	-
4.	Manufacture of paper & paper products & printing, publishing & allied industries	-0.752	0.974*** (2.138)	-0.063 (-1.626)	0.434	0.378	0.111	3.463	1.571
5.	Manufacture of alcohol, beverages, tobacco & tobacco products	6.326	0.290 (0.513)	0.035 (1.260)	0.473	0.420	0.178	4.033	1.656
6.	Manufacture of machinery, machine tools & parts (except electrical)	-12.374	2.004*** (1.892)	0.007 (0.251)	0.639	0.603	0.160	7.960**	1.867
7.	Manufacture of cotton textiles	16.617	-0.747 (-1.064)	0.040 (1.756)	0.267	0.193	0.141	1.639	1.008
8.	Manufacture of textile products (including wearing apparel other than footwear)	2.199	0.749 (1.484)	-0.045 (0.741)	0.257	0.182	0.341	1.553	0.726
	Category III	-	-	-	-	-	-	-	-
9.	Manufacture of non-metallic mineral products	1.024	0.708** (2.706)	-0.004 (-0.281)	0.604	0.565	0.105	6.873**	1.547
10.	Manufacture of sugar, khandsari & gur	-0.702	0.935** (2.598)	-0.016 (-0.441)	0.652	0.617	0.214	8.410*	1.127
11.	Manufacture of wood & wood products, furniture and fixtures	0.608	0.761* (3.922)	0.007 (0.514)	0.720	0.691	0.124	11.535*	4.088

Appendix Table-5.6 (Contd...)

	1	2	3	4	5	6	7	8	9
12.	Manufacture of leather & leather & fur products	5.965	0.258 (0.486)	0.035 (1.095)	0.377	0.315	0.222	2.725	0.993
	Category IV	**-0.830**	**0.943*** **(5.101)**	**-0.002** **(-0.179)**	**0.882**	**0.871**	**0.088**	**33.717***	**1.440**
	Total Manufacturing	**-5.652**	**1.386*** **(5.243)**	**-0.017** **(-1.304)**	**0.849**	**0.834**	**0.085**	**25.319***	**1.838**

Source : Based on ASI Reports : Various Issues.

Note : Figures in parentheses are t values of the estimates.

V : value added; L : labour; K : capital; and t : time.

* Significant at 1 percent level of significance.

** Signifcant at 5 percent level of significance.

*** Significant at 10 percent level of significance.

Appendix Table-6.1 : Region-wise Indices of Patial Productivities, Capital Intensity and Total Factor Productivity: 1974-75 to 1985-86

Table-6.1.1 : Uttar Pradesh (Combined)

Year	*Labour Productivity Index (LPI)*	*Capital Productivity Index (KPI)*	*Index of Capital Labour Ratio (IKLR)*	*Kendrick Index (KI)*	*Solow Index (SI)*	*Translog Index (TI)*
1	2	3	4	5	6	7
1974-75	100.0	100.0	100.0	1.000	1.000	1.000
1975-76	91.59	91.15	100.49	0.914	0.913	0.910
1976-77	96.82	98.25	98.55	0.976	0.973	0.968
1977-78	101.79	106.71	95.39	1.043	1.037	1.033
1978-79	107.26	105.93	101.26	1.066	1.059	1.054
1979-80	101.94	98.89	103.09	1.004	0.996	0.992
1980-81	80.66	84.55	95.40	0.826	0.819	0.788
1981-82	82.69	78.89	104.82	0.807	0.813	0.783
1982-83	117.76	98.76	119.24	1.072	1.119	1.019
1983-84	142.79	97.65	146.23	1.154	1.241	1.116
1984-85	148.81	92.47	160.94	1.133	1.231	1.109
1985-86	195.13	112.71	173.13	1.419	1.567	1.365
Trend Growth Rate	**5.074** (2.99)**	**-0.009 (0.010)**	**5.084* (4.76)**	**2.145 (1.844)**	**3.099** (2.343)**	**1.767 (1.459)**

Table-6.1.2 : Western Region

Year	*(LPI)*	*(KPI)*	*(IKLR)*	*(KI)*	*(SI)*	*(TI)*
1	2	3	4	5	6	7
1974-75	100.0	100.0	100.0	1.000	1.000	1.000
1975-76	83.29	84.48	98.58	0.840	0.842	0.825
1976-77	86.14	87.84	98.07	0.872	0.873	0.855
1977-78	87.38	94.61	92.35	0.917	0.911	0.895
1978-79	86.18	90.64	95.08	0.889	0.883	0.868
1979-80	86.74	88.00	98.56	0.875	0.871	0.858
1980-81	67.71	74.32	91.11	0.716	0.712	0.676
1981-82	75.64	72.46	104.39	0.737	0.751	0.710
1982-83	101.07	99.85	101.25	1.003	1.014	0.927
1983-84	120.46	93.91	128.27	1.027	1.065	0.970
1984-85	121.96	88.68	137.53	0.991	1.035	0.944
1985-86	168.45	113.36	148.59	1.298	1.382	1.203
Trend Growth Rate	**4.141** (2.326)**	**0.601 (0.560)**	**3.519* (3.728)**	**1.829 (1.428)**	**2.359 (1.728)**	**1.218 (0.952)**

Table - 6.1.3 Central Region

Year	(LPI)	(KPI)	(IKLR)	(KI)	(SI)	(TI)
1	2	3	4	5	6	7
1974-75	100.0	100.0	100.0	1.000	1.000	1.000
1975-76	86.75	78.99	109.81	0.835	0.829	0.830
1976-77	89.10	85.30	104.46	0.876	0.860	0.863
1977-78	106.64	102.95	103.59	1.052	1.031	1.020
1978-79	111.80	104.23	107.26	1.087	1.064	1.052
1979-80	110.55	100.34	110.18	1.063	1.040	1.030
1980-81	86.47	82.15	105.26	0.847	0.827	0.788
1981-82	93.61	79.29	118.06	0.874	0.879	0.832
1982-83	89.56	71.04	126.07	0.812	0.827	0.786
1983-84	114.35	78.33	145.99	0.968	1.039	0.954
1984-85	129.80	81.99	158.32	1.056	1.156	1.053
1985-86	122.81	76.89	159.73	0.995	1.090	0.992
Trend Growth Rate	**2.114 (2.003)**	**-2.086 (2.225)**	**4.289* (6.175)**	**0.204 (0.218)**	**1.181 (1.161)**	**0.168 (0.166)**

Table 6.1.4 : Eastern Region

Year	(LPI)	(KPI)	(IKLR)	(KI)	(SI)	(TI)
1	2	3	4	5	6	7
1974-75	100.0	100.0	100.0	1.000	1.000	1.000
1975-76	115.19	118.41	97.28	1.165	1.163	1.153
1976-77	119.61	126.22	94.77	1.223	1.220	1.210
1977-78	145.45	144.79	100.47	1.452	1.450	1.411
1978-79	162.57	151.29	107.46	1.577	1.565	1.516
1979-80	185.19	128.30	105.36	1.323	1.318	1.250
1980-81	99.44	106.01	93.80	1.021	1.030	0.918
1981-82	78.63	82.51	95.30	0.802	0.810	0.699
1982-83	200.15	123.87	161.58	1.597	1.978	1.230
1983-84	255.52	127.54	200.35	1.808	2.28	1.390
1984-85	263.59	116.63	226.00	1.735	2.192	1.343
1985-86	395.68	161.55	244.93	2.477	3.193	1.822
Trend Growth Rate	**9.902* (3.219)**	**0.851 (0.530)**	**8.975* (4.697)**	**5.195** (2.328)**	**8.061* (3.06)**	**1.989 (0.936)**

Table 6.1.5 : Uttaranchal

Year	(LPI)	(KPI)	(IKLR)	(KI)	(SI)	(TI)
1	2	3	4	5	6	7
1974-75	100.0	100.0	100.0	1.000	1.000	1.000
1975-76	131.78	135.18	97.48	1.330	1.327	1.286
1976-77	230.69	225.52	102.29	2.289	2.295	1.971
1977-78	84.94	137.66	61.70	0.981	1.486	0.603
1978-79	128.75	111.88	115.08	1.223	1.605	0.691
1979-80	99.18	95.35	104.02	0.978	1.292	0.530
1980-81	147.58	144.92	101.84	1.466	1.928	0.744
1981-82	119.36	114.10	104.62	1.175	1.533	0.578
1982-83	151.28	134.55	112.44	1.450	1.910	0.702
1983-84	162.02	136.50	118.70	1.521	2.008	0.736
1984-85	202.50	141.13	143.49	1.757	2.346	0.839
1985-86	172.56	110.75	155.81	1.443	1.902	0.676
Trend Growth Rate	**3.722 (1.559)**	**-0.572 (0.291)**	**4.319** (2.859)**	**2.092 (0.977)**	**4.574** (2.596)**	**-4.935 (1.778)**

Table 6.1.6 : BundelKhand

Year	(LPI)	(KPI)	(IKLR)	(KI)	(SI)	(TI)
1	2	3	4	5	6	7
1974-75	100.0	100.0	100.0	1.000	1.000	1.000
1975-76	112.24	109.51	102.50	1.121	1.121	1.115
1976-77	135.40	132.23	102.40	1.353	1.353	1.324
1977-78	147.88	71.85	205.81	1.413	1.312	1.281
1978-79	220.74	105.04	210.14	2.105	1.952	1.785
1979-80	183.33	82.26	222.87	1.739	1.562	1.411
1980-81	174.45	83.89	207.93	1.665	1.520	1.367
1981-82	168.83	80.39	210.02	1.610	1.468	1.320
1982-83	274.30	131.34	208.85	2.618	2.386	1.962
1983-84	239.45	122.05	196.20	2.297	2.152	1.753
1984-85	193.70	85.83	225.68	1.835	1.591	1.294
1985-86	323.82	132.20	244.94	3.044	2.626	1.919
Trend Growth Rate	**8.777* (5.521)**	**0.896 (0.469)**	**7.812* (4.115)**	**8.231* (5.329)**	**6.917* (4.483)**	**4.167** (2.993)**

Source : Based on A.S.I. Reports: Various Issues.

Notes : Figures in parentheses are t values of the estimates.

* Significant at 1 percent level of significance.

** Significant at 5 percent level of significance.

Appendix Table - 6.2 : Region-wise Wage Rates, Rates of Return on Capital and Shares of Labour in Value Added-Growth Rates : 1974-75 to 1985-86

Region	*Wage Rate*	*Rate of Return on Capital*	*Share of Labour in Value Added*
1	2	3	4
Western	3.19*	1.16	-0.52
	(4.535)	(0.541)	
Central	3.90*	-5.78	3.05
	(5.988)	(1.517)	
Eastern	7.03*	2.38	-2.76
	(6.346)	(0.477)	
Uttaranchal	5.690*	-2.177	5.30
	(3.637)	(0.473)	
Bundelkhand	3.90*	24.87*	-2.06
	(7.090)	(3.354)	
U.P. Combined	**4.25***	**0.57**	**-0.85**
	(6.040)	**(0.240)**	

Source : Based on ASI. Reports : Various Issues.

Notes : 1. Cols. 2-3 : Trend growth rates; Col 4: Average Annual Growth Rates.

2. Figures in parentheses are t values of the estimates.

* Significant at 1 percent level of significance.

Appendix - Table 6.3 Region-wise Estimates of the Cobb-Douglas Production Function for Organised Industrial Sector 1974-75 to 85-86 - Model IV

No. of Observations : 12 *Dependent Variable : Log (V/L)*

Region	*Constant*	*Log (K/L)*	*Log L*	*t*	*R*	$\bar{R}^2$	*SE*	*F Value*	*D.W*
1	2	3	4	5	6	7	8	9	10
Western	-4.543	1.458 (1.225)	-0.151 (-0.128)	-0.005 (-0.066)	0.824	0.785	0.104	12.479*	2.210
Central	30.019	-0.400 (-0.383)	-1.456 (-1.160)	0.069 (0.985)	0.511	0.402	0.099	2.782	2.022
Eastern	10.121	0.983 (1.521)	-1.018 (-0.706)	0.009 (0.165)	0.891	0.867	0.157	21.889*	1.232
Uttaranchal	17.238	0.077 (0.090)	0.949 (-1.051)	0.069 (0.974)	0.498	0.387	0.211	2.649	1.596
Bundelkhand	-1.515	0.171 (0.573)	0.957 (0.829)	0.016 (0.265)	0.801	0.757	0.156	10.756*	2.541
U.P. Combined	**-10.507**	**1.565***** **(1.934)**	**0.224** **(0.200)**	**-0.033** **(-0.505)**	**0.889**	**0.864**	**0.086**	**21.413***	**1.623**

Source : Based on A.S.I. Reports : Various Issues.

Notes : Figures in parentheses are t values of the estimates.

V : value added; L : labour; K : capital ; and t : time.

* Significant at 1 percent level of significance.

*** Significant at 10 percent level of significance.

Appendix Table-6.4 : Region-wise Estimates of the Cobb-Douglas Production Function for Organised Industrial Sector : 1974-75 to 85-86 - Model V

No. of Observations : 12 *Dependent Variable : Log (V/L)*

Region	*Constant*	*Log (K/L)*	R^2	$\bar{R}^2$	*SE*	*F Value*	*D.W.*
Western	-5.360	1.354* (6.713)	0.804	0.804	0.109	40.966	1.727
Central	3.347	0.542** (2.864)	0.427	0.427	0.107	7.455	1.492
Eastern	-4.026	1.194* (8.700)	0.873	0.873	0.170	68.807	1.075
Uttaranchal	-0.591	0.866** (2.920)	0.437	0.437	0.224	7.754	1.745
Bundelkhand	0.581	0.817* (4.408)	0.639	0.639	0.210	17.666	2.124
U.P. Combined	**-2.987**	**1.124* (8.351)**	**0.864**	**0.864**	**0.096**	**63.405**	**1.325**

Source : Based on A.S.I. Reports : Various Issues.

Notes : Figures in parentheses are t values of the estimates.

V : value added; L : labour; K : capital.

* Significant at 1 percent level of significance.

** Significant at 5 percent level of significance.

Appendix Table - 6.5 : List of Backward Districts in Uttar Pradesh

Category - A	*Category - B*	*Category - C*
1. Banda*	1. Ballia	1. Azamgarh
2. Fatehpur*	2. Basti	2. Badaun
3. Hamirpur*	3. Faizabad	3. Bahraich
4. Jalaun*	4. Jhansi	4. Barabanki
5. Jaunpur*	5. Rae Bareli	5. Bulandshahr
6. Sultanpur*	6. Lalitpur	6. Deoria
7. Kanpur (Dehat)*		7. Etah
8. Almora		8. Etawah
9. Chamoli*		9. Farrukhabad
10. Pauri Garhwal*		10. Ghazipur
11. Tehri Garhwal*		11. Gonda
12. Uttar Kashi*		12. Hardoi
13. Pithoragarh		13. Mainpuri
14. Dehradun		14. Mathura
15. Nainital		15. Moradabad
		16. Pilibhit
		17. Pratapgarh
		18. Rampur
		19. Shahj ahanpur
		20. Sitapur
		21. Unnao

Source : Government of Uttar Pradesh, Draft Annual Plan, 1987-88, Vol.II, p.168.

Note : 1. * Zero Industry Districts.

2. Kanpur (Dehat) is excluded from our analysis owing to non-availability of data.

Appendix Table-6.6 : Industrial Base of Districts in Uttar Pradesh : 1985-86

Districts	*Industries with Iij > 1*
1	2
Agra (15)	Manufacture of edible oil and vanaspati ghee (7.88); leather and leather and fur products (6.30); non-metallic mineral products (8.51); basic metals and alloys industries (2.41); machinery, machine tools and parts (except electrical) (2.45); other manufacturing industries (1.79); repair services (including repair of motor, motor cycles and scooter) (1.42).
Aligarh (14)	Manufacture of food products (1.13); edible oil and vanaspati ghee (17.89); cotton textiles (3.38); paper and paper products and printing, publishing and allied industries (3.27); non-metallic mineral products (1.77); metal products (except machinery and transport equipment) (7.42); trasport equipment and parts (1.97); repair services (1.95).
Bareilly (8)	Manufacture of food products (2.29); sugar, khandsari and gur (1.37).
Bijnor (4)	Manufacture of sugar, khandsari and gur (4.22).
Badaun (1)	Manufacture of sugar, khandsari and gur (1.51).
Bulandshahr (10)	Manufacture of paper and paper products and printing, publishing and allied industries (1.57); non-metallic mineral products (2.26); basic metals and alloys (1.32); metal products (except machinery and transport equipment) (1.22); repair services (1.28).
Etah (1)	Manufacture of metal products (except machinery and transport equipment (3.13).
Etwah (2)	Manufacture of food products (17.48); manufacture of metal products (except machinery and transport equipment) (1.44).
Farrukhabad (2)	Manufacture of chemicals and chemical products (except products of petroleum and coal) (1.24).
Mainpuri (14)	Manufacture of food products (4.99); edible oil and vanaspati ghee (6.82); paper and paper products and printing, publishing and allied industries (1.06); non-metallic mineral products (6.67).
Mathura (9)	Manufacture of textile products (including wearing apparel other than footwear) (1.26); basic metals and alloys (2.05); metal products (except machinery and transport equipment) (5.33); other manufacturing industries (1.89).
Meerut (14)	Manufacture of sugar, khandsari and gur (1.88); cotton textiles (3.60); rubber, plastic, petrolem and coal products (10.79); electrical machinery, apparatus, appliance and supplies and parts (1.15); other manufacturing industries (4.93).
Ghaziabad (18)	Manufacture of cotton textile (2.56); textile products (including wearing apparel other than footwear) (4.36); wood and wood products, furniture and fixtures (7.66); rubber, plastic, petroleum and coal products (2.64); chemicals and chemical products (1.97); basic metals and alloys (2.82); metal products (except machinery

1	2
	and transport equipment) (2.83); machinery, machine tools and parts (except electrical) (3.97); electrical machinery, apparatus, appliances and supplies and parts (2.89); transport equipment and parts (4.31).
Moradabad (8)	Manufacture of sugar, khandsari and gur (3.21); metal products and parts (except machinery and transport equipment) (3.49).
Muuzzafarnagar (11)	Manufacture of sugar, khandsari and gur (3.60); basic metals and alloys (1.66); other manufacturing industries (1.75).
Pilibhit (2)	Manufacture of food products (1.38); sugar, khandsari and gur (4.27).
Rampur (4)	Manufacture of paper and paper products, printing, publishing and allied industries (1.17).
Saharanpur (3)	Manufacture of food products (2.14); sugar, khandsari and gur (1.38); paper and paper products, printing, publishing and allied industries (2.05).
Shahjahanpur (3)	Manufacture of food products (6.00), sugar, khandsari and gur (2.83).
Barabanki (2)	Manufacture of leather and leather and fur products (1.88).
Fatehpur (1)	Manufacture of food products (21.37).
Kanpur (17)	Manufacture of food products (1.09); cotton textiles (13.52); jute, hemp and mesta textiles (8.41); leather and leather and fur products (4.08); chemicals and chemical products (except products of petroleum and coal) (1.48); metal products (except machinery and transport equipment) (1.30); manufacture of machinery, machine tools and parts (except electrical (1.44); other manufacturing industries (2.41); repair services (2.55).
Kheri (2)	Manufacture of sugar, khandsari and gur (4.48).
Lucknow (13)	Manufacture of paper and paper products, printing, publishing and allied industries (3.55); chemicals and chemical products (except products of petroleum and coal) (1.42); basic metals and alloys (1.51); manufacture of transport equipment and parts (7.47); other manufacturing industries (3.11); repair services (2.34).
Rae Bareli (4)	Manufacture of cotton textiles (6.76); electrical machinery, apparatus, appliance and supplies and parts (12.64).
Sitapur (4)	Manufacture of sugar, khandsari and gur (3.09); edible oil and vanaspati ghee (2.50); cotton textiles (1.04).
Unnao (5)	Manufacture of wool, silk and synthetic fibre textiles (23.06); leather and leather and fur products (12.52); basic metals and alloys (6.83).
Allahabad (11)	Manufacture of cotton textile (3.30); paper and paper products, printing, publishing and allied industries (3.34); non-metallic mineral products (1.14); basic metals and alloys (1.91); electrical machinery, apparatus, appliances and supplies and parts (5.08); repair services (1.57).

1	2
Azamgarh (6)	Manufacture of cotton textile (2.85); repair services (4.13).
Bahraich (1)	Manufacture of food products (except sugar, khandsari and gur) (9.13).
Basti (2)	Manufacture of sugar, khandsari and gur (1.93); rubber, plastic, petrol and coal products (4.65).
Deoria (1)	Manufacture of sugar, khandsari and gur (4.36).
Faizabad	Manufacture of food products (1.66).
Ghazipur (1)	Repair services (2.61).
Gonda (2)	Manufacture of food products (3.43); sugar, khandsari and gur (3.40).
Gorakhpur (10)	Manufacture of wood and wood products, furnitures and fixtures (8.10); paper and paper products, printing, publishing and allied industries (1.5); manufacure of chemical and chemical products (3.29); basic metals and alloys (2.02); repair services (1.70).
Janupur (3)	Manufacture of texile products (including wearing apparel other than footwear) (5.21); basic metals and alloys (3.60); machinery, machine tools and parts (except electrical) (6.70).
Mirzapur (4)	Manufacture of textile products (including wearing apparel other than footwear) (8.40); non metallic mineral products (3.23).
Varanasi (14)	Manufacturing of wool, silk and synthetic fibre textiles (27.66); textile products (including wearing apparel other than footwear) (6.63); paper and paper products, printing, publishing and allied industries (1.06); chemical and chemical products (except products of petroleum and coal) (1.61); machinery, machine tools and parts (except electrical) (1.63); electrical machinery, apparatus, appliances and supplies and parts (1.84); other manufacturing industries (1.44); repair services (1.78).
Almora (1)	Manufacture of chemicals and chemical products (except products of petroleum and coal) (8.04).
Dehradun (5)	Manufacture of paper and paper products, printing, publsihing and allied industries (2.38); chemical and chemical products (except products of petroleum anc coal) (13.05); electrical machinery, apparatus, appliances and supplies and parts (2.01); repair services (2.32).
P. Gharwal (1)	Manufacture of food products (15.16).
Nainital (7)	Manufacture of food products (2.92); sugar, khandsari and gur (1.38); cotton textiles (7.46); paper and paper products, printing, publishing and allied industries (2.91); repair services (3.11).
Banda (1)	Manufacture of food products (4.14).

Source : Based on A.S.I. Reports : 1985-86.

Note : 1. Figures in parentheses against the district name indicate the total number of industry groups for which data is available.

2. Figures in parentheses against names of industry groups are the respective Iij's (location quotents).

Bibliography

Abramovitz, M., 'Resource and Output Trends in the United States since 1870', *American Economic Review, Paper and Proceedings*, Vol.46, No.2, May, 1956.

Ahluwalia, I.J., *Industrial Growth in India: Stagnation SInce the Mid-Sixties*, Oxford University Press, Delhi, 1985.

Ahluwalia, I.J., 'Industrial Growth in India: Problems and Prospects', *Journal of Development Economics*, Vol. 23, 1986.

Ahluwalia, I.J., 'Role of Policy in Industrial Development', in P.R. Brahmananda and V.R. Panchmukhi (eds.), *The Development Process of the Indian Economy*, Himalaya Publishing House, Bombay, 1987.

Alai-Parviz, D., 'Trends in Productivity Growth across Large Scale Manufacturing Industries in India, 1973/74-1978-79' *Indian Economic Review* Vol. 22, No. 2, July-Dec. 1987.

Appavadhanulu, V., 'Firm Size and Saving Rate in Inda', *Indian Economic Review*, Vol. 9, October, 1974.

Arrow, K., 'The Economic Implications of Learning by Doing', *Review of Economic Studies*, Vol.29, No.3, June, 1962.

Arrow, K., Chenery, H.B., Minhas B.S. and Solow, R.M., 'Capital-Labour Substitution and Economic Efficiency', *Review of Economics and Statistics*, Vol. 43, No.3, August, 1961.

Aukrust, O. and Bjerke, J., 'Real Capital and Economic Growth in Norway, 1900-1956', in *The Measurement of National Wealth*, Income and Wealth, Series VIII, Bowes and Bowes, London, 1959.

Baer, W., 'Technology, Employment and Development : Empirical Findings', *World Development*, Vol. 4, No.2, 1976.

Banerji, A., 'Productivity Growth and Factor Substitution in Indian Manufacturing', *Indian Economic Review*, (New Series), Vol.6, No.1, April, 1971.

Banerji, A., *Capital Intensity and Productivity in Indian Industry*, Macmillan, Delhi, 1975.

Baran, P., *Political Economy of Growth*, New York, 1962.

Barna, T., 'On Measuring Capital', in F.A. Lutz and D.C. Hague (eds.), *The Theory of Capital*, Macmilan, London, 1961.

Bhalla, A.S. (ed.), *Technology and Employment in Industry,* ILO, Geneva, 1975.

Bhasin, V.K. and Seth, V.K., 'Estimation of Production Functions for Indian Manufacturing Industries', *Indian Journal of Industrial Relations*, Vol. 15, No.3, January, 1980.

Bidkar, I.R., 'The Paradox of Indian Economic Development: A Schumpeterian Perspective', *Indian Economic Journal,* Vol.35, No.3, January-March, 1988.

Bliss, C.J., *Capital Theory and Distribution of Income,* North Holland Publishing Co., Amsterdam, 1975.

Boon, G.K., 'Technological Choice in Metal working: With Special Reference to Mexico', in A.S. Bhalla (ed.), *Technology and Employment in Industry,* ILO, Geneva, 1975.

Bosworth, D.L. (ed.), *The Employment Consequences of Technological Change,* Macmillan, London, 1983.

Brown, M., *On the Theory and Measurement of Technological Change,* Cambridge University Press, Cambridge, 1966.

Brown, M. and deCani, J.S., 'Technological Change and the Distribution of Income', *International Economic Review,* Vol.4, September, 1963.

Brown, M. and Popkin, J., 'A Measure of Technological Change and Returns to Scale', *Review of Economics and Statistics,* November, 1962.

Bruton, H., 'Productivity Growth in Latin America', *American Economic Review,* December, 1967.

Buchanan, N.S., *International and Domestic Welfare,* New York, 1945.

Budhraja, J.C., Singh, V.S. and Dutta, R., *Regional Disparities in Uttar Pradesh and Proposed Strategies for their Reduction,* Area Planning Division, State Planning Institute, Lucknow, 1984.

Cairncross, A., and Puri, M. (eds). *Employment, Income Distribution and Development Strategy: Problems of Developing Countries,* Macmillan, London, 1976.

Chakraborty, D., 'CES Production Function: A Review of Recent Literature', *Artha Vijnana,* Vol. 24, No.3, September, 1982.

Champernowne, D.G., 'The Production Function and the Theory of Capital', *Review of Economic Studies,* Vol.21, 1953-54.

Chaturvedi, D.N., 'Problems of Estimation of Gross Fixed Capital Formation at State Level', *Journal of Income and Wealth,* Vol.4, No.1, January, 1980.

Chenery, H.B., 'The Application of Investment of Criteria', *Quarterly Journal of Economics,* February, 1953.

Chenery, H.B., 'Patterns of Industrial Growth', *American Economic Review,* September, 1960.

Christensen, L.R., Cummings, D., and Jorgenson, D.W., 'Economic Growth, 1947-73: An International Comparison', in J.W. Kendrick and B.N. Vaccara (eds.) *New Development in Productivity Measurement and Analysis,* NBER, Vol. 44, 1980.

Christensen, L.R., Jorgenson, D.W., and Lau, L.J., 'Conjugate Duality and the Transcedental Logarithmic Production Function', *Econometrica,* Vol.39, No.4, July, 1971.

Christensen, L.R., Jorgenson, D.W., and Lau L.J., Transcedental Logarithmic Production Frontiers, *Review of Economics and Statistics* Vol.55, No.1. February, 1973.

Clark, C., *The Conditions of Economic Progress,* Macmillan, London, 1940.

Cobb, C.W. and Douglas, P.H., 'A Theory of Production', *American Economic Review* (Supplement), March, 1928.

Coombs, R., Saviotti, P., and Walsh, V., *Economics and Technological Change,* Macmillan Education, Houndmills, 1987.

Cooper, C.M., and Clark, J., *Employment, Economics and Technology: The Impact of Technological Change on Labour Market*, Wheatsheaf Books, Great Britain, 1982.

Datta Roy Choudhury, U., 'Industrial Breakdown of Capital Stock in India', *The Journal of Income and Wealth,* Vol.1, No.2, April, 1977.

David, P.A., 'The Deflation of Value Added', *Review of Economics and Statistics,* 1962.

Denison, E.F., 'Theoretical Aspects of Quality Change, Capital Consumption and Net Capital Formation', in *Problems of Capital Formation,* NBER, Vol. 19, 1957.

Denison, E.F., 'Measurement of Labour Input: Some Questions of Definition and Adequacyof the Data', in *Output, Input and Productivity Measurment,* NBER, Vol.25, 1961.

Denison, E.F., *The Sources of Economic Growth in The U.S. and Alternatives Before Us,* Committee for Economic Development, New York, 1962a.

Denison, E.F., 'United States Economic Growth', *Journal of Business,* Vol.35, April, 1962b.

Denison, E.F., *Why Growth Rates Differ: Postwar Experience in Nine Western Countries,* The Brookings Institution, Washington D.C., 1967.

Denison, E.F/, 'Some Major Issues in productivity Analysis: An Examination of Estimates by Jorgensen and Griliches', *Survey of Current Business,* May, 1969.

Denison, E.F., *Accounting for United States Economic Growth,* 1929 to 1969, The Brooking Institution, Washington D.C., 1974.

Dhillon, S.S., 'Productivity Trends and Factor Substitutability in Manufacturing Sector in Karnataka', *Margin,* Vol.16, No.1, October, 1983.

Dholakia, B.H., *The Sources of Economic Growth in India,* Good Companions, Baroda, 1974.

Dholakia, B.H., 'Sources of Output Growth in Indian Iron and Steel Industry', *Indian Journal of Industrial Relations,* Vol.12, No.3, January, 1977.

Dholakia, B.H., 'Measurement of Capital Input and Estimation of Time Series Production Functions in Indian Manufacturing', *Indian Economic Journal,* Vol.24, No.3, January-March, 1977.

Dholakia, R.H., 'An Inter-State Analysis of Capital and Output in Registered Manufacturing Sector', *Indian Journal of Industrial Relations,* Vol.15, No.1, July, 1979.

Dholakia, R.H., and Patel, P.M., 'On Estimating Net Fixed Capital Formation at Constant Prices in Registered Manufacturing Sector at State Level', *Journal of Income and Wealth,* Vol.4, No.1, January, 1980.

Diwan, R.K., 'Returns to Scale in Indian Industry: A Comment', *The Econometric Annual of the Indian Economic Journal*, Vol.15, 1968.

Diwan, R.K. and Gujarati, D.N., 'Employment and Productivity in Indian Industries', *Artha Vijnana*, Vol.10, No.1, March, 1968.

Domar, E.D., 'Soviet Model of Growth', in *Essays in the Theory of Economic Growth*, New York, 1957.

Domar, E.D., 'On the Measurement of Technological change', *Economic Journal*, Vol.77, December, 1961.

Domar, E.D., 'The Capital-Output Ratio in the United States: Its Variations and Stability', in F.A. Lutz and D.C. Hague (eds.) *Theory of Capital*, Macmillan, London, 1961.

Dutta Majumdar, D., 'Productivity of Labour and Capital in Indian Manufacturing during 1951-61', *Arthaniti*, January-July, 1966.

Dutta, M.M., 'The Production Function for Indian Manufacturing', *Sankhya*, Vol. 15, 1955.

Enos, J.L., 'Invention and Innovation in Petroleum Refining Industry', In *The Rate and Direction of Inventive Activity: Economic and Social Factors*, Princeton University Press, Princetion, 1962.

Ezekiel, H., 'The Pattern of Investment and Economic Growth', *Indian Economic Journal*, Vol.8, No.2, October-December, 1965.

Fabricant, S., 'Economic Progress and Economic Change', *34th Annual Report of the National Bureau of Economic Researh*, New York, 1954.

Fel'dman, 'On the Theory of National Income Growth', *Planovoc Khoziaistvo*, November-December, 1928.

Ferguson, C.E., 'Time Series Production Functions and Technological Progress in American Manufacturing Industry', *Journal of Political Economy*, Vol. 25, April, 1965.

Ferguson, C.E., 'Substitution, Technical Progress and Returns to Scale', *Americal Economic Review, Association Paper'*, Vol.55, May, 1965.

Fie, J.C.H. and Ranis, G., 'Innovation, Capital Accumulation and Economic Development', *American Economic Review*, Vol.53, No.3 June, 1963.

Fie, J.C.H. and Ranis, G., *Development of the Labour Surplus Economy*, Yale University, 1964.

Fisher, A.G.B., 'Capital and Growth of Knowledge', *Economic Journal*, September, 1933.

Fisher, A.G.B., 'Production: Primary, Secondary and Tertiary', *Economic Record*, June, 1939.

Forsyth, D.J.C., McBain, N.S. and Solomon, R.F., 'Technical Rigidity and Appropriate Technology in Less Development Countries, *World Development*, Vol.8, 1980.

Fransman, M., *Technology and Economic Development*, Wheatesheaf Books, Great Britain, 1986.

Freeman, C., Clark, J. and Soete, L., *Unemployment and Technical Innovation: A Study of Long Waves and Economic Development*, Frances Pinter, London, 1982.

Galenson, W. and Leibenstien, H., 'Investment Criteria, Productivity and Economic Development', *Quarterly Journal of Economics*, August, 1955.

Gillis, M., Perkins, D.H., Roemer, M. and Snodgrass, D.R., *Economics of Development*, W.W. Norton, New York, 1983.

Gold, B. (ed.) *Research, Technological Change and Economic Analysis,* D.C. Heath and Co., U.S.A., 1977.

Goldar, B.N., 'Productivity Trends in Indian Manufacturing Industry, 1951-1978', *Indian Economic Review,* Vol.18, No.1, January-June, 1983.

Goldar, B.N., *Productivity Growth in Indian Industry,* Allied Publishers, New Delhi, 1986.

Goldsmith, R.W., 'A Perpetual Inventory of National Wealth', in *Studies in Income and Wealth,* NBER, Vol.14. 1951.

Gollop, F.M. and Jorgenson, D.W., 'U.S. Productivity Growth by Industry, 1947-73', in J.W. Kendrick and B.N. Vaccara (eds.), *New Developments in Productivity Measurement and Analysis,* NBER, 1980.

Government of India, *The Second Five year Plan, 1956-61.* Planning Commission, New Delhi.

Government of India, *The Third Five Year Plan, 1961-66,* Planning Commission, New Delhi.

Government of India, *The Fourth Five Year Plan, 1969-74,* Planning Commission, New Delhi.

Government of India, *Draft Fifth Five Year Plan, 1974-79,* Vol.II, Planning Commission, New Delhi.

Government of India, *The Sixth Five Year Plan, 1980-85,* Planning Commission, New Delhi.

Government of India, *The Seventh Five Year Plan, 1985-90,* Vol.II, Planning Commission, New Delhi.

Government of India, *Estimates of Capital Stock of Indian Economy : As on 31st March, 1981,* Central Statistical Organisation, Ministry of Planning, 1988.

Government of India, *Annual Survey of Industries, 1974-75, Summary Results for Census Sector,* Central Statistical Organisation, Ministry of Planning.

Government of India, *Reserve Bank of India Bulletins,* Various Issues.

Government of Uttar Pradesh, *Sixth Five Year Plan,* 1980-85, Planning Department.

Government of Uttar Pradesh, *Draft Annual Plan, 1987-88,* Vol.II, Planning Department.

Government of Uttar Pradesh, *Draft Eight Five Year Plan, 1990-95, and Annual Plan, 1991-92,* Vol.I, Planning Department.

Government of Uttar Pradesh, *State of the Economy,* Planning Department, December, 1987

Government of Uttar Pradesh, *Status Paper on Industrial Sector,* Perspective Planning Division, State Planning Institute, Lucknow, July, 1988.

Government of Uttar Pradesh, *Annual Survey of Industries,* Economics and Statistics Division, State Planning Institute, Lucknow, Various Issues.

Government of Uttar Pradesh, *Statistical Abstracts,* Economics and Statistics Division, State Planning Institute, Lucknow, Various Issues.

Griliches, Z., 'Hybrid Corn: An Exploration in the Economics of Technological Change', *Econometrica,* November, 1957.

Griliches, Z., 'The Sources of Measured Productivity Growth : United States Agricultures, 1940-60', *Journal of Political Economy,* August, 1963.

Griliches, Z. and Ringstad, V., *Economies of Scale and the Form of the Production Function,* North Holland Publishing Co., Amsterdam, 1971.

Gujarati, D., 'A Test of the ACMS Production Function: Indian Industries, 1958', *Indian Journal of Industrial Relations,* Vol. 2, 1966.

Gujarati, D., 'Sources of Output Growth in Indian Manufacturing, 1946-58', *Indian Journal of Industrial Relations,* Vol.3, No.1, 1967.

Gupta, D., 'Productivity Trends and Factor Substitutability in Manufacturing Sector of Maharashtra', *Margin,* Vol. 17, No.4, July, 1985.

Gupta, G.S. and Patel, K., 'Production Function in Indian Sugar Industry', *Indian Journal of Industrial Relations,* Vol.11, No.3, January, 1976.

Habakkuk, *American and British Technology in the Nineteenth Century,* Cambridge University Press, 1962.

Hahn, F.H. and Mathews, R.C.O., 'The Theory of Economic Growth: A Survey', *Economic Journal,* December, 1964.

Hajra, S., *Capital and Technological Progress in the Indian Economy, 1950-51-1980-81,* Radiant Publishers, New Delhi, 1985.

Hajra, S. and Kumar, A., *Production Function in Indian Industry,* Economic and Scientific Research Foundation, 1977.

Harcourt, G.C. and Liang, N.F. (eds.). *Capital and Growth,* Penguin Modern Economics Readings, 1971.

Harrod, R.F., *Towards a Dynamic Economics,* Macmillan, London, 1948.

Hashim, S.R. and Dadi, M.M., *Capital-Output Relations In Indian Manufacturing (1946-64),* M.S. University of Baroda, Baroda, 1973.

Heathfield, D.F., *Production Functions,* Macmillan, London, 1971.

Hebden, J., *Statistics for Economists,* Indian Edition, Heritage Publishers, 1982.

Heertje, A., *Economics and Technical Change,* Weidenfeld and Nicolson, London, 1977.

Hennigs, K.H., 'Capital as a Factor of Production', in J. Eatwell, M. Milgate and P. Newman (eds.), *The New Pelgrave: A Dictionary of Economics,* Vol.I, Macmillan, London, 1987.

Hicks, J.R., *The Theory of Wages,* Macmillan, London, 1932.

Hicks, J.R., 'Measurement of Capital in Relation to the Measurement of other Economic Aggregates', in F.A. Lutz and D.C. Hague (eds.), *The Theory of Capital,* Macmillan, Londn, 1961.

Hirschman, A.O., *The Strategy of Economic Development*, Yale University Press, New Haven, 1960.

Hoffman, W.G., *The Growth of Industrial Economies*, Manchester University Press, 1958.

Hollander, S., *The Sources of Increased Efficiency: A Study of Du Pont Rayon Plants*, MIT Press, Cambridge (Mass.), 1965.

Hussain, A., 'Theoretical Approches to the Effects of Technical Change on Unemployment', in D.L. Bosworth (ed.) *The Employment Consequences of Technological Change*, Macmillan, London, 1983.

Jackson, D. and Turner, H.A., 'How to Provide More Employment in a Labour Surplus Economy', *International Labour Review*, Vol.107, 1973.

Johansen, L., *Production Functions: An Integration of Micro and Macro, Short Run and Long Run Aspects*, North Holland Publishing Co., Amsterdam, 1972.

Jones, D., 'Technological Change, Demand and Employment', in D.L. Bosworth (ed.), *The Employment Consequences of Technological Change*, Macmillan, London, 1983.

Jorgenson, D.W., 'Productivity and Economic Growth in Japan and United States', *American Economic Review*, Vol. 78, No.2, May, 1988.

Jorgenson, D.W. and Griliches, Z., 'The Explanation of Productivity Change', *Review of Economic Studies*, July, 1967.

Kahn, A.E., 'Investment Criteria in Development Programmes', *Quarterly Journal of Economics*, February, 1951.

Kaldor, N., 'A Model of Economic Growth', *Economic Journal*, Vol. 67, December, 1957.

Kaldor, N. and Mirlees, J.A., 'A New Model of Economic Growth', *Review of Economic Studies*, Vol. 29, No. 3, June, 1962.

Katsoulacos, Y., *The Employment Effect of Technical Change : A Theoretical Study of New Technology and the Labour Market*, Wheatsheaf Books, Great Britain, 1986.

Kendrick, J.W., 'Productivity Trends : Capital and Labour', *Review of Economics and Statistics*, August, 1956.

Kendrick, J.W., *Productivity Trends in the United States*, NBER, 1961.

Kendrick, J.W., *Post-War Productivity Trends in the United States, 1948-1969*, NBER, New York, 1973.

Kendrick, J.W. and Vaccara, B.N. (eds.), *New Developments in Productivity Measurement and Analysis*, Studies in Income and Wealth, NBER, Vol. 44, 1980.

Kennedy, C. and Thirlwall, A.P., 'Surveys in Applied Economics : Technical Progress', *Economic Journal*, Vol. 82, March, 1972.

Khan, A.H. and Siddiqui, R., 'On the Measurment of Technical Progress', *International Journal of Development Planning Literature*, Vol. 5, No.1, January, 1990.

Khatkhate, D.R., 'Investment Pattern, Techniques and Growth', *Economia Interazionale*, February, 1961.

Kindleberger, C.P., and Herrick, B., *Economic Development*, McGraw Hill Kogakusha, Tokyo, 1977.

Krishna, K.L., 'Total Factor Productivity : Concept and Measurement', *Productivity*, Vol. 10, No. 4, Janaury-March, 1970.

Krishna, R. and Mehta, S.S., 'Productivity Trends in Large Scale Industries', *Economic and Political Weekly*, October 26, 1968.

Kumar, V., 'Productivity Trends in Selected Industries in India', *Indian Labour Journal*, Vol. 24, No. 1. January, 1983.

Lal, R.N., *Capital Formation and its Financing in India*, Allied Publishers, 1977.

Lall, S., *Developing Countries in the International Economy*, Macmillan, London, 1981.

Lewis, W.A., *The Theory of Economic Growth*, 12th Edition, Allen & Unwin, London, 1978.

Lutz, F.A. and Hague, D.C. (eds.), *The Theory of Capital*, Macmillan, London, 1961.

Lynn, F., 'An Investigation into the Rate of Development and Diffusion of Technology in our Modern Industrial Society', *The Employment Impact of Technological Change*, Washington, 1962.

MacDonald, S., Lamberton, D.McL, Mandeville, T.D., *The Trouble With Technology : Explorations in the Process of Technological Change*, Frances Printer, London, 1983.

Maddison, A., *Economic Progress and Policy in Developing Countries*, Allen & Unwin, London, 1970.

Mahalanobis, P.C., *The Approach of Operational Research to Planning in India*, Asia Publishing House, Bombay, 1963.

Mansfield, E., Technical Change and the Rate of Imitation, *Econometrica*, October, 1961.

Mansfield, E., 'Technological Change : Measurement, Determinants and Diffusion', in *The Employment Impact of Technological Change*, Washington, 1962.

Mansfield, E., *The Economics of Technological Change*, W.W. Norton, New York, 1968.

Massell, B.F., 'Capital Formation and Technological Change in U.S. Manufacturing', *Review of Economics and Statistics*, 1960.

Mathur, G., 'The Economics of True Employment', *Hindustan Times*, July, 1972.

Mathur, G., 'A Microeconomic Growth Model', in L.K. Sen (ed.), *Readings on Micro-Level Planning and Growth Centres*, National Institute of Community Development, Hyderabad, 1974.

Mehta, S.S., *Productivity, Production Function and Technical Change : A Survey of Some Indian Industries*, Concept Publishing Company, New Delhi, 1980.

Mishra, R.P., Sundaram, K.V. and Prakasha Rao, V.L.S., *Regional Development Planning in India : A New Strategy*, Vikas Publishing House, Delhi, 1974.

Moore, F.T., Technological Change and Industrial Development : Issues and Opportunities'., *World Bank Staff Working Papers, No. 613*, Washington D.C., 1983.

Morawetz, D., 'Employment Implications of Industrialisation in Developing Countires : A Survey', *Economic Journal*, Vol. 84, No. 335, September, 1974.

Morawetz, D., 'Elasticities of Substitution in Industry : What Do We Learn from Econometric Estimates?', *World Development*, Vol. 4, No. 1, 1976.

Mountjoy, A.B., *Industrialisation and Developing Countries*, 5th Edition, Hutchinson and Co., London, 1982.

Murty, V.N. and Sastry, V.K., 'Production Functions for Indian Industry', *Econometrica*, Vol. 25, April, 1957.

Myrdal, G., *Economic Theory and Underdeveloped Regions*, Duckworth, London, 1957.

Nadiri, M.I., 'Some Approaches to the Theory and Measurement of Total Factor Productivity : A Survey', *Journal of Economic Literature*, Vol. 8, No. 4, December, 1970.

Nadiri, M.I., 'International Studies of Factor Inputs and Total Factor Productivity : A Brief Survey'. *Review of Income and Wealth*, June, 1972.

Nain, J.S., 'Industrial Development with Special Emphasis on Employment Generation & Technological Change', *Manpower Journal*, Vol. 20, No. 3, October - December, 1984.

Narasimham, G.V.L., and Fabrycy, M.Z., 'Relative Efficiencies of Organised Industries in India, 1949-1958', *The Journal of Development Studies*, January, 1974.

Nelson, R.R. 'Research on Productivity Growth and Productivity Differences : Dead Ends and New Departures', *Journal of Economic Literature*, September, 1981.

Nerlove, M., 'Recent Empirical Studies of the CES and Related Production Functions', in M. Brown (ed.), *The Theory and Empirical Analysis of Production*, Studies in Income and Wealth, NBER, Vol. 31, New York, 1967.

Niitamo, O. 'The Development of Productivity in Finnish Industry, 1925-52', *Productivity Measurement Review*, November, 1958.

Nurkse, R., *Problems of Capital Formation in Underdeveloped Countries*, 3rd Edition (Indian Reprint), Oxford University Press, New Delhi, 1980.

Pack, H., 'The Employment - Output Trade - off in LDCs — A Microeconomic Approach', *Oxford Economic Papers*, November, 1974.

Pandey, R.C., *Growth of Factories in U.P. and the Need for their Planned Development*, Economics and Statistics Division, Uttar Pradesh, 1951.

Pandey, R.L., *Employment Implications of Industrialisation in India*, Mittal Publications, Delhi, 1987.

Papola, T.S., 'Spatial Diversification of Manufacturing Industries : A Study of Factory Industries in Uttar Pradesh', in T.S. Papola, V.N. Mishra, H.S. Verma, R.C. Sinha and A. Joshi (eds.), *Studies on Development of Uttar Pradesh*, Giri Institute of Development Studies, Lucknow, 1979.

Papola, T.S., Mishra, V.N., Verma, H.S., Sinha, R.C. and Joshi, A. (eds.), *Studies on Development of Uttar Pradesh*, GIDS, Lucknow, 1979.

Pasinetti, L.L. and Scazzieri, R., 'Capital Theory : Paradoxes', in J. Eatwell, M. Milgate and P. Newman (eds.), *The New Pelgrave : A Dictionary of Economics*, Vol. I, Macmillan, London, 1987.

Pigou, A.C., *The Economics of Welfare*, 4th Edition, London, 1932.

Polak, J.J., 'Balance of Payment Problems of Countries Reconstructing with the Help of Foreign Loans', *Quarterly Journal of Economics*, February, 1963.

Raj, K.N., 'Some Observations on Economic Growth in India over the Period 1952-53 to 1982-83', *Economic and Political Weekly*, Vol. 19, No. 41, October, 1984.

Rajalakshmi, K., 'A Production Function Analysis of Non-Metallic Mineral Products and Non-Ferrous Basic Metal Industries of Rajasthan', *Indian Journal of Regional Science*, Vol. 8, No. 1, January, 1981.

Rajalakshmi, K., 'Sources of Growth in the Total Manufacturing Sector in Rajasthan and at All India Level', *Indian Journal of Industrial Relations*, Vol. 19, No. 1, July, 1983.

Rajalakshmi, K., 'A Time Series Analysis of Productivity of Electrical Machinery Industry in Three Leading States of India', *Indian Journal of Regional Science*, Vol. 15, No. 2, 1983.

Ranis, G., 'Factor Proportions in Japanese Economic Development', *American Economic Review*, Vol. 47, No. 5, September, 1957.

Ranis, G., 'Production Functions, Market Imperfections, and Economic Development', *Economic Journal*, Vol. 72, June, 1962.

Reddaway, W.B. and Smith, A.D., 'Progress in British Manufacturing Industries in the Period 1948-54'. *Economic Journal*, March, 1960.

Reddy, M.G.K. and Rao, S.V., 'Functional Distribution in Large Scale Manufacturing Sector in India', *Artha Vijnana*, Vol. 4, 1962.

Robinson, J., 'The Production Function and the Theory of Capital', *Review of Economic Studies*, Vol. 21, 1953-54.

Robinson, S., 'Sources of Growth in Less Developed Countries : A Cross Section Study', *Quarterly Journal of Economics*, August, 1971.

Rosen, G., *Industrial Change in India*, Asia Publishing House, Bombay, 1959.

Rosenberg, N. (ed.), *The Economics of Technological Change*, Penguin Modern Economics Readings, 1971.

Rosenberg, N., *Perspectives on Technology*, Cambridge University Press, Cambridge, 1976.

Rosenberg, N., *Inside the Black Box : The Technology and Economics*, Cambridge University Press, Cambridge, 1982.

Rosenstein-Roden, P.N., 'Notes on the Theory of the 'Big Push'', in H.W. Ellis (ed.), *Economic Development for Latin America*, Macmillan, London, 1961.

Rostow, W.W., *The Stages of Economic Growth*, 2nd Edition, Cambridge University Press, 1971.

Rothwell, R. and Zegveld, W., *Technical Change and Employment*, Frances Printer, London, 1979.

Ruggles, R. and Ruggles, N., 'Concepts of Real Capital Stoks and Services', in *Output, Input and Productivity Measurement*, Studies in Income and Wealth, NBER, Vol. 25, 1961.

Ruttan, V., 'Usher and Schumpeter on Invention, Innovation and Technolocial Change', *Quarterly Journal of Economics*, November, 1959.

Sadhak, H., *Industrial Development in Backward Regions in India*, Chugh Publications, Allahabad, 1986.

Salter, W.E.G., *Productivity and Technical Change*, Cambridge (Mass.), 1960.

Sakong, I.L. and Narasimhan G.V.L., 'Inter-Industry Resource Allocation and Technological Change : The Situation in Indian Manufacturing', *The Developing Economies*, June, 1974.

Samuelson, P.A., 'Prices of Factors and Goods in General Equilibrium', *Review of Economic Studies*, Vol. 21, No. 1, 1953.

Samuelson, P.A., 'Parable and Realism in Capital Theory : The Surrogate Production Function', *Review of Economic Studies*, Vol. 39, June, 1962.

Sandesara, J.C., 'Scale and Technology in Indian Industry', *Bulletin of the Oxford University Institute of Economics and Statistics*, Vol. 28, No. 3, August, 1966.

Sandesara, J.C., 'Industrial Growth in India — Performance and Prospects', *Indian Economic Journal*, Vol. 30, October —December, 1982.

Sankar, U., 'Elasticities of Substitution and Returns to Scale in Indian Manufacturing Industries', *International Economic Review*, Vol. 2, October, 1970.

Schumacher, E.F., *Small is Beautiful : A Study of Economics as if People Mattered*, Radha Krishna Prakashan, New Delhi, 1977.

Schumpeter, J., 'The Instability of Capitalism', *Economic Journal, 1928.*

Schumpeter, J., *The Theory of Economic Development*, Harvard University Press, 1934.

Schumpeter, J., *Business Cycles*, McGraw Hill, New York, 1939.

Sen, A.K., 'Some Notes on the Choice of Capital Intensity in Development Planning', *Quarterly Journal of Economics*, November, 1957.

Sen, A.K., *Employment, Technology and Development*, (A Study Prepared for the ILO), Claredon Press, 1975.

Shivamaggi, Rajgopalan and Venkatachalam, 'Wages, Labour Productivity and Costs of Production', *Economic and Political Weekly*, May, 1968.

Singh, A.K., 'Relative Growth Performance of the U.P. Economy' in R.T. Tewari and A. Joshi (eds.), *Development and Change in India*, Ashish Publishing House, New Delhi, 1988.

Singh, L., 'Productivity Trends and Factor Substitutabilty in Punjab Industry', *Indian Journal of Economics*, Vol. 67, No. 266, January, 1987.

Singh, L. and Singhal, K.C., 'Economies of Scale and Technical Change', *Productivity*, Vol. 27, No. 1, October - December, 1987.

Singh, R.R., 'Productivity Trends and Wages', *Eastern Economist*, April, 1966.

Sinha, J.N. and Sawhney, P.K., *Wages and Productivity in Indian Industries*, Vikas Publications, Delhi, 1970.

Smithies, A., 'In Reply to Solow', *American Economic Review* (Supplementary), May, 1962.

Solow, R.M., 'A Contribution to the Theory of Economic Growth', *Quarterly Journal of Economics*, 1956.

Solow, R.M. 'Technical Change and the Aggregate Production Function', *Review of Economics and Statistics*, August, 1957.

Solow, R.M., 'Investment and Technical Progress', in K. Arrow, S. Karlin and P. Suppes (eds.), *Mathematical Methods in Social Sciences*, Stanford University Press, 1960.

Solow, R.M., 'Technical Progress, Capital Formation and Economic Growth', *American Economic Review*, Vol. 52, 1962.

Solow, R.M., *Capital Theory and Rate of Return*, North Holland Publishing Co., Amsterdam, 1963.

Somayajulu, V.V.N, and George, J., 'Production Function Studies of Indian Industires — A Survey', *Artha Vijnana*, Vol. 25, No. 4, December, 1983.

Sraffa, P., *Production of Commodities by Means of Commodities*, Cambridge University Press, 1960.

Srinivasamurthy, A.P., *Investment Allocation in Indian Planning*, Himalaya Publishing House, Bombay, 1981.

Srivastava, S.C. and Lal, B., *Capital Formation in the Economy of the Uttar Pradesh : A Study of Development Head-wise Estimates, 1969-70 to 1978-79*, State Planning Institute, Lucknow, 1978.

Steward, F., 'Technology and Employment in LDCs', *World Development*, Vol. 2, No. 3, March, 1974.

Steward, F., 'Capital Goods in Developing Countries', in A. Cairncross and M. Puri (eds.), *Employment, Income Ditribution and Development Strategy : Problems of Developing Countries*, Macmillan, London, 1976.

Steward, F., 'Manufacture of Cement Blocks in Kenya' in A.S. Bhalla (ed.), *Technology and Employment in Industry*, ILO, Geneva, 1975.

Steward, F., *Technology and Underdevelopment*, Macmillan, London, 1977.

Steward, F. and Streeten, P., 'New Strategies for Development : Poverty, Income and Growth', *Oxford Economic Papers (New Series)*, Vol. 28, November, 1976.

Stoneman, P., *The Economic Analysis of Technological Change*, Oxford University Press, New York, 1983.

Subramaniam, K., *Capital Theory and Economic Analysis*, Gian Publishing House, Delhi, India, 1987.

Subramaniyan, G., 'Measurement of Productivity and Production Functions in Indian Sugar Industry — A Regional Analysis', *Indian Journal of Regional Science,* Vol. 11, No. 2, 1979.

Subramaniyan, G., 'An Inter-State Production Study for Indian Sugar Industry : An Econometric Approach', *Indian Journal of Economics,* Vol. 61, No. 242, January, 1981.

Sutcliffe, *Industry and Underdevelopment*, Addison, Wesley, London, 1971.

Tewari, R.T., 'Inter-Regional pattern of Industrialisation in India : 1971-81' in R.T. Tewari and A. Joshi (eds.), *Development and Change in India*, Ashish Publishing House, New Delhi, 1988.

Tewari, R.T. and Joshi, A. (eds.), *Development and Change in India*, Ashish Publishing House, New Delhi, 1988.

Thirlwall, A.P., *Growth and Development : With Special Reference to Developing Economies*, 3rd Edition, ELBS/Macmillan, 1983.

Usher, A.P., *A History of Mechanical Inventions,* 2nd Edition, Hardvard University Press, 1954.

Venkataswami, T.S., *An Empirical Investigation into Production Functions and Technical Change in Indian Manufacturing Industries,* Boston University, Ph.D. Thesis, 1968.

Venkataswami, T.S., 'Production Functions and Technical Change in Indian Manufacturing Industries', *Indian Journal of Economics,* April, 1975.

Verma, P.C., 'Production Structure of Jute Industry in India', *Indian Economic Journal, Vol. 33,* No. 2, October - December, 1985.

Wallis, K.F., *Topics in Applied Econometrics*, Gray-Mills Publishing, London, 1973.

White, L.J., 'The Evidence on Appropriate Factor Proportions for Manufacturing in Less Developed Countries : A Survey', *Economic Development and Cultural Change*, Vol. 27, No. 1, October, 1978.

Williamson, J.G., 'Regional Inequality and the Process of National Development : A Description of Patterns', *Economic Development and Cultural Change,* Vol. 13, July, 1965.

Yeh, Yeong Her, 'Economies of Scale for Indian Manufacturing Industries', *Econometric Annual of the Indian Economic Journal,* Vol. 14, 1966.

Yotopoulos, P.A. and Nugent, J.B., *Economics of Development : Empirical Investigations*, Harper and Row, New York, 1976.

Zarembka, P.A., *Towards a Theory of Economic Development*, Holden — Day Inc., San Francisco, 1972.

Zuvekas, C., *Economic Development : An Introduction,* Macmillan, London, 1979.

Index